Land Grabs in Asia

Although there is no universally accepted definition of the term 'land grabbing', ordinary people whose livelihoods are adversely affected by land grabbing know exactly what it is. It involves the physical capture and control of land and homes, including the usurpation of the power to decide how and when these will be used and for what purposes – with little or no prior consultation or compensation to the displaced communities.

This thought-provoking book defines land grabbing, and examines aspects of the land grabs phenomenon in six Asian countries, researched and written by country-specific legal scholars. The book provides unique perspectives on how and why land grabbing is practised in Cambodia, China, Indonesia, Malaysia, Myanmar and Vietnam, and explores the surprising role that law plays in facilitating and legitimizing land grabs in each country. In contrast to most of the literature which focuses on foreign investors' rights under international law, here the focus is on domestic laws and legal infrastructures. Finding that Asian states need to move beyond existing regimes that govern land to a regime that encourages more equitable land rights allocation and protection of stakeholders' rights, the book urges further research in the nexus between the use of law to facilitate development.

Land Grabs in Asia is the first book to explore land grabbing in multiple jurisdictions in Asia. As such, it will appeal to students and scholars of law and development, law and society, and international relations, as well as being essential reading for development policy makers and government ministers.

Connie Carter is Professor of Law & International Business in the Faculty of Management at Royal Roads University, Victoria, Canada. Her research focuses on law and development, foreign direct investment and corporate social responsibility in China and South-East Asia.

Andrew Harding is a Professor in the Faculty of Law, National University of Singapore, where he is also Director of the Centre for Asian Legal Studies and Director of the Asian Law Institute. He is a leading scholar in the fields of Asian legal studies and comparative constitutional law, on which he has published widely.

Routledge Contemporary Asia Series

1 Taiwan and Post-Communist Europe
Shopping for allies
Czeslaw Tubilewicz

2 The Asia-Europe Meeting
The theory and practice of interregionalism
Alfredo C. Robles, Jr

3 Islamic Legitimacy in a Plural Asia
Edited by Anthony Reid and Michael Gilsenan

4 Asian-European Relations
Building blocks for global governance?
Edited by Jürgen Rüland, Gunter Schubert, Günter Schucher and Cornelia Storz

5 Taiwan's Environmental Struggle
Toward a green Silicon Island
Jack F. Williams and Ch'ang-yi David Chang

6 Taiwan's Relations with Mainland China
A tail wagging two dogs
Su Chi

7 The Politics of Civic Space in Asia
Building urban communities
Edited by Amrita Daniere and Mike Douglass

8 Trade and Contemporary Society Along the Silk Road
An ethno-history of Ladakh
Jacqueline Fewkes

9 Lessons from the Asian Financial Crisis
Edited by Richard Carney

10 Kim Jong Il's Leadership of North Korea
Jae-Cheon Lim

11 Education as a Political Tool in Asia
Edited by Marie Lall and Edward Vickers

12 Human Genetic Biobanks in Asia
Politics of trust and scientific advancement
Edited by Margaret Sleeboom-Faulkner

13 East Asian Regionalism from a Legal Perspective
Current features and a vision for the future
Edited by Tamio Nakamura

14 Dissent and Cultural Resistance in Asia's Cities
Edited by Melissa Butcher and Selvaraj Velayutham

15 Preventing Corruption in Asia
Institutional design and policy capacity
Edited by Ting Gong and Stephen Ma

16 Expansion of Trade and FDI in Asia
Strategic and policy challenges
Edited by Julien Chaisse and Philippe Gugler

17 Business Innovation in Asia
Knowledge and technology networks from Japan
Dennis McNamara

18 Regional Minorities and Development in Asia
Edited by Huhua Cao and Elizabeth Morrell

19 Regionalism in China–Vietnam Relations
Institution-building in the Greater Mekong subregion
Oliver Hensengerth

20 From Orientalism to Postcolonialism
Asia-Europe and the lineages of difference
Edited by Sucheta Mazumdar, Kaiwar Vasant and Thierry Labica

21 Politics and Change in Singapore and Hong Kong
Containing contention
Stephan Ortmann

22 Inter-Ethnic Dynamics in Asia
Considering the Other through ethnonyms, territories and rituals
Edited by Christian Culas and François Robinne

23 Asia and Latin America
Political, economic and multilateral relations
Edited by Jörn Dosch and Olaf Jacob

24 Japan and Africa
Globalization and foreign aid in the 21st century
Edited by Howard P. Lehman

25 De-Westernizing Communication Research
Altering questions and changing frameworks
Edited by Georgette Wang

26. Asian Cities, Migrant Labor and Contested Spaces
Edited by Tai-Chee Wong and Jonathan Rigg

27. Diaspora Literature and Visual Culture
Asia in flight
Sheng-mei Ma

28. Alterities in Asia
Reflections on identity and regionalism
Edited by Leong Yew

29. Soft Power in Japan–China Relations
State, sub-state and non-state relations
Utpal Vyas

30. Enhancing Asia-Europe Co-operation through Educational Exchange
Georg Wiessala

31. History Textbooks and the Wars in Asia
Divided memories
Edited by Gi-Wook Shin and Daniel C. Sneider

32. The Politics of Religion in South and Southeast Asia
Edited by Ishtiaq Ahmed

33. The Chinese / Vietnamese Diaspora
Revisiting the boatpeople
Edited by Yuk Wah Chan

34. The Dynamics of Social Capital and Civic Engagement in Asia
Vibrant societies
Edited by Amrita Daniere and Hy Van Luong

35. Eurasia's Ascent in Energy and Geopolitics
Rivalry or partnership for China, Russia and Central Asia?
Edited by Robert E. Bedeski and Niklas Swanström

36. Asian Popular Culture in Transition
Edited by John A. Lent and Lorna Fitzsimmons

37. Sexual Diversity in Asia, c. 600 – 1950
Edited by Raquel Reyes and William G. Clarence Smith

38. Asia's Role in Governing Global Health
Edited by Kelley Lee, Tikki Pang and Yeling Tan

39. Asian Heritage Management
Contexts, concerns, and prospects
Edited by Kapila D. Silva and Neel Kamal Chapagain

40. Genocide and Mass Atrocities in Asia
Legacies and prevention
Edited by Deborah Mayerson and Annie Pohlman

41. Child Security in Asia
The impact of armed conflict in Cambodia and Myanmar
Cecilia Jacob

42. Vietnamese–Chinese Relationships at the Borderlands
Trade, tourism and cultural politics
Yuk Wah Chan

43. Asianism and the Politics of Regional Consciousness in Singapore
Leong Yew

44. Disaster Relief in the Asia Pacific
Agency and resilience
Edited by Minako Sakai, Edwin Jurriëns, Jian Zhang and Alec Thornton

45. Human Trafficking in Asia
Forcing issues
Edited by Sallie Yea

46.Democracy or Alternative Political Systems in Asia
After the strongmen
Edited by Michael Hsin-Huang Hsiao

47. European Studies in Asia
Contours of a discipline
Georg Wiessala

48. Corporate Social Responsibility and Human Rights in Asia
Robert J. Hanlon

49. Irregular Migration and Human Security in East Asia
Edited by Jiyoung Song and Alistair D. B. Cook

50. Renewable Energy in East Asia
Towards a new developmentalism
Christopher M. Dent

51. East Asian Development Model
21st century perspectives
Edited by Shiping Hua and Ruihua Hu

52. Land Grabs in Asia
What role for the law?
Edited by Connie Carter and Andrew Harding

53. Asia Struggles with Democracy
Evidence from Indonesia, Korea and Thailand
Giovanna Maria Dora Dore

54. China-Malaysia Relations and Foreign Policy
Razak Abdullah

Land Grabs in Asia

What role for the law?

Edited by
Connie Carter and Andrew Harding

Routledge
Taylor & Francis Group
LONDON AND NEW YORK

First published 2015
by Routledge
2 Park Square, Milton Park, Abingdon, Oxon OX14 4RN

and by Routledge
711 Third Avenue, New York, NY 10017

First issued in paperback 2017

Routledge is an imprint of the Taylor & Francis Group, an informa business

British Library Cataloguing in Publication Data
A catalogue record for this book is available from the British Library

Library of Congress Cataloging in Publication Data
A catalog record for this book has been requested

ISBN: 978-1-138-55412-2 (pbk)
ISBN: 978-1-138-90401-9 (hbk)

Typeset in Times New Roman
by Taylor & Francis Books

Contents

Table

Preface

This book had its genesis in a workshop organized by the Centre for Asian Legal Studies (CALS) at the National University of Singapore, Faculty of Law in 2013.

Andrew Harding conceived the idea for the event as a result of a conference organized by Qianfan Zhang (one of the contributors here) at Beijing University in August 2011. After a full day of discussion on land grabs (the conference was actually entitled 'Constitutional protection of peasant land in China'), he returned to the hotel to find that the first three items on the television news covered land grabs in Cambodia, Vietnam and India. This, coupled with further conversations with other academics, made him realize that land grabbing was an issue not just for China, but for almost every country across the region, and so it appeared to be an important issue to look at comparatively.

A lot of work has been done on this issue, for example in conferences and special issues of journals. However, that work has generally stopped at the point where this book begins, in asking what the role of the law is in dealing with the problems that land grabs present. The topic of land grabs is therefore understudied in a specifically legal context. It seemed as though CALS could make a valuable contribution to the ongoing discussion at both national and international levels on this issue.

One issue that arises immediately, and which we discussed extensively in the workshop, is that there is no clear definition of 'land grab'. The phrase carries a connotation of illegality or illegitimacy, but one person's land grab may be another person's perfectly legitimate acquisition of real property. This issue is addressed squarely in Chapter 1 of this book, where we attempt to set out our own definition of 'land grab', a definition which builds on the discussion at the workshop and acknowledges the varied experiences of the phenomenon as observed by the participants in light of their individual research and perspectives.

The discussion of the substantive issues that followed was creative, and focused on how and why land grabs happen. These are elaborated upon in the following chapters, which reveal the complex and intractable nature of this problem, which is, as we saw, fundamental to development in Asia, with potentially damaging and destabilizing effects. It is not just affected smallholder farmers and villagers who have an interest in this issue being dealt with: governments and investors, too, see the need to find a way of protecting fundamental socio-economic interests without impeding the overall trajectory of development across Asia.

Following the workshop, Connie Carter stepped forward to join Andrew Harding in editing this book, writing Chapter 1 as well as adding her own contribution on Myanmar. We thank CALS for hosting a visit to the National University of Singapore (NUS) by Connie Carter which enabled her to work on the book. We thank the contributors, all the participants at the 2013 workshop, the publishers, and the staff of CALS, especially Regana Mydin, for facilitating and advancing our discussion, and bringing our answers to the light of day. We also thank PhD candidates Wilson Tay and Katherine Southwick for helpful comments on early drafts of several chapters, as well as the students in NUS' Asian Legal Studies Colloquium in 2014, for their very useful responses. We hope that this book will in some way contribute to discussion and law reform to prevent land grabs and safeguard Asian people's legitimate rights to their land and its use.

Andrew Harding and Connie Carter

List of contributors

Laurens Bakker is Assistant Professor in the Department of Sociology and Anthropology at the University of Amsterdam, Netherlands. He holds a PhD in law from the University of Leiden. His research focuses on land law and land conflict in South-East Asia, as well as on the influence of informal militias in South-East Asian local politics, society and economy. His publications include *Who Owns the Land? Looking for Law and Power in Reformasi East Kalimantan* (Radboud University Nijmegen, 2009), and a variety of contributions to edited volumes and journals.

Connie Carter is Professor of Law & International Business in the Faculty of Management at Royal Roads University, Victoria, Canada. She is also a Barrister of Lincoln's Inn, London, currently non-practising. She holds a PhD in law from the School of Oriental & African Studies, University of London. Her current research focuses on special economic zones in China and Myanmar. Her publications include *Law and Economic Development in Singapore* (Kluwer, 2001), *Fighting Fakes in China: Legal Protection of Trademarks and Brands in China* (Intellectual Property Institute, London), and *Special Economic Zones in Asian Market Economies* (as co-editor, Routledge, 2011).

Sumithra Dhanarajan is an international development practitioner, specializing in the impact of the private sector on poverty reduction and human rights protection. She is a Trustee to the Business & Human Rights Resource Centre, a member of SustainAbility's Council and of the World Economic Forum's Global Agenda Council 2012/14. She holds an MA in Understanding & Securing Human Rights from the University of London and an LLM in Asian Legal Studies from National University of Singapore, where she is currently a doctoral candidate.

Daniel Fitzpatrick is Professor of Law at Australian National University (ANU). He has been a Visiting Professor at New York University School of Law, National University of Singapore, and a Distinguished Visitor at the University of Toronto. He served as United Nations land rights adviser in post-conflict Timor and post-tsunami Indonesia, and has consulted widely with international nongovernmental organizations (NGOs). He holds a PhD in Law from ANU.

Andrew Harding is a Professor in the Faculty of Law, National University of Singapore, where he is also Director of the Centre for Asian Legal Studies (CALS) and Director of the Asian Law Institute (ASLI). He is a leading scholar in the fields of Asian legal studies and comparative constitutional law, on which he has published widely. He is co-founding editor of Hart Publishing's book series *Constitutional Systems of the World*, a major resource for constitutional law in context, and has authored the books on Malaysia (2011) and Thailand (2012) in that series.

Toan Le is a Lecturer in the Department of Business Law and Taxation, Monash Business School, Monash University. His research and teaching interests focus on East Asian legal systems from the perspective of law and society. He has written various book chapters on land disputes in Vietnam and his writing has appeared in the *Journal of World Trade.*

Mariam N. Munang holds an LLM in International Human Rights Law and Criminal Justice from Utrecht University, Netherlands. She is a Barrister of Lincoln's Inn, London, and of the High Court of Malaysia. Her book *Indigenous Rights: Development, Land and Identity – Law and Policies Relating to the Rights of Indigenous Peoples in Sabah* was published by Malaysia Environmental NGO in 2012.

Jing Qian is a doctoral candidate in the law and society programme at the University of Victoria, Canada. His research focuses on judicial roles in authoritarian regimes, and development of the rule of law in transitional states. His current empirical research focus is land grabs-related administrative litigation in China.

Gustaaf Reerink is an Attorney-at-law in Jakarta. He holds a PhD in law from the University of Leiden, Netherlands. His book *Tenure Security for Indonesia's Urban Poor: A Socio-legal Study on Land, Decentralization and the Rule of Law in Bandung*, was published by Leiden University Press in 2011.

Surya P. Subedi is Professor of International Law at the University of Leeds and Barrister of the Middle Temple, London. He has been serving as the UN Special Rapporteur for human rights in Cambodia since March 2009, for which he has produced four substantive reports on judicial, parliamentary and electoral reform, and on the impact of economic and other land concessions on people's lives. He holds a DPhil in Law from the University of Oxford.

Yogeswaran Subramaniam is an Advocate and Solicitor of the High Court of Malaysia. He serves on the Human Rights Committee and Committee for

Orang Asli Rights at the Malaysian Bar Council. He holds a PhD in law from the University of New South Wales, Australia.

Qianfan Zhang holds a PhD in Government from the University of Texas at Austin, USA. He teaches Constitutional Law at Beijing University where he is also Director of the Center for the People's Congress and Parliamentary Studies, and Senior Deputy Director of the Constitutional and Administrative Law Center. He has published extensively on comparative and Chinese constitutional law.

1 Consent not coercion

Rethinking the taking of land for 'development'

Connie Carter

This chapter aims to make a modest contribution in satisfying the need to agree on a working definition of land grabs, with a focus on putting the phenomenon in the legal context of how and why land grabbing is happening in Asia. It provides a background to the discourses in subsequent chapters which explore land grabbing in Cambodia, China, Indonesia, Malaysia, Myanmar and Vietnam. It challenges the mainstream framing of land grabs and puts them in the wider context of economic development in which host states play a key role. Drawing on the advent of fifteenth- and sixteenth-century European colonialists who ventured to distant lands and claimed them as their own for economic gain, and on lessons from the English land enclosure system of the seventeenth to nineteenth centuries, which facilitated the industrialization of agriculture in England, the chapter posits that land grabbing is nothing new, and that both colonialism and the enclosure system helped shape land tenure law, policies and issues in most of contemporary Asia.

This chapter argues that then as now, land grabbing was often facilitated by law, often in the name of 'development', and, as some of the subsequent chapters document, land grabbing catalyses transformative change among peoples and communities. The chapter provides an overview of the sources of law as they relate to land grabs and concludes with recommendations to policy makers in Asia who craft economic development plans based on industrialization and urbanization.

Towards an inclusive definition: what lawyers need to know about land grabbing

Many lawyers say that the term land grabbing is devoid of any legal meaning, and they offer no definition.[1] In truth, even outside the legal corridors, there is no universally accepted definition of the term. Writing about large-scale investments for industrial agriculture, De Schutter (2011) the former UN rapporteur on the right to food, states that 'the phenomenon referred to as "land-grabbing" – [is] the acquisition or long-term lease of large areas of land by investors'. Similarly, White *et al.* (2012: 619), in their excellent introduction to a collection of essays on land deals in a political economy perspective, say they 'explore the rapid growth of large-scale land deals in recent years – the phenomenon popularly known as "land grabbing", the large-scale acquisition of land or land-related rights and resources by corporate (business, non-profit or public) entities'. As discussed below, these definitions are woefully inadequate as they seem to use the terms land grabs, large-scale land acquisition and land deals synonymously. Furthermore, they reflect the media-dominated framing of the phenomenon (during the 2007–08 global food price crisis and the Western financial meltdown) as the rush of wealthy nations to acquire huge areas of land in the global South to grow food, feed and fuel for export to their own people back home. These narratives do not adequately capture the trends in land takings and the complexities of what was and is still happening on the ground in many developing nations. For instance, as documented in subsequent chapters in this volume, in some Asian states huge areas of land are seized by forced eviction under the cover of law, while in others legal reclassification of land renders current occupiers homeless, often without prior consultation, or compensation for displacement, dispossession and involuntary land loss.

An analysis of the narratives of ordinary people whose livelihoods are adversely affected by land grabbing illuminates the phenomenon poignantly. To them, land grabbing is the physical taking or capture for possession, and control of their land and homes, including the usurpation of the power to decide how and when these will be used and for what purposes – with little or no prior consultation or compensation to them, to the displaced communities or dispossessed individuals.

The Tirana Declaration, which grew out of a conference held in the Albanian capital in May 2011, offers a definition that more closely reflects reality (International Land Coalition 2011). The conference, which was convened to discuss land rights and land regulation, was attended by governments, international aid organizations, nongovernmental organizations (NGOs), civil society groups and other partners of the International Land Coalition.[2] While denouncing all forms of land grabbing – whether national or international – the Tirana Declaration defines land grabs as any land deals that are one or more of the following:

1 in violation of human rights, particularly the equal rights of women;
2 not based on free, prior and informed consent of the affected land users;
3 not based on a thorough assessment, or are in disregard of social, economic and environmental impacts, including the way they are gendered;
4 not based on transparent contracts that specify clear and binding commitments about activities, employment and benefits sharing; and
5 not based on effective democratic planning, independent oversight and meaningful participation.

The editors of this book agree and, for emphasis, add that any land deals that fulfil one or more of the Tirana stipulations – irrespective of their size or manner of appropriation or acquisition – will qualify as land grabs.

Many civil society groups seem to accept the Tirana Declaration's definition unconditionally, while others make a distinction between land grabs and land deals. For example, according to Action Aid (2014), citing Land Matrix, an online public database, which partners with the International Land Coalition, land deals:

- entail a transfer of rights to use, control or ownership of land through sale, lease or concession;
- cover an area of 200 hectares or more; and
- imply the potential conversion of land from smallholder production, local community use or important ecosystem service provision to commercial use.

The authors find it problematic to distinguish between land grabs and land deals based solely on the land deal criteria listed above since issues such as transparent contracts, corruption, meaningful partnership and so on are ignored. Five specific issues are considered.

First, we examined some of the deals that 'entail a transfer of rights to use, control or ownership of land through sale, lease or concession', and found that government policies and new, overly investor-friendly laws are often complicit in facilitating the sales, leases or concessions of *occupied* land without due regard to current occupiers, many of whom have traditional land tenure or other land use rights which have been ignored for the benefit of investor land deals.

Second, research indicates that contracts for the large-scale sale, lease or concession of land are either not disclosed or are not transparent (see, for example, Smaller and Mann 2009), which means that they would be in violation of several of the stipulations of the Tirana Declaration discussed above.

Third, in several cases, for example in Cambodia (Chapter 5 in this volume), Myanmar (Chapter 7) and Malaysia (Chapters 8 and 9), laws are often enacted to reclassify *occupied* land as wasteland or fallow and virgin land, thus making it 'available' for other use even though such land is often occupied by small household farmers, pastoralists or forest dwellers. In our view, such contracts of sales, leases and concessions should therefore be considered void *ab initio*, on the grounds that the object of the contract is not legally viable. Under such circumstances, it is possible that a state which insisted on enforcing such contracts could be held liable for a wrongful act under international law as posited by Dhanarajan in Chapter 11.

Fourth, we do not distinguish between large-scale land grabs/deals of '200 hectares or more' and deals for smaller areas of land comprising scattered, individual plots or strips which can be and often are specifically 'enclosed' (reminiscent of the old English enclosure system) to form large-scale properties. A land deal should be a land deal irrespective of its size: the contract and method of acquisition should decide. Similarly, a land grab is a land grab irrespective of the size of the land grabbed, for it is the unjust, often deceitful, use of law, the taking with impunity and the impact on the livelihoods of the displaced people that are key.

Fifth, we recognize that whether through deals or grabs, all land is usually converted 'from smallholder production, local community use or important ecosystem service provision' to other uses, sometimes commercial, but oftentimes they are labelled 'for development in the public interest' and taken by eminent domain or other legal instrument before being sold off to private investors for personal gain by government cronies.

Therefore, in our view, all land grabs will involve an element of illegality or at least specious legality or deceit – even when they are conducted in the name of a state's economic development plans and for the public good. That is also why land grabs are often done with the involvement, collusion or acquiescence of state officials, and sometimes by the government itself, whose policies and laws call for development through foreign direct investment (FDI), industrialization and urbanization. Similarly, all land deals that involve an element of illegality, specious legality or deceit, forced eviction, and lack of transparency, consultation and compensation for the displaced are more appropriately termed land grabs.

On the ground, the result is the same: smallholder subsistence farmers, pastoralists, forest dwellers and other rural and poor urban communities involuntarily lose their lands and homes to: large-scale agriculture; special economic zones (SEZs) and industrial parks; residential blocks; new infrastructure like roads, rail, ports, power generation and so on, designed to support industrialization and urbanization; carbon cap-and-trade programmes or REDD initiatives (reducing emissions from deforestation and degradation); large-scale resource extraction; and speculation in land through old and new financial instruments such as real estate investment trusts (REITs), pension funds, hedge funds and other asset management tools.

'Known unknowns and known knowns': the scope, pace and causes of modern land takings in Asia

As already indicated, all over the world, the modern taking of large swaths of land – whether legally or illegally – is often linked to host states' push for modernization or economic development. This, many say, is best achieved through industrialization and urbanization, by attracting FDI, and ultimately through being integrated into the global economy – especially by participating in supply chain capitalism (Graham 2004; Ota 2003), often through special economic zones (Carter and Harding 2011). This development model has been tried in many countries, and its success – especially in Asia – is widely acclaimed (World Bank 2008b). One only has to think of China or Vietnam during the past three decades, and of the Asian tigers before them which the World Bank proclaimed the 'East Asian miracles' (World Bank 1993).

However, what constitutes 'development' is rarely agreed upon within each state, and its costs are rarely quantified. An analysis of this topic is beyond the scope of this chapter, but what is known and can be observed globally is that development often involves taking lands occupied and used by traditional smallholder farmers and indigenous peoples, or lands that provide an important ecosystem service, and putting them into the service of big investment projects which are incentivized or operated by wealthy local elite, corporate or government-led entities, sovereign wealth funds, multilateral institutions such as the Organisation for Economic Co-operation and Development (OECD), World Bank, and other United Nations (UN) bodies such as the Food and Agriculture Organization (FAO), and so on.

What is also known is that the land takings and conversions are extensive, growing rapidly and often lead to forced evictions, human rights violations, lost livelihoods, divided communities, and destruction of culturally significant sites, wetlands, wildlife refuges and other ecosystems (Action Aid 2014; Cotula 2012; Anseeuw *et al.* 2012; Oxfam 2013; TNI 2012; Zoomers 2010; Cotula *et al.* 2009; Grain 2008). In some areas, air and water pollution and other environmental damage are rampant (Weis 2010).

However, so far, the scope, pace and extent of large-scale land deals and land grabs have eluded serious empirical investigation. First, as indicated above, there is no consensus on what constitutes land grabs and land deals. Second, even if there were consensus on the definition, there is no known methodology – how and what would we count?

Grain, a Spanish-based NGO, was first to monitor and attempt to quantify land grabbing and so-called legitimate land transfer cases based on media reports. Its report (Grain 2008) documents land transactions at various stages of negotiations, but was unable to provide an accurate, comprehensive picture since many cases are not reported in the media. Besides, it remains unclear whether any or how many of the 'legitimate land transfers' or 'land deals' would be rendered 'land grabs' because they violated any of the Tirana Declaration stipulations discussed above.

Similarly, as mentioned above, the Land Matrix database seeks to record all land deals of 200 hectares or more that 'imply the potential conversion of land from smallholder production, local community use or important ecosystem service provision to commercial use'. However, the *average size* of land contracts recorded on its database when accessed in July 2014 was 8,701 hectares. The database itself admits that it is not a true reflection of reality: numbers change frequently, deals get cancelled, some are never reported to begin with, and some fail. Besides, as Smaller and Mann (2009) point out, the contracts for acquiring land, whether by purchase, lease or concession, are often not disclosed at all, and those which are, are not transparent. It is therefore difficult, if not impossible, to evaluate accurately the scope, pace, extent and even exact location of land deals/grabs.

Cotula's (2012) critical study served only to confirm the confusion, since all sources and fact gathering, and therefore conclusions, reflected varying time spans and different definitions of land grabs and land deals. For example, the World Bank (2011) estimated that, worldwide, about 40 million hectares were under large-scale land deals (while claiming that over 440 million hectares are 'available'[3]). The estimate of the International Land Coalition (2011) puts land deals at 80 million hectares, while Oxfam's (2013) estimate is 227 million hectares. Thus Cotula's study concluded that 'the phenomenon is massive and growing' (Cotula 2012: 33). It is estimated that about 40 percent of these acquisitions relate to sub-Saharan Africa, while just over 30 percent of documented land deals occur in South-East Asia (Action Aid 2014). However, Action Aid's source is Land Matrix, which admits to having somewhat unreliable data.

If quantifying the known targets of investment is (relatively) unknown, then perhaps we can know who the investors are with greater certainty. From the Land Matrix website, we know that the top five investors countries of origin for all concluded land investments – domestically and globally – are the USA (with 7.09 million hectares), Malaysia (3.35 million hectares), the UK (2.96 million hectares), United Arab Emirates (2.82 million hectares), and India (1.99 million hectares). Singapore is next with 1.88 million hectares, while China features tenth with only 1.34 million hectares, despite its popular-press image as neo-colonial rogue land grabber number one. It is unknown whether these relatively low China numbers are genuine or whether the real ones are shrouded in secrecy, since it is well known that many Sino-foreign contracts and transactions are undisclosed. Besides, do the statistics focus on land acquired solely for large-scale agriculture and ignore land acquired for other purposes – resource extraction and SEZs, for example? This too is an unknown, although the World Bank's (2011) study suggests that their statistics reflect only land acquired for investment in industrialized agriculture. The next section attempts to untangle the drivers of large-scale land acquisition.

Known knowns: drivers and context

A report written by Schaffnit-Chatterjee (2012) for Deutsche Bank Research, puts investors in large-scale agricultural land into three categories: 1 governments seeking to acquire land in other countries in order to secure food and energy supplies; 2 agricultural companies and agribusinesses seeking to expand or to integrate into the supply chain; and 3 financial investors, who – in light of the 2007–08 financial meltdown – see land as a safer object of investment than stocks and bonds, because as Mark Twain allegedly said, 'buy land; they don't make it any more' (although Singapore public servants might disagree).

Clearly, the German report has followed the popular framing, and focused on the acquisition of agricultural land predominantly for use in large-scale farming or land speculation. However, as subsequent chapters of this book show, in addition to these land- and revenue-seeking investors, there are many investments from other sectors such as tourism, the extractive industries, timber plantations, industrial parks, infrastructure development and so on.

However, in terms of foreign *incentives*, Schaffnit-Chatterjee's observations are probably correct: the main drivers are related to industrialized agriculture and food security. For in recent years the global North, aided and abetted by international aid agencies, multilateral banks, think tanks and so on, have found that it suits their purposes to support large-scale industrialized agriculture as the potential solution to poverty in the global South. The example below illustrates this.

The New Vision for Agriculture was launched at the World Economic Forum in 2010 to stimulate public-private partnerships for investment in industrial agriculture. According to Action Aid (2014: 16):

> At a global level New Vision has partnered with the G8 and G20 and facilitated high-level informal dialogues that have spawned subsequent initiatives, such as the New Alliance for Food Security and Nutrition … At the regional and country level, it has catalysed multi-stakeholder partnerships in 14 countries in Africa, Asia and Latin America, including a regional partnership called Grow Africa, that between them have mobilized over USD 5.7 billion in agricultural investment commitments in the next 3–5 years …

Grow Africa (growafrica.com/about) sees itself as:

> … a partnership platform that seeks to accelerate investments and transformative change in African agriculture … [by] supporting partner countries in developing investment blueprints, building a pipeline of investments, and strengthening cross-sector collaboration.

The plan is to establish several large agricultural hubs or 'growth corridors' – are these SEZs for agriculture? – with which to attract foreign investment. In this scenario, the host state, incentivized by foreign donors, will offer a package of FDI incentives including tax breaks, land and regulatory incentives, infrastructure and so on, to attract foreign investors. The plan supports large-scale agriculture in preference to small-scale farming, and 'the pipeline of investments' will lead from G8 and G20 countries to developing nations, or from the global North to the global South with a profit motif as the primary driver and poverty alleviation secondary.

A similar platform is planned for South and South-East Asia, which will be launched under the auspices of the Association of Southeast Asian Nations (ASEAN), to facilitate partnerships for agricultural investments in the region (World Economic Forum 2014 website). So the launch of 'Grow Asia' was probably imminent during the Myanmar presidency of the ASEAN community in 2014. Already in June 2013, the World Economic Forum's New Vision for Agriculture had inaugurated the Myanmar Agriculture Network in which 30 companies and organizations, including government ministries, were charged with the task of exploring potential collaboration on specific crops and other issues (Action Aid 2014: 17). A similar body, the Vietnam Public-Private Task Force on Sustainable Agriculture, was formed in that country in 2010 to focus on tea, coffee, fruit, vegetables and fisheries (ibid.).

One key issue that remains untouched by the new enablers is whether large-scale farming is better for the local population, economically and socially, than small-scale farming. There has been a documented rise in local food insecurity and, ultimately, increased poverty in areas where large-scale industrial agriculture has replaced small-scale farming (Action Aid 2014; TNI 2012). However, causation is always difficult to prove – whether this is because alien monocultures have replaced local botanical species, or because cash crops are grown for export only, or some other reason involving productivity, no one knows for sure. Few empirical studies have been conducted. Peter Gibbon's review of the historical evidence on the productivity and job-creation record of plantations and large-scale farming in twentieth-century sub-Saharan Africa concluded that large-scale farms have not always been less productive, or less labour absorbing than small farms but that they generally provided lower-quality employment (Gibbon 2011). Anecdotal evidence in some Asian countries suggests that promises of jobs for the displaced farmers and communities rarely materialize – see, for example, Chapter 7 of this volume on Myanmar, and Chapter 10 on Vietnam.

The debate about large- versus small-scale farming is ongoing and, as discussed in White *et al.* (2012: 625–26), has its roots in a wider political discourse between Marxists and agrarian populists (Lenin 1960 [1899]; Chayanov 1966 [1925]), which influenced most of the debate in the 1970s, 1980s and beyond. A discussion is beyond the scope of this chapter; however, suffice it to say that, as yet, there are no winners or losers (of the debate), and even the World Bank is riding both horses as its much criticized[4] reports, *Agriculture for Development* (World Bank 2008a) and the follow-up, *Rising Interest in Global Farmland: Can it Yield Sustainable and Equitable Benefits?* (World Bank 2011), attest.

It has been argued that 'only large farms or smallholder out-growers hooked into large agribusiness nuclei can compete, and meet the standards required for successful export' (White *et al.* 2012: 626). Many advocates of large-scale corporate land deals envisage the development of a dualistic agrarian economy in which large-scale farms engage in 'capitalist production often for export, while smallholder farms gradually disappear or are incorporated as part of contract-farming arrangements, with the former peasantry proletarianized, providing low paid labour to the new estates and plantations' (ibid.: 625). Either way, many governments in developing countries seem to be convinced that their agricultural futures lie in one form or other of industrialized farming, in which they revert to the old well-tried colonial role of supplier to the metropolis.

Finally, it has been said that these interventions often result in a breakdown in community relationships and confuse the roles of family members (Feldman and Geisler 2012; Kenny-Lazar 2012). Women, who in many countries undertake most of the household food production, are often left far worse off than they were before the land was taken and converted to large-scale farming or other 'development' projects (White and White 2012; Sustainable Development Solutions Network 2013). This dispossession of women is particularly unfortunate since it comes at a time when most UN agencies, civil society and others agree that the empowerment of women is a key to poverty alleviation in the global South.

Domestic laws, international laws, hard laws, soft laws: which laws are relevant?

From the foregoing, it is obvious that we are witnessing the commodification of land, and an industrialization of agriculture nationally and globally. The question that this book poses is, what role is there for the law? Each chapter that follows provides nuanced and diverse answers. First, though, the next section gives an overview of which laws are relevant and might be applicable in these circumstances of mixed domestic and global land transactions and possible land grabs.

It is commonly known that many countries in the global South have weak legal institutions and even weaker land governance regimes. Indeed, this fact is probably one of the drivers of land takings and their rapid increase. For instance, as nearly all the chapters illustrate, but especially Cambodia (Chapter 5), Myanmar (Chapter 7), Malaysia (Chapters 8 and 9) and Vietnam (Chapter 10), countries whose legal systems are characterized by weak, ill-defined or unclear land rights for occupiers and customary land users, and weak, unclear or insufficiently robust laws governing water rights, the environment, human rights and so on, are most vulnerable to unjust land takings or takings with impunity.

Ironically, a perceived weak domestic regulatory regime is also one reason why foreign investors demand the cushion supplied by international law. As discussed below, foreign investors often have opportunities to get protection many times over, namely through their international commercial contracts (often signed with governments of states, or other state entities), and through international investment agreements (IIAs) such as bilateral investment treaties (BITs), which are biased in favour of foreign investors.[5]

Four main sources of law are relevant to land-related foreign investments and development. These are: 1 domestic law; 2 international investment contracts; 3 international investment agreements; and 4 international human rights conventions. Smaller and Mann (2009: 8–19) provide an overview of the first three and illustrate ways in which those sources might interact to mediate risk for the foreign investor, often to the detriment of the host state and the subsistence farmer. However, much depends on the wording of the contracts that have been agreed between the parties, leaving Smaller and Mann to admit that 'few concrete conclusions can be drawn because agricultural investment contracts are not publicly available' (ibid.). The following section builds on their analysis. However, for a more nuanced discussion of international law response to land grabbing in Asia, and an analysis of how states could be held responsible for human rights violations resulting from global land grabs, see Chapters 2 and 11, respectively, in this volume.

Domestic law

It is obvious that in the context of land, FDI and development, a sovereign state will have, or at least will need to have, an array of domestic laws designed to regulate a range of issues relating to property rights (even though, as Chapter 3 shows, China did not have a property law until 2007), contractual rights, foreign investment incentives, tax, infrastructure, the environment, and workers' health, safety and well-being, etc.

As the subsequent chapters illustrate, all states in the case studies have enacted numerous laws that make provisions for most of these domestic issues. Indeed, most states start promisingly by declaring the protection of property and other rights in their constitution. However, as the findings document, for example in the case of China (Chapter 3), Cambodia (Chapter 5) and Myanmar (Chapter 7), it is often the actual design of these laws that creates pathways for land grabbing by the local elite or other agents of foreign and domestic investors. In other cases, for instance in China (Chapter 4) and Malaysia (Chapters 8 and 9), enforcement is the issue, since statutory provisions do exist but they are often ignored and can remain unenforced since government agencies, judicial institutions and sometimes even the plaintiffs collude to bypass formal law. Sometimes, as in the case of Myanmar (Chapter 7) and Vietnam (Chapter 10), it is the laws themselves that appear to be inappropriate or unjust, as they provide state officials with unbridled discretion for implementation and enforcement.

International investment contracts

As is the case in every country, a contract will set out all the details of the land transaction agreed between the contracting parties: that is, the host state entity and the foreign investor. Apart from the obvious issues of price, quantity and duration, the contract will probably also include terms regarding incentives such as tax holidays, exemptions from import duties on equipment, export of production, arrangements to hire expatriate staff, foreign currency management, repatriation of profits, environmental protection, workplace safety, labour conditions, jurisdiction, form of dispute resolution, and so on. In any event, domestic law will apply where the contract is silent.

However, as discussed below, there are huge advantages to being a foreign investor as opposed to being a domestic one, and this has given rise to nationality shopping. For example, a Chinese investor who registers in the United Kingdom and returns to China to invest as a foreign investor is entitled to legal protection and dispute settlement under an international tribunal or under the laws of England and Wales.

Sometimes a contract between a foreign investor and a host state includes a so-called stabilization clause, which is a risk-management device that investors insert in investment contracts. As Smaller and Mann (2009) explain:

> These are clauses … that either preclude the application of, or require compensation for, new or changed regulatory measures that affect the investment. They may apply for a certain period, or for the full life of the contract and any renewal period.

The use of stabilization clauses is more prevalent in the global South than in the global North, and they are widespread across all sectors of industry (Shemberg 2009: v). In her comprehensive study, Shemberg found that many stabilization clauses:

> … were drafted in a way that can either insulate investors from having to implement new environmental and social laws or to provide investors with an opportunity to be compensated for compliance with such laws.
>
> (Shemberg 2009: v)

She also found that none of the contracts that she analysed from OECD countries offered exemptions from new laws, and that they very rarely allowed an opportunity for the other party to seek compensation for compliance with the same breadth of social and environmental laws as offered in non-OECD countries (Shemberg 2009). This obvious imbalance has caused many developing countries to question the propriety and utility of including such clauses. They have become so hated, that some people have dubbed them 'stabilization curses' (Okinabirhie n.d.). On the other hand, it could be argued that these clauses are inserted to help manage the risk of investing in unstable environments with weak rule of law, and this would not apply to OECD countries. So perhaps instead of seeking to eliminate stabilization clauses altogether, they should be rendered inapplicable to laws that are introduced specifically to meet universally recognized goals such as environmental protection, workplace safety and so on.

International investment agreements

IIAs are treaties between states which can be bilateral, multilateral or regional. Their objective is to provide special legal protection to investors of one state that invest in the territory of another state, or states in the case of multilateral agreements. The most popular IIAs are BITs between two states. These have proliferated in recent years – so much so, that according to

Akhtar and Weiss (2013), well over 3,000 have been signed, even though not all are in force. In addition, there are many free trade agreements (FTAs), which are regional trade agreements such as the North American Free Trade Agreement (NAFTA), ASEAN, the European Union (EU, which has grown into a political union), and so on. Still on the drawing board are FTAs such as the Trans-Pacific Partnership (TPP) and the Transatlantic Trade and Investment Partnership (TTIP). What most IIAs, especially the newer BITs, seem to have in common is an incorporation of the Chapter 11 or similar investment protection clause that was created for NAFTA, the 1994 FTA between the USA, Canada and Mexico. Many developing countries that have signed BITs seem to have lost their appetite for them because of the onerous nature of these clauses, and because they find it difficult to comply with some of the general provisions and principles of the World Trade Organization (WTO) treaty, which are incorporated into IIAs. For a discussion, see Smaller and Mann (2009); Sauvant and Sachs (2009); and Mann (2013, 2008, 2003).

International human rights conventions

International human rights conventions relate to land grabbing and foreign investment both directly and indirectly. As Subedi argues in Chapter 2 of this volume, at its founding, the Universal Declaration of Human Rights (UDHR) recognized all individuals' right to property. However, Cold War politics resulted in the International Bill of Human Rights (the International Covenant on Civil and Political Rights, or ICCPR, and the International Covenant on Economic, Social and Cultural Rights, or ICESCR) not guaranteeing the right to property. No other international human rights treaty guarantees the right to property either.

However, upon close reading, many lawyers may agree that Article 17 of the UDHR provides international recognition of land grabs as a violation of the basic human right not to be arbitrarily deprived of property. As the UDHR has acquired the character of customary international law (CIL), it is binding on all states. Indeed, as Subedi relates in Chapter 2, '[w]hen the 192 UN nations met in New York in 2005, they agreed that the UDHR was a binding legal document'.

The problem is that many cases, for example as Fitzpatrick points out in Chapter 5 with regard to land grabs in Cambodia, involve *ab initio denial* of land rights rather than arbitrary deprivation of rights recognized by law. Those occupying land are often classified as illegal occupiers with no *de jure* property rights for arbitrary deprivation. Or, as is the case in Myanmar (Chapter 7) the land itself is reclassified so that *de facto* occupiers become illegal and are evicted, sometimes forcibly.

Similarly, as Chapters 8 and 9 attest in the case of Malaysia, the application of other international human rights law such as the 2007 UN Declaration on the Rights of Indigenous Peoples is questioned. Article 10 clearly states:

> Indigenous peoples shall not be forcibly removed from their lands or territories. No relocation shall take place without free, prior and informed consent of the indigenous peoples concerned and after agreement on just and fair compensation and, where possible, with the option of return.

However, such clear statements are regularly ignored by member states that have ratified the instruments because they remain non-binding.

The 1979 UN Convention Eliminating all forms of Discrimination against Women (CEDAW), the UN Convention on Biodiversity, and the UN Convention against Corruption, are all potentially applicable in this area. All of these (with the exception of the Convention on Biodiversity) are regarded as soft law instruments, and they do not have an effect unless or until their principles are enshrined in domestic law. Even when enacted as hard law mechanisms, such rules and regulations are and often will be difficult to enforce in many developing countries.

Finally, there is a host of voluntary guidelines which, if followed, can help mediate some of the dire human rights consequences of land grabbing. The most prominent among them (discussed in Chapter 2) is the UN Guiding Principles on Business and Human Rights, which the UN Human Rights Council (HRC) unanimously agreed upon in 2011. It is also called the UN's Protect, Respect, Remedy Framework, as it asserts three pillars: the state's *duty to protect* against human rights abuses, the corporate responsibility to *respect* the human rights of all peoples, and the parties' obligation to ensure access to effective remedies when protection fails.

However, like all other voluntary codes of conduct, compliance is not guaranteed, which is why '[i]n September 2013 Ecuador proposed that the UN Human Rights Council establish an intergovernmental working group to negotiate … a treaty instrument, and some 600 NGOs formed a "treaty alliance" to support it' (Ruggie 2014: 8). The HRC adopted the proposal on 26 June 2014, and negotiations were expected to start in 2015. However, as Ruggie explains, success will not be easy, if it is achieved at all.

Another important international soft law instrument is the Voluntary Guidelines on Responsible Governance on Tenure of Land, Fisheries and Forests in the Context of National Food Security, which was adopted by the UN Committee on World Food Security in May 2012. The use of these guidelines could also help. For example, paragraph 3(2) requires that:

> States, in accordance with their international obligations, should provide access to effective judicial remedies for negative impacts on human rights and legitimate tenure rights by business enterprises. Where transnational corporations are involved, their home States have roles to play in assisting both those corporations and host States to ensure that businesses are not involved in abuse of human rights and legitimate tenure rights. States should take additional steps to protect against abuses of human rights and legitimate tenure rights by business enterprises that are owned or

> controlled by the State, or that receive substantial support and service from State agencies.

However, as discussed, voluntary principles and codes are often ignored by the contracting parties when land transactions are being negotiated or enforced.

Seeing the future through the past: neo-colonialism and English enclosures

Land grabbing is nothing new. The biggest land grabs known in recent history were perpetrated by European colonialists who, starting in the fifteenth century, ventured to far-away lands and claimed them as their own – often with little or no compensation, regularly with violence, resistance and social conflict. This includes the dispossession of native peoples in the Americas, Canada, Africa and Australasia. When Vasco da Gama found a new trading route to Asia, by rounding the Cape of Good Hope, he started what would become a four and a half-century Western domination of Asia. World War II heralded withdrawal, but by then the impact and changes had been embedded. Land had been seized and transferred using processes not unlike the English enclosure system, discussed below. In most Asian countries, prior to colonial settlement, land was held in common by the community, the clan or the family under customary tenure. The Western concept of individual property rights as it relates to land was alien to most Asian communities; although, as Chapter 10 shows, that was not the case in Vietnam, where individual land rights were recognized in Imperial times – a practice that French colonialists continued and built upon until it was overthrown by socialist ideology and laws. As Quizon (2013: 9) explains:

> The colonial powers introduced systems of land administration and land-based revenue collection in order to support the costs of colonial expansion … Vast lands outside of permanent settlements and permanently cultivated areas were brought under foreign ownership or declared to be 'public domains'. Landholdings carved out from these domains were then brought under state-controlled cultivation, or else sold or leased for use as private plantations. The introduction of new land registration systems further disenfranchised and marginalized local populations.

However, there is also abundant evidence of occupied land being classified as 'unowned', so that by default, the state became the legal owner (Wily 2012), which then sold or leased the land to private players (mostly foreign) for large-scale farm plantations. When the colonial powers withdrew after World War II, the newly independent nations, assisted by the World Bank and other development agencies, introduced land reforms. These helped to convert most of the colonial-held lands into state property, which was then redistributed to tenants and landless workers, sometimes with the objective of forming relatively homogenous small family farms (Ghose 1983), and sometimes as the first step towards socialist collectives. In some cases, the newly available land was used as a tool for patronage to the local elite.

During the 1950s and most of the second half of the twentieth century, the World Bank supported the breakup of large corporate, colonial-style plantations in favour of small, native farmer-based agricultural development strategies. However, those policies and strategies in favour of small-scale farmers were reversed during the 1980s and 1990s as the World Bank, International Monetary Fund and other agencies put in place structural adjustment and neoliberal reform programmes designed to curb the energy-related indebtedness of the global South and countries of the former Soviet Union.

Such programmes promoted new, market-driven, free-trade enclosures and the privatization of state-owned or state-supported farms, large and small. Privatization and the new free-trade mantra triggered the spate of land transactions experienced during the 1980s and 1990s, when many multinational companies, driven by the notion of comparative advantage, invested in large-scale production of indigenous crops for export, and established mechanisms such as 'contract farming'[6] and factories that served the needs of industrialized agriculture.

The investments and land grabs that are being experienced now, and which accelerated during 2007–08, are more akin to the immediate post-World War II foreign takings and deals. According to Peluso and Lund (2011: 672), the only aspects that are new or different in today's land grabs are the 'mechanisms of land control, their justifications and alliances for "taking back" the land, as well as the political economic context of neo-liberalism'.

Another dimension is that after four and a half centuries of colonialism, many peoples of those previously exploited lands still suffer the trauma of upheaval and dispossession and the repercussions of social, economic, political and other displacements (Wily 2012; Woodhouse 2012; Tanner 2010). For, as Upham (2014: 36) points out:

> … land not only has economic value … but also provides the basis for social relations and in many ways constitutes those relationships through the creation of individual, group, and community identities.

This is as true today as it was during colonialism. For even when they are conducted legally, most large-scale land transfers can create havoc among the usually close-knit groups and communities of people whose livelihoods are being transformed to make way for the new. Several chapters in this book bear witness to this phenomenon.

In an ironic twist, in the modern-day versions of land grabbing, the offspring of some of the previous victims of colonial land grabs are now the perpetrators. For instance, during the past decade and a half, multinational companies from Malaysia, China, India, Japan, South Korea and Singapore have led the way in large-scale land acquisitions in other Asian countries as well as in Africa and South America. While many of these land acquisitions were undoubtedly made in legal contracts of purchase or long-term leases and concessions, some were undoubtedly made or implemented under dubious circumstances and therefore would qualify as land grabs under our definition. The problem is that the lack of transparency and the non-disclosure of these contracts also prevent serious study and consideration of their legality or the perceived illegitimacy of these land transactions.

However, colonialism is not the only historical example of land grabbing. Even at home in England, land grabbing through the 'enclosure' system was well under way during the seventeenth century. In common usage, 'enclosure' literally meant encircling or shutting off a piece of land with a hedge, fence or wall so that its new 'owner' gained sole control over its use and access to it.[7] This often involved the removal of communal rights, and in the earliest days, the land was also enclosed through mutual agreement among villagers. It is worth spending a little time to understand the English enclosure system, for its implementation is reminiscent of what currently happens in rural areas throughout many Asian countries.

In the Middle Ages in England, an open field system of agriculture operated whereby each small farmer farmed several narrow strips of land scattered around the village, in large, unfenced fields, supplemented by common or community-owned wasteland used for grazing, fishing, hunting, foraging and so on.

However, if at least 75 percent of the villagers agreed, community land could be fenced, and individual farmers could swap their strips so as to bring them together into large plots to be controlled by one farmer. If such agreement was reached, a petition was drawn up asking Parliament to pass an Enclosure Act for that particular village. A notice would be posted on the church door to inform all villagers of the intention to enclose. During the seventeenth century and beyond such local agreements became very popular and were supported by individual Acts of Parliament. Studies show that the enclosure procedure itself was conducive to collusion, cronyism and widespread abuse by small- and large-scale farmers and officials in charge of implementing the enclosures (Thompson 1963). It is not difficult to imagine how small farmers could be coerced into giving up their strips of land and getting promises of jobs or smaller, less fertile strips in return; or how villagers could be coerced into agreeing to enclosure of village lands, to ensure the required 75 percent approval.

Enclosures, whether by mutual agreement or individual Acts of Parliament, are therefore a good example of large-scale land grabbing, facilitated by legislation. By the eighteenth century, Parliament regulated all enclosures – a separate Enclosure Act was required for each village that 'wished' to enclose its land. Indeed the decade between 1770 and 1780 saw no fewer than 660 Enclosure Acts in England. However, in 1801, Parliament passed the General

Enclosure Act, which allowed any English village to enclose its land where 75 percent of the landowners agreed.

According to Quizon (2013: 11), 'Asia is home to 75 percent of the world's farming households, 80 percent of whom are small-scale farmers and producers'. It is not difficult to imagine how parallels to the enclosure system, including coercion and widespread dispossession, would work in these Asian rural environments. Indeed, the chapters on Myanmar (Chapter 7), Indonesia (Chapter 6) and Malaysia (Chapters 8 and 9) give examples of modern-day enclosure procedures.

Conclusion and recommendations

As a universal definition of land grabbing remains elusive, this chapter has sought to provide a definition that is more nuanced than popular mainstream media allow. It has also aimed to provide greater legal clarity to assist in the future framing of the phenomenon with the aim of prevention.

Large contractual deals for land, incentivized and facilitated by host states in the global South, supported by players from the global North and the political elite at home in the global South, are problematic because they are often negotiated and concluded in secrecy, they cause widespread displacement of rural communities and small-scale farmers, often without consultation, consent and compensation or safeguards for alternative livelihoods. Since the contracts are often not disclosed to the public, they cannot be analysed and the lack of access creates uncertainties and raises questions about their legality. In many cases, governments of host states use domestic law as a pathway that facilitates land grabs by reclassifying various forms of occupied land as wasteland, farmland, state land or land required for development for the public good. With the new classification in hand, such land can then be allocated for other projects, including 'development' and what the World Bank (2011) claims is land 'available' for industrialized agriculture – with no safeguards for the occupiers who will be displaced and dispossessed.

International law also plays crucial roles in regulating contractual relationships between state parties and foreign investors, and as a mechanism for preventing or remedying human rights violations. However, while international contracts and treaties provide ample legal protection for foreign investors, soft law mechanisms for preventing or remedying human rights violations related to land grabs are often ignored and remain unenforced. The hope is that corporations and other entities will apply voluntary corporate social responsibility (CSR) initiatives and self-regulate their way to providing social and environmental justice.

However, policy makers cannot afford to trust in hope alone. The next section is an attempt to share lessons and experiences that policy makers in Asia might wish to consider and adopt in an effort to facilitate sustainable development in their countries. The recommendations draw on discourses from a range of stakeholders in Asian countries – scholars, debaters and concerned citizens of the world, among them De Schutter (2011), Action Aid (2014), Peters (2013), Smaller and Mann (2009), White *et al.* (2012), Woods (2014) and the World Bank (2011). History should not be allowed to repeat itself by merely replacing old colonial players in land enclosure games with neo-colonial ones. The style and substance of what is deemed 'development' and the implementing tools must be redefined and transformed to accommodate a focus on what is equitable and sustainable. Specifically, this means that governments should:

1 Not use law to deny or erode people's rights to customary and traditional communal lands. On the contrary, governments should use law to recognize and institutionalize customary land rights within communities where they operate. For example, governments in India, Nepal and the Philippines have enacted and are implementing new laws and policies that define and recognize community land rights. A beneficial outcome of recognizing customary land regimes can be the perpetuation of good husbandry and ecosystem management knowledge, the use of which will likely result in more sustainable development.
2 Move towards more inclusive and equitable governance and sharing of natural resources and the profits gained from their exploitation. This means respecting, securing and enforcing land tenure and property rights of all stakeholders and engaging in free, prior, informed consent for all projects that involve land use.
3 Use law to ensure that those in occupation of land cannot be arbitrarily denied their right to occupy, and that they cannot be arbitrarily deprived of their property rights.
4 Not provide incentives for foreign investments that fuel land grabs for large-scale agriculture, extractive industries and so on. Incentives should be employed to establish pilot projects designed to help local farmers improve their farming methods and sustainable ecosystem management techniques.
5 Demand the reform of the international legal framework for FDI, and recognize the links between FDI and sustainable development, which the current regime of IIAs undermines.
6 Reconsider the overall utility of signing IIAs and providing incentives for FDI, since there is consensus in the literature suggesting that the effect of IIAs in attracting investment into the global South is minimal at best, and more likely non-existent (UNCTAD 2009; Sauvant and Sachs 2009; Hallward-Driemeier 2003).
7 Demonstrate zero tolerance for land grabs and put in place a mechanism that dis-incentivizes and punishes corruption among its agents.
8 Reconsider the 'one size fits all' proposals of the World Bank, the OECD and other international agencies. The evidence that large-scale farming produces better and more sustainable outcomes than small-scale farming is scant to non-existent. Therefore, as De Schutter (2011) suggests,

governments should develop strategies in which they reorient agricultural investment away from industrialized agriculture towards small-scale family farms and local markets.

9 Reject the World Bank's analysis and recommendations based on 'yield gap' calculations which, as White *et al.* (2012: 638) explain, are flawed since they 'compare the productivity of long-neglected, resource- and infra-structure-starved peasantries with that of well-supported high-input agriculture'. Instead, governments should focus on 'the really relevant comparison: comparing the productivity, employment potential and long term sustainability of industrial capitalist agriculture with that of a well-supported smallholder farming' (ibid.).
10 Ensure participation and inclusiveness by consulting with *all stakeholders* before starting any new projects that will affect the livelihoods and social status of the occupiers of land.
11 Stop authorization of any project that violates the principles of the Tirana Declaration on land grabs.
12 Put on hold any project that risks violating the principles of the Tirana Declaration, until suitable laws and policies derived from the Tenure Guidelines can be implemented to protect the land rights of communities and women.
13 Publish all contracts for large-scale land transactions, and ensure transparency of all land deals.
14 Ensure fair, democratic and professional oversight of large-scale land transactions during all phases of acquisition, including representation of all affected parties and stakeholders.
15 Listen to those who protest the illegal taking of land. Make safe spaces for them and ensure that they are not intimidated, and that their rights to free speech and assembly are not encroached upon.
16 Submit to project monitoring by civil society groups, ensuring safe spaces for them to conduct advocacy concerning land grabbing issues.

Notes

1 An exception is India's Andhra Pradesh Land Grabbing (Prohibition) Act, 1982, where Section 2(d) defines 'land grabber', while Section 2(f) defines land grabbing as: '… every activity of grabbing of any land belonging to the government, local authority, religious or charitable institution or endowment including wakf or any other private person, by a person or group of persons without any lawful entitlement and with a view to possess illegally or enter into or create illegal tenancies or lease and license agreements in respect of such lands, or to construct unauthorized structures thereon for sale or hire or give such lands to any person on rental or lease and license basis for construction or use and occupation of unauthorized structures and the term "to grab land" shall be construed accordingly.'

2 The International Land Coalition is a global alliance of civil society and farmers' organizations, United Nations agencies, NGOs and research institutes. According to its website, it comprises about '152 organisations representing 56 countries,

working together to promote secure and equitable access to land for rural people, mainly through capacity building, knowledge sharing and advocacy'. See www.landcoalition.org/en/who-we-are/history (accessed September 2014).

3 The World Bank's controversial designation of 'available' land is based on an analysis of 'currently non-cultivated area suitable for cropping that is nonforested, nonprotected, and populated with less [sic] than 25 persons/km^2 (or 20 ha/household) …' (World Bank 2011: xxxiv). There is no mention of safeguards for those fewer than 25 persons/km^2 who currently occupy the land.

4 For criticism, see, for example, Akram-Lodhi 2008; Oya 2009; Li 2009; Borras *et al.* 2007; and White *et al.* 2012.

5 For an excellent analysis of the evolution of international investment treaties, see Mann 2013.

6 Contract farming is an agreement between farmers or farming collectives on one side and processing or marketing firms on the other, for the production and supply of agricultural produce under forward contracts, usually at set prices. For a discussion, see FAO 2001.

7 For a discussion and historical perspective, see Sharman 1989; Kain *et al.* 1975; Neeson 1993; Thompson 1963; Yelling 1977.

References

Action Aid (2014) *The Great Land Heist: How the World is Paving the Way for Corporate Land Grabs*, Johannesburg, South Africa: Action Aid International.

African Union (2009) *Declaration on Land Issues and Challenges in Africa, Assembly of the African Union, Thirteenth Ordinary Session*, Doc. Assembly/AU/Decl.1(XIII), 1–3 July.

Akhtar, S.I. and Weiss, M.A. (2013) *US International Agreements: Issues for Congress*, Washington, DC: Congressional Research Service.

Akram-Lodhi, H. (2008) '(Re)imagining Agrarian Relation? The World Development Report 2008: Agriculture for Development', *Development and Change* 39(6): 1145.

Anseeuw, W., Alden Wily, L., Cotula, L. and Taylor, M. (2012) *Land Rights and the Rush for Land: Findings of the Global Commercial Pressures on Land Research Project*, Rome: International Land Coalition.

Borras, S.M. and Franco, J.C. (2010a) 'Contemporary Discourses and Contestations around Pro-poor Land Policies and Land Governance', *Journal of Agrarian Change* 10(1): 1–32.

Borras, S.M. and Franco, J.C. (2010b) 'From Threat to Opportunity? Problems with the Idea of a "Code of Conduct" for Land-grabbing', *Yale Human Rights and Development Law Journal* 13: 507–523.

Borras, S., Kay, C. and Lahiff, E., eds (2007) *Market-led Agrarian Reform: A Critique*, London: Routledge.

Carter, C. and Harding, H., eds (2011) *Special Economic Zones in Asian Market Economies*, London and New York: Routledge.

Chayanov, A. (1966 [1925]) *The Theory of Peasant Economy*, Homewood, IL: American Economic Association.

Cotula, L. (2012) 'The International Political Economy of the Global Land Rush: A Critical Appraisal of Trends, Scale, Geography and Drivers', *Journal of Peasant Studies* 39(3–4).

Cotula, L., Vermeulen, S., Leonard, R. and Keeley, J. (2009) *Land Grab or Development Opportunity? Agricultural Investment and International Land Deals in Africa*, Rome and London: UN FAO.

De Schutter, O. (2011) 'How Not to Think about Land Grabbing: Three Critiques of Large-scale Investments in Farmland', *The Journal of Peasant Studies* 38(2): 249–279.

FAO (2001) *Contract Farming: Partnerships for Growth*, UN Food and Agriculture Organization.

Feldman, S. and Geisler, C. (2012) 'Land Expropriation and Displacement in Bangladesh', *Journal of Peasant Studies* 39(3–4): 971–994.

Fu, H. and Gillespie, J., eds (2014) *Resolving Land Disputes in East Asia: Exploring the Limits of Law*, Cambridge: Cambridge University Press.

Ghose, A. (1983) *Agrarian Reform in Contemporary Developing Countries*, London: Palgrave Macmillan.

Gibbon, P. (2011) *Experiences of Plantation and Large-scale Farming in 20th Century Africa*, Working Paper 2011: 20, Copenhagen: Danish Institute for International Studies.

Graham, E. (2004) 'Do Export Processing Zones Attract FDI and its Benefits? The Experience from China', *International Economics and Economic Policy* 1: 87–103.

Grain (2008) 'Seized! The 2008 Land Grab for Food and Financial Security', www.grain.org/briefings_files-2008-en.pdf.

Hallward-Driemeier, M. (2003) *Do Bilateral Investment Treaties Attract Foreign Direct Investment? Only a Bit and they Could Bite*, World Bank Policy Research Working Paper 3121, papers.ssrn.com/sol3/papers.cfm?abstract_id=636541.

International Land Coalition (2011) *Tirana Declaration*, www.landcoalition.org/about-us/aom2011/tirana-declaration.

Kain, R.J.P., Chapman, J. and Oliver, R.R. (1975) *The Enclosure Maps of England and Wales, 1595–1918*, Cambridge: Cambridge University Press.

Kenny-Lazar, M. (2012) 'Plantation Rubber, Land Grabbing, and Social Property Transformation in Southern Laos', *Journal of Peasant Studies* 39(3–4): 1017–1038.

Kramer, T. and Woods, K. (2012) *Financing Dispossession: China's Opium Substitution Program in Northern Burma*, Transnational Institute (TNI).

Lenin, V. (1960 [1899]) *The Development of Capitalism in Russia*, Volume 3, *Collected Works*, London: Lawrence & Wishart.

Li, T., ed. (2009) 'Forum: Reading the World Development Report: Agriculture for Development', *Journal for Peasant Studies* 36(3): 591–661.

Mann, H. (2003) *International Investment Agreements: Building the New Colonialism?* 97 ASIL Proc. 247.

Mann, H. (2008) *International Investment Agreements, Business and Human Rights: Key Issues and Opportunities*, International Institute for Sustainable Development (IISD).

Mann, H. (2013) 'Reconceptualizing International Investment Law: Its Role in Sustainable Development', *Lewis & Clarke Law Review* 17(2): 521–544.

McElroy, W. (2012) 'The Future of Freedom Foundation, "The Enclosure Acts and The Industrial Revolution"', WEB, 23 April 2014.

Neeson, J. (1993) *Commoners: Common Rights, Enclosure and Social Change in England 1700–1820*, Cambridge: Cambridge University Press.

Okinabirhie, T.O. (n.d.) 'A Stabilization Clause or a Stabilization Curse? A Look at the Effect of Stabilization Clauses on Host Countries by Measuring the Effect of the LNG Act on the Nigerian Economy', University of Dundee.

Osborne, M. (1986) *China's Special Economic Zones*, Geneva: OECD.
Ota, T. (2003) *Industrial Policy in a Transitional Economy: The Role of China's SEZs in Economic Development*, Tokyo: Tokyo University.
Oxfam (2013) *Poor Governance, Good Business: How Land Investors Target Countries*, February, www.oxfam.org/en/grow/pressroom/pressrelease/2013-02-07/poorly-governed-countries-targeted-land-investors#sthash.y7r4PPFH.dpuf.
Oya, C. (2009) 'The World Development Report 2008: Inconsistencies, Silences, and the Myth of Win-win Scenarios', *Journal of Peasant Studies* 36(3): 593–601.
Peluso, N. and Lund, C. (2011) 'New Frontiers of Land Control: Introduction', *Journal of Peasant Studies* 38(4): 667–681.
Peters, P. (2013) 'Land Appropriation, Surplus People and a Battle Over Visions of Agrarian Futures in Africa', *Journal of Peasant Studies* 40(3): 537–562.
Quizon, A. (2013) *Land Governance in Asia: Understanding the Debates on Land Tenure Rights and Land Reforms in the Asian Context*, Rome: International Land Coalition, Framing the Debate Series #3.
Rama, R. and Wilkinson, J. (2008) 'Foreign Direct Investment and Agri-food Value Chains in Developing Countries: A Review of the Main Issues', in *FAO Commodity Market Review 2007–2008*, Rome: Food and Agriculture Organization of the United Nations, pp. 51–66.
Ruggie, J. (2014) 'Regulating Multinationals: The UN Guiding Principles, Civil Society and International Legalization', in C. Rodriguez-Garavito (ed.) *Business and Human Rights: Beyond the End of the Beginning*, New York: Norton.
Sauvant, K. (2008) 'The Rise of International Investments, Investment Agreements and Investment Disputes', ccsi.columbia.edu/files/2014/01/AppealsMechanisminInternationalInvestmentDisputes-ToC_000.pdf.
Sauvant, K. and Sachs, L., eds (2009) *The Effect of Treaties on Foreign Direct Investment: Bi-lateral Investment Treaties, Double Taxation Treaties and Investment Flows*, Oxford: Oxford University Press.
Schaffnit-Chatterjee, C. (2012) *Foreign Investment in Farmland: No Low-hanging Fruit*, New York: Deutsche Bank DB Research.
Sharman, F. (1989) 'An Introduction to the Enclosure Acts', *The Journal of Legal History* 10(1): 45–70.
Shemberg, A. (2009) *Stabilization Clauses and Human Rights*, Washington, DC: World Bank (IFC).
Smaller, C. and Mann, H. (2009) *A Thirst for Distant Lands: Foreign Investment in Agricultural Land and Water*, Ottawa: International Institute for Sustainable development (IISD).
Sustainable Development Solutions Network (2013) 'Achieving Gender Equality, Social Inclusion and Human Rights for All: Challenges and Priorities for the Sustainable Development Agenda', unsdsn.org/resources/publications/achieving-gender-equality-social-inclusion-and-human-rights-for-all-challenges-and-priorities-for-the-sustainable-development-agenda/.
Tanner, C. (2010) 'Land Rights and Enclosures: Implementing the Mozambican Land Law in Practice', in W. Anseeuw and C. Alden (eds) *Struggles Over Land in Africa: Conflicts, Politics and Change*, Cape Town: Human Sciences Research Council, pp. 105–130.
Thompson, E.P. (1963) *The Making of the English Working Class*, London: Gollancz.
TNI (Transnational Institute) (2012) 'The Global Land Grab: A Primer', www.tni.org.

UNCTAD (2009) 'The Role of International Investment Treaties in Attracting Foreign Direct Investment to Developing Countries', unctad.org/en/Docs/diaeia20095_en.pdf.

Upham, F. (2014) 'Property Rights, Commodification, and Land Disputes in Contemporary Socialist Asia', in H. Fu and J. Gillespie (eds) *Resolving Land Disputes in East Asia: Exploring the Limits of Law*, Cambridge: Cambridge University Press, 35–51.

Weis, T. (2010) 'The Accelerating Biophysical Contradictions of Industrial Capitalist Agriculture', *Journal of Agrarian Change* 10(3): 315–341.

White, B., Borras, S., Hall, R., Scoones, I. and Wolford, W. (2012) 'The New Enclosures: Critical Perspectives on Corporate Land Deals', *Journal of Peasant Studies* 39(3–4): 619–647.

White, J. and White, B. (2012) 'Gendered Experiences of Dispossession: Oil Palm Expansion in a Dayak Hibun Community in West Kalimantan', *Journal of Peasant Studies* 39(3–4): 995–1016.

Wily, L.A. (2012) 'Looking Back to See Forward: The Legal Niceties of Land Theft in Land Rushes', *Journal of Peasant Studies* 39(3–4): 751–776.

Woodhouse, P. (2012) 'New Investment, Old Challenges: Land Deals and the Water Constraint in African Agriculture', *Journal of Peasant Studies* 39(3–4): 777–794.

Woods, K. (2014) 'A Political Anatomy of Land Grabs', *Myanmar Times*, 10 March.

World Bank (1993) *The East Asian Miracle: Economic Growth and Public Policy*, Washington, DC: World Bank.

World Bank (2008a) *World Development Report 2008: Agriculture for Development*, Washington, DC: World Bank.

World Bank (2008b) *Land Law Reform: Achieving Development Policy Objectives*, World Bank Law, Justice, and Development Series, Washington, DC: World Bank.

World Bank (2011) *Rising Interest in Global Farmland: Can it Yield Sustainable and Equitable Benefits?* Washington, DC: World Bank.

World Bank, UNCTAD, FAO and IFAD (2010) *Principles of Responsible Agricultural Investments*, Washington, DC: World Bank.

Yelling, J. (1977) *Common Field and Enclosures in England 1450–1850*, London: Macmillan.

Zoomers, A. (2010) 'Globalization and the Foreignization of Space: Seven Processes Driving the Current Global Land Grab', *Journal of Peasant Studies* 37(2): 429–444.

2 International law response to land grabbing in Asia

Surya P. Subedi

Introduction

Land grabbing by rich and powerful individuals, whether economically, politically or militarily, and by the state, whether national or local, is rampant in many countries across Asia, especially those in transition, whether politically or economically. While countries like Cambodia and Myanmar are in the process of both economic and political transition, other countries such as China and Vietnam have been in the process of economic transition for some time. After the demise of communism in Europe, the collapse of the Soviet Union and China's decision to embark on the road to economic liberalization, land rights and land disputes returned to occupy centre stage in domestic policy making in countries with socialist tendencies. This is because some form of individual right to property or land has been recognized in these countries with the opening up of the economy.

When these countries were under a communist system of governance they witnessed the introduction of collective farming, or commune or state ownership of land. A fundamental change has taken place in these countries with their decision to liberalize the economy and recognize ownership of private property. However, land grabbing by individuals and land acquisition by the government or local councils for various social and economic purposes under schemes such as economic land concessions – which lack in transparency, accountability, due process and adequate compensation, and involve forcible eviction of especially the poor, the indigenous and traditional communities, and those on the margins of the society – has posed its own challenges. The situation in countries such as China, Cambodia and Vietnam is particularly illustrative of the challenges for a number of historical, political and social reasons.

The main method used for land grabbing or land acquisition in these countries has been economic and other land concessions, including not only acquisition of land for agri-industry (for example, rubber, sugar, acacia and cassava plantations), but also for mining, oil and gas, forestry, and for the purposes of tourism, property development and large-scale development projects, such as hydro-electric power dams. A land concession is a contract between the government and a state or private actor which gives that actor specific rights (for example, exclusive rights to manage and harvest the land) normally for a long period of time, but not ownership (Cotula *et al.* 2009; Barney 2007; Borras *et al.* 2011; De Schutter 2011; Hall 2011; FAO 2012; Zoomers 2010).

It should be recognized that as developing countries, these countries in transition may wish to utilize their land and natural resources in order to develop and become more prosperous. Nevertheless, the problem arises when land concessions are not granted and managed within a sound legal and policy framework, with due consideration for and consultation with those who will be affected, and with the sustainable use of natural resources in mind. The current climate of development in these countries – characterized by uneven transparency, inadequate consultation and participation that is not inclusive – is unsustainable and likely to hamper future national economic growth.

This is because the human cost of many such concessions has been high and the poorest of the poor have suffered the most. It is not clear how many of the people in these countries have actually benefited from land concession, and many such concessions often have a dimension of corruption because they operate behind a veil of secrecy. There are far too many land disputes associated with economic or other land concessions that remain unresolved, and they are having a negative impact on the lives and livelihoods of the rural and urban poor, indigenous people and other traditional communities.

The governments in these countries should be transparent in dealing with economic and other land concessions and protect the lives and livelihood of such people when negotiating concessions with companies, both foreign and national, and hold them accountable over land disputes. It should be recognized that the development of land and natural resources of these countries could have a positive impact on the lives of all the people in the country if done in a sustainable and equitable manner and within the framework of the state's human rights obligations. However, this does not seem to be case in most of these countries.

In spite of the gravity of the problem of land grabbing across Asia and in countries in Africa and elsewhere, and its impact on the people in society, the response to this problem is that law, both national and international, has remained weak. There is no specific 'hard law' instrument in international law to deal with the challenges posed by land grabbing. All we have is an assortment of provisions in various 'soft law' instruments which touch on certain aspects of the problem of land grabbing. This chapter aims to analyse the response of international law to the challenges posed by land grabbing. It will begin with an assessment of different possible approaches to the problem of land grabbing in international law. Next will be an examination of various provisions in international legal instruments relating to land rights, and the chapter will conclude with some recommendations.

Land grabs and the right to property in international law

What is at stake with regard to the problem of land grabs is the right to property itself. The Magna Carta, the English Bill of Rights, and American and French Revolutions were inspired by the people's right to property against state interference. This right is at the heart of the rule of law, democracy and human rights. Under international law, the right to property (especially of foreigners or foreign investors) has been protected for a long time. The land belonging to individuals can be taken by the state only under certain conditions recognized in international law. The conditions for the acquisition, expropriation or nationalization of land are as follows:

- compensation must be given;
- it must be carried out in a non-discriminatory manner;
- it must be carried out with due process of law; and
- it must be for a bona fide public purpose.

The Universal Declaration of Human Rights (UDHR) recognized all individuals' right to property. However, Cold War politics resulted in the International Bill of Human Rights (International Covenant on Civil and Political Rights, or ICCPR, and International Covenant on Economic, Social and Cultural Rights, or ICESCR) not guaranteeing the right to property. The UDHR is now widely regarded to have acquired customary international law character and is binding on all states, endorsed by the 192 members states of the United Nations (UN) meeting in New York in 2005, and agreeing that the UDHR is a binding legal document.

Many countries do welcome foreign investment to develop land. Under international law, foreign investors have greater protection than national investors. Foreign investors tend to engage in nationality shopping to get the best deal possible. For instance, it is possible for a Chinese investor to register his/her business in the United Kingdom and return to China as a foreign investor with a view to obtaining better legal protection. Disputes with foreign investors can be required to be settled before an international tribunal or under UK law.

Across Asia, land is typically divided into four categories:

- state public land, which is protected by law and difficult to encroach upon;
- state private land, which the state can sell off to individuals and companies;
- private land, which is owned by private individuals; and
- community land, which is owned by indigenous or other peoples, which the state cannot encroach upon.

In many countries, state public land is being converted into state private land. State public land belongs to the people, but when it is reclassified as state private land, legal protection is stripped from the land and the state obtains the power to sell it. Problems also arise when governments sell off land that is national park, wildlife sanctuary, a protected area, a multiple-use area, a national heritage site, marine park or which has biosphere resources. Pursuant to international conventions on the protection of such lands, states do conserve large tracts, and with growing demand, there has been a tendency across Asia to encroach on and reclassify these lands. However, there is no hard law instrument to guide states on how to harness their land resources and neither is there an effective dispute resolution mechanism for individuals seeking legal redress. When disputes arise, foreign investors can sue the host government before an international tribunal, but this facility is not available to individuals. National mechanisms are not strong enough because the right to property is not well protected in national legal systems.

Within the UN human rights system, none of the 9–10 treaty bodies is competent to deal with issues related to land grabbing. None of the 130 international human rights instruments has a clear mandate to deal with land grabs. UN special rapporteur reports are submitted recommendations to governments through the UN Human Rights Council (HRC) but, from experience, in the absence of a proper follow-up mechanism, these recommendations are not translated into law.

Relevant international legal instruments

The UN Declaration on the Rights of Indigenous Peoples (UNDRIP)[1] is a major 'soft law' instrument that provides an international normative foundation for the legal framework on the recognition and registration of indigenous peoples and their rights to collective land title. The adoption of the declaration was the result of a culmination of decades of advocacy for indigenous peoples' rights, and explicitly lays out rights to land, culture, livelihood and consultation, among others.

Another instrument of significance is the Basic Principles and Guidelines on Development-based Displacement and Evictions of 2007, developed by the special rapporteur on adequate housing. It provides a baseline standard related to the relocation of people affected by land concessions.[2] The guidelines recommend that states explore all possible alternatives to evictions and ensure full consultation and participation of affected communities throughout the entire process, as well as provide adequate compensation and restitution.[3]

An international instrument of major significance is the Guiding Principles on Business and Human Rights, adopted unanimously by the HRC in June 2011 (UNHRC 2011).[4] While not a legally binding document, this endorsement established the Guiding Principles as the authoritative global reference point, clarifying business accountability and the responsibilities of the state. It should be noted that the concept of business and human rights includes efforts of corporate social responsibility but international standards impose obligations that are neither voluntary nor ad hoc.[5]

The Guiding Principles are grounded in the recognition of states' existing obligations to respect, protect and fulfil human rights and fundamental freedoms. Therefore, the standards on business and human rights are directly relevant to Cambodia through their international legal commitments and domestic law. The Guiding Principles apply to all business enterprises, both transnational and others, regardless of their size, sector, location, ownership and structure. Therefore, *all* businesses involved in land concessions in Cambodia (the host state), including businesses operations from foreign countries (the home states) bear the responsibility to protect against human rights violations.

The Guiding Principles are a set of 31 standards to support the implementation of the UN 'Protect, Respect and Remedy' policy framework.[6] They are the product of six years of research and extensive consultations involving governments, businesses and associations, civil society, affected individuals and communities, and investors. They highlight what steps states should take to foster businesses' respect for human rights, providing a standard for stakeholders to monitor and assess these steps, and show how businesses can become aware and demonstrate to others that they respect human rights and reduce the risk of causing or contributing to human rights harm. They also stipulate what both states and businesses should do to enhance access to effective remedies for those whose rights have been harmed.

The UN Working Group on Business and Human Rights has undertaken the promotion of the Guiding Principles, which they explain have led to a convergence of global standards and initiatives on business and human rights, including a link with the standards of the International Standardization Organization (ISO) Guidance on Corporate Responsibility, Organisation for Economic Co-operation and Development (OECD) Guidelines for Multinational Enterprises, UN Global Compact, and the International Finance Corporation (IFC) Sustainability Framework, among others (UNHRC 2012).

The 2011 IFC Policy and Performance Standards on Environmental and Social Sustainability acknowledges 'an emerging international consensus that the private sector has a responsibility to respect human rights', including trying to close the gap in protection against forced evictions. The Association of Southeast Asian Nations (ASEAN) announced that the first thematic study by its relatively new Intergovernmental Commission on Human Rights would focus on business and human rights in a manner that is fully compliant with the UN frameworks, especially the Guiding Principles.[7] The convergence of these standards is directly applicable to the situation of land grabbing in the countries in transition, given the large number of business enterprises (including international and domestic, and those wholly or partly owned by the state) involved in land concessions.[8]

Other human rights standards

There are myriad other standards that set out the international legal obligations of states for addressing the environmental and social impacts of economic or other land concessions. Business enterprises are internationally obliged to carry out 'due diligence' – that is, to identify, prevent, mitigate and account for how they address their adverse human rights impacts.[9] Not only do businesses have this responsibility, but it is the duty of the state to ensure proper management and monitoring of this function. As noted earlier, states have the duty to protect against human rights abuses by third parties in their country or area of jurisdiction. Moreover, they are obligated in their international human rights obligations to exercise adequate oversight when they contract with or legislate for business enterprises.

The process for both states and businesses should include assessing the actual and potential human rights impacts, integrating and acting upon the findings, tracking responses, and communicating how such impacts are addressed. This applies to all state- and donor-operated projects and to all business enterprises, regardless of size (whether transnational corporations, conglomerates, or small or medium-sized enterprises), sector, structure, ownership, or country of domicile or operation (national or foreign). In the context of land concessions, it may refer directly to the environmental and social impact – carrying out assessments with good faith participation of all those affected.

Moreover, the assessment of the impact should be participatory and development planning should be inclusive of all those potentially affected. The ICCPR and ICESCR both recognize the right of all individuals and peoples to 'freely pursue their economic, social and cultural development'. The UN Declaration on the Right to Development[10] laid the foundation for participation and consultation in development processes, which was complemented by references in UNDRIP Article 32(2), which upholds free, prior and informed consent.[11] This language has been incorporated into other international standards, for example the 2011 update on IFC Policy and Performance Standards on Environmental and Social Sustainability.[12] In addition to the international human rights obligations of states and businesses, there are practical, operational and logistical reasons for incorporating these requirements in business and development activities, and many governments have incorporated these standards into their national laws and policies, and companies into their standard operations.[13]

With regard to access to an effective remedy, there are several non-judicial and quasi-judicial mechanisms for dispute resolution, including the various levels of the cadastral system. However, the time-consuming administrative and procedural burden, financial costs associated with submitting a complaint (although there are no official fees, as with courts, transportation, lost wages, legal assistance, and so on, can prove costly for individuals), and a lack of faith in the system means that these mechanisms are being used inconsistently.

What is more, experience has demonstrated that decisions by such bodies are inconsistent, irregular and subject to political interference.

Most of the countries in transition have no independent national human rights institution. Owing to an uneven application of the relatively well-developed legal framework governing land rights, and an inadequate access to remedies, communities are becoming increasingly frustrated and disillusioned by formal judicial and administrative processes. Demonstrations and protests by affected communities are increasing and have become more violent. The proliferation of displays of discontent around the country related to land disputes point to inadequate consultation and negotiation with those affected. Early and inclusive consultation can address the tensions before they escalate and contribute to preventing disputes. The UN Guiding Principles on Business and Human Rights promote the use of 'operational-level' grievance mechanisms to facilitate addressing disputes early and directly. These mechanisms should be accessible directly to individuals and communities that may be adversely impacted by business activities, and are typically administered by business enterprises alone or with the collaboration of local authorities and civil society organizations.[14] Some concession companies have set up procedures to deal with local-level disputes and complaints, which can be an effective way of directly addressing misinformation and addressing tensions before they escalate.

Implementation of legal standards

The majority of the challenges in the countries in transition with regard to the granting and management of economic and other land concessions derive from a failure to apply the domestic legal framework properly – that is, the laws, policies and regulations that the government itself has developed. The granting and management of economic and other land concessions in these countries suffer from a lack of transparency and adherence to existing laws. Much of the legal framework on these matters is relatively well developed on paper, but the challenge is implementation in practice.

Further, a pervasive problem that exists in this regard is uneven access to information, which has contributed to concessions benefiting only a minority, as well as a proliferation of land-related conflicts, which has the potential to contribute to instability. The governments in these countries should be transparent in granting land concessions, and rigorous in monitoring them, especially when negotiating concession agreements with both foreign and national companies, avoid conflicts of interest, hold concession companies to account by exercising oversight over their activities, and resolve land disputes. In particular, the absence of transparency in such matters has bred suspicion of corruption at all levels of the government, and has fuelled resentment on the part of many citizens in these countries.

The current climate of development in these countries is characterized by low transparency and uneven access to information, inadequate consultation and participation that is not inclusive, and, in my view, is unsustainable and likely to hamper future national economic growth. Of course, some cases of land concessions seem to have had positive impacts for the people of these countries in terms of job creation, stimulation of the local economy, generation of revenue to finance public services, and overall contribution to national growth. However, the human cost of many concessions has been high, and human rights considerations should be at the heart of the granting and management of land concessions in order for them to have a positive impact.

The development of land and other natural resources of these countries could have a positive impact on the lives of all people if undertaken in a sustainable and equitable manner and within the framework of human rights obligations. To this end, these governments should make publicly accessible all information concerning land investments, land deals and bidding processes, reviews of proposals for land concessions (and the decision-making criteria for acceptance or denial of proposals), and future plans (including on commencement of concession activity). Such information could be made available on public display at the provincial level and on official governmental websites.

All relevant government bodies and businesses should adhere to the legal requirements for public consultation. Such consultations should be meaningful, inclusive and accessible to affected people. Communities on land to be affected by the granting of a land concession should be consulted at the earliest stage on the land use plan and included in the decision-making process. Due consideration should be given to the current livelihood activities of the community and all efforts be made to avoid their disruption. Standards of free, prior and informed consent should be rigorously applied when consulting with all indigenous peoples.

Conclusions

Land concessions that are found to be exploitative, inactive or otherwise violating the conditions of the concession agreement should be cancelled, as per the relevant laws. Companies of all sizes, structures and modes of operation, both domestic and foreign, whether wholly or partly owned by the state, should address their human rights impact by practising due diligence, including implementing measures to identify, prevent and mitigate adverse human rights consequences, and account for their business activities. In the case of foreign-owned companies, the home states should ensure that representatives of private business enterprises under their jurisdiction do not contribute to adverse human rights impacts by regular monitoring and oversight. Finally, given the seemingly intractable status of long-standing land disputes and the proliferation of new disputes, efforts should be made to enhance effective and legitimate operational level grievance mechanisms, and involve communities and their representatives (communities may decide whether civil society organizations should be involved) at the early stages of the granting of a land concession and include them in the planning process.

However, many of these elements seem to be missing in the acquisition of land by governments in these countries, and there is no robust system of monitoring compliance by governments and local councils of the standards set out above. The response of international law to the challenges posed by land grabbing is weak and inadequate. Therefore, there is a need for negotiation and eventual adoption of a sector-specific binding international legal instrument to address the challenges posed by land grabbing, which can consolidate and strengthen the provisions to be found in some of the international 'soft law' instruments examined above and develop new principles vis-à-vis land grabbing and protection of the rights of the people evicted from their land or facing the threat of eviction. This would make states accountable for failures to comply with international law standards. Such an instrument should require consultation, participation and environmental and social impact assessments before granting land to national and international investors. There should be a dispute resolution mechanism for affected individuals, and there should be a complaints mechanism whereby individuals can petition UN treaty bodies, other UN bodies or other international bodies.

Land grabbing is a problem that is on the increase in Asia. Changes to national law will take time as each country has its own political cycle. International law has always been the guiding body of law for national law and if an international legal instrument were adopted, it would be likely to bring about change in the behaviour of governments in many states. Therefore, there is a need for an international treaty to govern land grabbing, with a provision for a separate treaty body empowered to receive individual petitions from the people affected. Now that communist regimes are essentially gone, the time has come to recognize the problem of land grabbing and negotiate a binding international treaty. If the adoption of a completely new treaty is not feasible at the moment, some of the objectives could be achieved by amending the ICCPR and ICESCR, or by adopting a separate protocol to the covenants to this effect.

It should be recognized that enforcing treaty compliance is difficult. Nevertheless, we should start the process of reform and create a legal mechanism so that lawyers, individuals, human rights defenders and academics have a concrete legal instrument on which to rest their case. Of course, new law is not always the answer to the problem at hand, but the law provides a context or a framework within which the problem of land grabbing could be addressed. Indeed, even with the proliferation of human rights instruments and bodies, the violation of human rights still goes on. However, governments are more willing to uphold human rights if there is international pressure underpinned by a legal basis. No country wants to be seen to be violating international law. Having a law is better than not having a law. Having an international treaty would spark massive education campaigns to make governments and people in power aware of the illegality of their actions, motivating them not to take the risk and violate the law.

The very existence of an international legal instrument would give advocates a language to speak and to use so that governments cannot continue their denial, as is the case in many countries at the moment. Such an instrument would empower domestic courts to invoke it when providing remedy to the victims of land grabbing. The judiciaries of India, Pakistan and the Philippines have led the way in giving force to soft law instruments, although in doing so they have been criticized for judicial activism.

To conclude, it should be acknowledged that a treaty to this effect will not be created overnight. The international community could first accept the idea in principle. A soft law declaration might then be adopted before a hard law instrument. It is to be hoped that publications of this nature, such as the present volume, will further stimulate the debate in this area and act as a catalyst for acceptance of the idea in principle, laying the path for a declaration and a legally binding treaty with a treaty body.

Notes

1 General Assembly resolution 61/295, UN Doc. A/61/PV.107 (13 September 2007).
2 Basic Principles and Guidelines on Development-based Evictions and Displacement, Annex 1 of the report of the special rapporteur on adequate housing as a component of the right to an adequate standard of living, A/HRC/4/18.
3 The Office of the UN High Commissioner for Human Rights in Cambodia published in December 2009 the 'United Nations Commentary and Guidelines on Eviction and Resettlement' in both English and Khmer, available at: cambodia.ohchr.org/WebDOCs/DocPublications/EvictionsGuidelines/EvictionGuidelines-EN.pdf.
4 The Guiding Principles on Business and Human Rights are contained in the annex to the special representative's 2011 report to the Human Rights Council (A/HRC/17/31), available at: www2.ohchr.org/english/bodies/hrcouncil/docs/17session/A.HRC.17.31_en.pdf.
5 The Office of the UN High Commissioner for Human Rights in Cambodia, published in December 2011, the 'Guiding Principles on Business and Human Rights: Implementing the United Nations "Protect, Respect and Remedy" Framework', available at: cambodia.ohchr.org/WebDOCs/DocPublications/Business-and-HR Guidelines/Business%20and%20Human%20Rights_English.pdf.
6 The 'Protect, Respect and Remedy' policy framework was unanimously welcomed in 2008 by the HRC. See *Protect, Respect and Remedy: A Framework for Business and Human Rights*, Report of the Special Representative of the Secretary-General on the issue of human rights and transnational corporations and other business enterprises (A/HRC/8/5); Summary of Five Multi-stakeholder Negotiations (A/HRC/8/5/Add.1), 23 April 2008.
7 Remarks by Rafendi Djamin, Indonesian representative to the ASEAN Intergovernmental Commission on Human Rights, at the Asia Pacific Forum of National Human Rights Institutions Regional Conference on Business and Human Rights, 11–13 October 2011, Seoul, South Korea.
8 Note also that the Committee on the Elimination of Racial Discrimination, in its concluding observations in 2010, encouraged business entities engaging in economic land concessions 'to take into consideration their corporate social

responsibility as it relates to the rights and well-being of local populations'. See United Nations CERD Comm. 2010.

9 Guiding Principles on Business and Human Rights, at 17–24.

10 General Assembly resolution 41/128, UN Doc. A/RES/41/128 (4 December 1986), Article 1 states that everyone is 'entitled to participate in, contribute to, and enjoy economic, social, cultural and political development'.

11 For a practical guide on free, prior and informed consent, see Oxfam 2010.

12 IFC, performance standard 7.

13 For commentaries on the utility of human rights policies for businesses, see Business and Human Rights Resource Centre, 'Commentaries on Human Rights Policies', www.business-humanrights.org/ToolsGuidancePortal/Policies/Commentaries; and for a list of companies that have incorporated human rights into their statements, see 'Company Policy Statements on Human Rights', www.business-humanrights.org/Documents/Policies. For a list of member companies of the Global Business Initiative on Human Rights, see www.global-business-initiative.org/Members.html. Of these members, at least Chevron, Sime Darby, General Electric, Unilever, Coca-Cola, Novo Nordisk, and Total operate in Cambodia.

14 Guiding Principles on Business and Human Rights, at 28–31.

References

Barney, K. (2007) *A Note on Forest Land Concessions, Social Conflicts, and Poverty in the Mekong Region*, Proceedings: International Conference on Poverty Reduction and Forests, Proceedings of the International Conference on Poverty Reduction and Forests, Bangkok.

Borras, S.M. Jr, Hall, R., Scoones, I., White, B. and Wolford, W. (2011) 'Towards a Better Understanding of Global Land Grabbing: An Editorial Introduction', *The Journal of Peasant Studies* 38(2): 209–216.

Cotula, L., Vermeulen, S., Leonard, R., Keeley, J. (2009) *Land Grab or Development Opportunity? Agricultural Investment and International Land Deals in Africa*, Rome and London: IIED/FAO/IFAD.

De Schutter, O. (2011) 'How Not to Think of Land-grabbing: Three Critiques of Large-scale Investments in Farmland', *The Journal of Peasant Studies* 38: 249.

Food and Agriculture Organization of the UN (FAO) (2012) *Voluntary Guidelines on the Responsible Governance of Tenure of Land, Fisheries and Forests in the Context of National Food Security*, Rome: FAO.

Hall, R. (2011) 'Land Grabbing in Southern Africa: The Many Faces of the Investor Rush', *Review of African Political Economy* 38: 193.

Oxfam (2010) *Guide to Free, Prior and Informed Consent*, 27 July.

United Nations Human Rights Council (UNHRC) (2011) *Human Rights and Transnational Corporations and Other Business Enterprises*, UN Doc. A/HRC/17/L.17/Rev.1.

United Nations Human Rights Council (UNHRC) (2012) *Report of the United Nations Working Group on Business and Human Rights*, UN Doc. A/HRC/20/29, www.ohchr.org/Documents/Issues/Business/A.HRC.20.29_AEV.pdf.

United Nations CERD Comm. (2010) *Concluding Observations: Cambodia*, 17, UN Doc. CERD/C/KHM/CO/8-13.

Zoomers, A. (2010) 'Globalisation and the Foreignisation of Space: Seven Processes Driving the Current Global Land Grab', *The Journal of Peasant Studies* 37: 429.

3 How land grabs are made 'constitutional' in China

Qianfan Zhang

Introduction

Land grabbing is perhaps a universal problem, but it is probably most acutely felt in China, where it has been dubbed 'where to demolish' (拆哪儿 *chai'-na'er*). In fact, land grabbing is the very process by which urbanization and urban renewal are carried out, and the people in China have paid dearly for the high speed of economic development. Over the last two decades, land grabbing in the cities and villages has created massive social dislocation, cultural destruction and official corruption. For years it has been listed consistently as the very top cause for both official corruption and civilian grievance petitions (上访 *shangfang*). In the historic city of Nanjing, the capital of Jiangsu province, as much as three quarters of the old city has been demolished in order to build commercial and residential establishments (Xie 2009). Whenever a land acquisition or house demolition is carried out, tension erupts between the people and the government, which is often obliged to use armoured police in order to secure peace and order.

Land grabbing is defined here as an illegitimate compulsory act of government that takes the land right originally owned by the people. A typical example in China is where a local government takes the rural land collectively owned by a village without informed consent and just compensation based on a fair measure of the land value (more below). Since land in the city is usually owned by the 'state', it is usually understood that the urban residents own the right to use the land rather than the land itself. Still, the demolition of urban houses involves not only the taking of the infrastructure, but also the taking of the right to use the land, which is usually uncompensated and thus constitutes another form of land grab. Indeed, from both international standards and the Chinese legal definition itself, it may plausibly be argued that 'state ownership' is in essence the ownership of the whole people, so that when the government as the land manager comes in and takes hold of the urban (i.e. 'state-owned') land owned by the people, there *is* taking, and doing so without compensation does constitute a land grab.

This chapter discusses the constitutional origin of the land grab in China. It will first review the history of land ownership and focus on the issue of whether the sudden categorization of urban land as 'state owned' under Article 10 of the 1982 Constitution constitutes a wholesale confiscation by the state. It then moves on to explore the serious consequences of compensation below the market value standard, which has led to many conflicts and tragedies in China, epitomized in the self-immolation of Tang Fuzhen at the end of December 2009. The tragedy urged the State Council to enact a new Taking and Compensation Regulation in 2011. The new regulation was an improvement over the previous one, as it applied to urban land and property, but the problems related to the taking of rural land remain unresolved. The chapter then examines the root causes of land grabs in China, and concludes with a proposal for reinterpreting Article 10 of the constitution in a way that will make it consistent with international standards and practices.

A brief history of land ownership in China

Before 1949, land in China was predominantly privately owned. However, the Chinese Communist Party (CCP) saw private property as the principal bourgeois evil that needed to be eradicated. Above all, under orthodox Marxist ideology, land ownership, the 'primary means of production', must be firmly controlled in the hands of the state under 'proletarian dictatorship'. Enterprises (also a 'means of production') of the 'nation' and the petit bourgeois, many of whom supported the communist takeover in 1949, were spared from confiscation during the initial transition period. However, urban land and enterprises were gradually taken over by the state, and rural land, which the CCP had promised to the peasants to gain their support since its early difficult times in the revolutionary border areas, was taken away and merged into the People's Communes almost overnight during the upheaval of the Great Leap Forward in 1957–58.

Despite ideological hostility, private land ownership persisted in urban China. After the communist takeover in 1949, the government confiscated land belonging to counter-revolutionaries such as alleged imperialists, traitors and war criminals. However, the state did not own all land. The regime was unstable at the time, and had to make concessions to various classes of people. Enacted in 1949, Article 3 of the Common Programme claimed to protect the private property of workers, peasants and the national bourgeoisie. Thus land ownership remained largely a private right during most of the 1950s. The situation began to change when the government bought factory land from capitalists and converted it to public land. However, there remained a good deal of private land in cities, especially the land underneath private dwelling houses. This situation continued up until 1954, when the first Communist Constitution was codified, and lasted through the Cultural Revolution (1966–76) and the 1975 Constitution. The 1978 Constitution provided that the state could take urban or rural land where necessary, implying that at least some urban land remained privately owned. It also provided for state ownership of land containing natural resources, mountains and minerals.

Quite a different picture is painted in the countryside. In exchange for power and stability, the communists had promised that the peasants would get their own land from the landlords, and that promise was by and large fulfilled in the early 1950s. That did not last long, however. The Great Leap Forward, initiated by Mao Zedong in 1958, turned virtually all peasant land into collective land owned by communes, so that the peasants quickly lost their privately owned land. By the late 1970s, the People's Communes began to crumble and give way to the current responsibility system, in which peasant families gained the right to use and derive profits from rural land.

Things became interesting when the current constitution was made in 1982. Article 10 defines the land system and makes all land public. Although successive constitutional amendments gradually enhanced the status of the 'private economy', whose contribution to the gross domestic product (GDP) has long surpassed that of the public sector, public land ownership remains the ultimate touchstone for the 'socialist' character of the 1982 Constitution. All forms of social conflict and tragedy have arisen from the potential for abusing the public power which is hidden in the fantasy of public ownership, coupled with the official imperative to promote development and the GDP figure, from which the ruling party derives its legitimacy. To make things worse, the public land system defined in the 1982 Constitution is a dual – as opposed to a single – ownership system, divided into state-owned land and collectively owned land. While land in the rural area is collectively owned by villagers, land in the city is owned by the state, which is equivalent to 'the whole people' (全民 *quanmin*).

Compared with the village ownership of rural land, the state ownership of urban land is a more ambiguous concept, which could comprise the people, the government, or a mixture of both. On the common view that Article 10 resulted in an overnight confiscation of private land in the cities, this seems to constitute a wholesale land grab by the state. Although the state is equivalent to the people in the Chinese and perhaps all socialist constitutions, it is not meaningful to talk about 'the people' and public ownership in this sense, especially in a large country like China, since it is impossible for 'the people' meaningfully to exercise such property rights. A representative or manager is needed to exercise the relevant rights effectively. While it is conceivable that the National People's Congress (NPC) could act as such a representative, laws require that the State Council exercise the power to regulate land rights on behalf of the people. Thus, even though the state should be defined in terms of the people, for practical reasons it is defined as the government with power to administer the use of land.

Such power has been further delegated to various levels of local government in China, since the central government (i.e. the State Council) cannot possibly manage all land in such a vast country. The provincial, city and county governments all possess different degrees of power to regulate land use. Since nobody actually owns the land, these governments, by exercising their managerial powers, sit in the chair of the owner. This is precisely the attitude of the government, as indicated by enacted laws. For example, residents and developers who want to use land for residential and commercial buildings lease it from the government for a maximum of 70 years. Substantive ownership, which includes the right to use the land, is thus limited to 70 years, after which it reverts back to the government.

This understanding of the city land system was convenient for governments, because they could use the land whenever they wanted to. According to conventional wisdom of the government and mainstream society, the government was effectively the owner and could take the land back at any time on the payment of compensation. The taking seems always to be legitimate because the land belonged to the government in the first place. This understanding makes sense, however, only if Article 10 of the constitution is interpreted to have confiscated the urban land since, by 1982, there remained isolated pockets of private land (e.g. dwelling houses) that had certificates of land rights.

Legal developments before and after the Tang Fuzhen incident

Article 10 of the constitution was enacted and interpreted at the beginning of the reform period, when ordinary people were not sufficiently informed, conscious and active in order to protect their property rights effectively. In the past three decades, China has witnessed a dramatic rise of public consciousness of individual rights, reflected above all in the rapidly revived consciousness of property rights. With disenchantment with the socialist ideology, ownership of private property is no longer a sign of depraved bourgeoisie, but a source of social recognition and personal pride. In the aftermath of the Sun Zhigang (孙志刚) incident,[1] the constitutional amendment in 2004 not only generally requires the state to 'respect and protect human rights', but declares more specifically that 'the lawful private property of citizens is inviolable' (Art. 13), only a slight step below the 'socialist public property' (Art. 12), which is 'sacrosanct' (神圣不可侵犯 *shensheng buke qinfan*). For the first time private property can be taken for public use only if the state 'pay[s] compensation in accordance with the law' (Art. 13).

Such a provision may seem less than impressive, even meaningless, since compensation of some sort is almost always paid in land takings or demolition of houses, as in the Tang Fuzhen case (on which more below). It is *just compensation* that should have been required, and it was the very absence of such requirement that caused Tang Fuzhen's death and many more similar tragedies. Nevertheless, the constitutional amendment does reflect the emerging public consensus on a vital principle for China's social harmony and provides an anchor, as it were, for further legal developments.

A major development is the Property Law enacted by the NPC in 2007, after a year-long delay caused by Professor Gong Xiantian of Peking

University, who challenged the provisions in the law for violating the 'socialist character' of the 1982 Constitution by conferring largely equal protection for private and public property. The Property Law, essentially a part of the larger Civil Code which will be enacted in future, provides comprehensive protections for various types of property, but proves marginally useful for the protection of land rights against taking without just compensation. Article 42 reiterates the constitutional requirement for 'compensation in accordance with the law', but the legally defined compensation may well be below the fair market value of the land or property (e.g. houses) on the land that will be taken. The fact is that even a requirement for just compensation may not be effectively enforced by a court whose personnel appointments and finance depend on the local government, the main driving force behind the taking. In February 2002, for example, over 10,000 evicted residents in Beijing brought an administrative class action against the demolitions, yet the court declined to review the case (Duan 2004). Although the Supreme People's Court required the lower courts to hear the cases, the local courts often narrowed the scope of review on their own initiative to eschew such 'sensitive' cases.

To be sure, the people do make use of better laws to protect their rights. On the same day as the NPC passed the Property Law, for instance, the court of Jiulongpo district in Chongqing municipality issued its 'ultimatum' for final relocation to the 'most robust nail house', whose occupants refused to move for years even though the surrounding houses had long been demolished, leaving the house an isolated island, without water and power supply.[2] However, benefiting from the propitious timing of the passing of the new Property Law, the residents succeeded in obliging the Chongqing government to make an offer to their satisfaction, after which they peacefully moved out. Unfortunately, such a happy ending remains the exception, which cannot save thousands of victims like Tang Fuzhen.

By the end of 2009, the Sun Zhigang tragedy found itself duplicated in a different context. On 23 December, Tang Fuzhen (唐福珍), a Chengdu resident who had forcibly resisted the demolition team from tearing down her house for hours, lost control and poured petroleum over her body, setting herself on fire. Despite prompt rescue, she died in hospital several days later (163 News 2009). The news spread instantly on the internet, fuelled by a video taken by a neighbour using a mobile phone, which vividly recorded the self-immolation. Like the Sun Zhigang event, the news created a massive public uproar, followed by five law professors from Peking University petitioning the NPC Standing Committee to review the constitutionality of the Regulation on the Demolition of City Houses, which authorized urban renovation projects. Although the regulation was not strictly applicable to Tang's house, allegedly an 'illegal construction' located in a 'village within the city' (城中村 *chengzhongcun*), minor details made little difference, and public pressure for abolishing the Urban Demolition Regulation was overwhelming.

Like the Sun Zhigang case, the Tang Fuzhen tragedy moved the central government to take prompt action. The Legislative Affairs Office (LAO), the

State Council's legal department, responded quickly to public pressure. Following several meetings with legal scholars, it managed to publish a draft revision of the old regulation that eliminated a number of its constitutional infirmities.[3] Unlike the Detention and Repatriation Regulation, however, the revision of the Urban Demolition Regulation is a much more difficult task, since it has met serious resistance from local governments, which have been deriving a significant part of their fiscal revenue from lucrative takings by paying compensation at sub-market values.[4] Although the LAO expressed its willingness to require just compensation and narrow the scope of 'public interest' in the new regulation, it did not appear confident enough to withstand the pressure of local governments, which are in charge of implementing most of the central laws and policies, and enjoy considerable discretion in deciding the extent of implementation. After a long delay, apparently having consulted the local governments, the LAO came up with a second draft of the Regulation on Taking and Compensation for Houses on State-owned Land, which made considerable concession to the local governments. Although the new draft affirmed the principle of just compensation and authorized compulsory taking only with court approval, it deleted several important provisions in the first draft that had enabled the interested parties to participate in deciding whether the proposed taking was required by the 'public interest' and that compensation satisfied the just compensation criterion. They may challenge compensation at the court, but it is uncertain how much protection the judiciary may provide them, given its present status.

Urbanization through taking? The rural land conundrum

Even if the new regulation may reduce the violent demolitions in the cities somewhat, it is inapplicable to land taking in rural areas, where the Tang Fuzhen tragedy took place. Article 10 of the 1982 Constitution not only provides for the state ownership of urban land, but also provides that 'land in the rural and suburban areas is owned by collectives', i.e. by villages, except those portions that belong to the state according to the law, thus instituting a dualist land ownership regime. Unlike urban land, which is commonly supposed already to have been owned by the state, rural land is owned by a non-state entity and thus requires taking if the state intends to gain ownership.

Owing to the mischievous interpretation of Article 10, however, the constitutional taking requirement has failed to secure the ownership of rural land in the hands of villagers. Indeed, several problems have made the piecemeal taking of rural land even worse than that of the wholesale confiscation of urban land.

First, ambiguity is necessarily present when dealing with a collective entity: is the land owned by the villagers as a whole, the villagers individually, the village community, or another village organization? Articles 10 and 13 set the preconditions for the taking of land: the demonstration of public interest and the provision of compensation. The requirement of compensation for taking was added to the constitution in 2004, but the provision is ambiguous because it did not require *just* compensation, even though Chinese scholars are increasingly inclined today to understand that compensation should be of a just amount according to market value.

Second, there is not really a 'market' for rural land to assess its market value since land cannot be freely transacted. Article 10 of the constitution stipulates that 'the right to use of the land may be transferred according to law', but the transactions of rural land are strictly limited to its own type and are prohibited from exchanges with urban land. The Law of Land Administration, enacted in 1986 and revised several times, is increasingly more rigorous in restricting the right to transfer property. The result is that the peasants are obliged to use the farmland for agricultural purposes. They may engage in the farm work themselves, or may lease the farm to others and collect rent, but they are forbidden from transferring the land to urban residents or using the rural land for any purpose other than agriculture. This restriction on the use of rural land removes an essential characteristic of a free market exchange. Strictly speaking there *is* a 'market' for rural land, but this market is completely separate from the national market for the transaction of urban land – or more accurately, the right to the use of urban land. Compared with the market value of urban land, the value of rural land has long been seriously depressed, making it entirely inadequate for the purposes of awarding just compensation.

Third, the prohibition on voluntary transactions between rural and urban land has created a double effect. On the one hand, housing prices in the cities have kept at high levels due to the scarce supply of urban land. On the other hand, the relatively cheap houses constructed on rural land cannot be sold for residential, commercial or industrial purposes due to the prohibition of the Law of Land Administration. However, despite the legal prohibition, these properties thrive because they are beneficial to peasants and urban residents alike. It is a way, if not *the* way for peasants to make extra money and for urban residents to reduce their living costs. Of course, these properties are *not* legally recognized or protected. They are called 'small property', as opposed to big property, which are legally constructed and acquired urban houses that have legal titles.

Lastly, rural land can be converted into urban land, but only through the process of land taking by local government. Constructions for industrial, residential or commercial purposes must not only obtain government approval, but also be preceded by the taking process which would convert the collectively owned land to state-owned land. The rationale is that rural land that is owned by the village must now be owned by the state, so the state must take the land before construction can be permitted. Thus, associated with the dualist regime is the common understanding (or misunderstanding) that change of ownership *requires* taking or confiscation, an interpretation that must have made all local officials rest assured since urbanization is now synonymous with taking. Whenever rural land is converted to industrial, commercial or urban residential use, the local government is constitutionally authorized to step in and take the land before selling it for a much higher price.

Under this interpretation, China is perhaps the only country in the world that equates urbanization with official land taking or government confiscation. This conceptual misunderstanding is the result of the dualistic land system. While urbanization through land taking provides for seemingly efficient development, it creates very high social costs. Local officials are now instinctively committed to 'development' by taking the rural land and converting millions of peasants into landless petitioners with unjust compensation. Compared with urban demolitions, rural land takings have produced many more conflicts and tragedies. In Zhucheng, Shandong province, for example, the local government goaded the peasants to move to storied apartment buildings in exchange for their rural homesteads (Tu 2010).

The rationale for such tight state control over rural land is purportedly to maintain food security. This rationale has been challenged by economists and others; nevertheless, the taking or grabbing continues apace. For instance, the Ministry of Land Resources has drawn a 'red line' around 1.8 billion acres of farm land, requiring that it be preserved, without giving an explanation about its necessity or future usage (Mao 2008).

Institutional causes of land grabbing in China

Despite the restrictions in the Land Administration Law, the land preservation objective has not been effectively realized because local officials have every incentive to confiscate village land and sell it to urban developers at a price that is many times what they paid at the taking, and peasants are in no position to defend themselves.

For example, in the case of the Tieben factory in Jiangsu, the land taking not only violated the peasants' rights because they were given insufficient compensation, but it also compromised land security since the local government authorities and the enterprise owner colluded to bypass the strict review and approval rules laid down by the central government. Legally, large projects such as the Tieben factory require State Council approval but by cutting the project into separate pieces, the enterprise owner was able to bypass the strict rules and gain provincial approval instead (He and Chen 2004: 77–86).

Since the central government often lacks the exact information of the local development projects and peasants are not empowered to defend their land rights, the local government and developers can easily make a corrupt deal at the expense of the interests of both peasants and farm land protection. Having recognized the scope and severity of these problems, the central government is in the process of revising the law. However, for several reasons, the revision is unlikely to change the Chinese model of development or halt the government land grabbing process.

First, China is a 'developmental state' driven by pressures for GDP growth, which has been the primary source of legitimate justification for a one-party monopoly since the crackdown of the Tiananmen Protest in 1989. In order to resuscitate economic reform when political reform had been suffocated, Deng Xiaoping had to take the 'southern tour' (南巡 *nanxun*) to Guangdong province, where he emphasized the theme of 'development is the solid reason'. Soon afterwards, new measures began to produce the expected effect of making officials (rather than the people) the driving force of social development in China. While China's GDP was increasing at a rate of nearly 10 percent each year over the last two decades, a 'great leap forward' in land grabbing and demolitions in the name of 'development' (发展 *fazhan*) was creating the 'China miracle', which also contributed to the 'solid' legitimacy of the Party. The speed of economic growth also became a primary indicator used to measure the 'performance' (政绩 *zhengji*) of local officials. Indeed, the concept of 'local GDP' was invented for that purpose. Since building modern infrastructure is the most efficient way of increasing local GDP, local officials have always found it irresistible to grab rural land or demolish urban buildings in order to make sure that the numbers for local economic development look good.

Second, for over a decade, the income from land grabs has become a major source of revenue for the majority of local governments in China. In many cities and counties, revenue from land sales constitutes about half of local governments' total revenue, resulting in the phenomenon called 'land finance' (土地财政 *tudi caizheng*) (Yu 2013). Local governments are compelled into 'land finance' by the fiscal pressure of the Divided Tax (分税制 *fenshuizhi*) scheme implemented in 1994. Although the tax reform was ostensibly a 'fiscal federalism' experiment, giving local governments more autonomy over their own taxes, the net result has been to increase dramatically the central government's share of the total revenue at the expense of local revenues, thus forcing local governments to find non-tax revenues to maintain the balance sheet.

Third, land finance is only possible in a legal system that does not require just compensation for land and property taking. The local governments' noncompliance with the just compensation standard has fuelled their incentive for taking, since substandard compensation makes taking a lucrative proposition. As a result, local governments are the largest beneficiary of taking without just compensation.

Finally, taking without just compensation affords the most abundant opportunities for rent seeking and corruption. Since land revenue is not a tax, it is subject to less formal supervision and control, and thus more open to embezzlement. The large-scale construction projects following the taking and demolition also produce corrupt bidding, which facilitates all sorts of bribery. Party and government officials are in the best position to use regulatory power in exchange for profits, which has been one of the quickest ways to make money.

In the past decade, land grabbing has simultaneously been the primary cause of official corruption and of civilian grievance petitions in China. On the one hand, local officials at all levels are obliged to take the people's land and property, both to increase local revenues and to add to their performances scores. On the other hand, land takings and demolitions have long been the culprits for social conflict and instability. Ministry of Construction statistics show that taking-related grievances have consistently ranked top in the number of petitions in recent years. In the first half of 2004, over 18,000 petitioners went to Beijing to seek relief, the majority of whom arrived in groups (Zhao 2004). On 20 April, for example, several hundred peasants from Tianjin municipality went before the Ministry of Land and Natural Resources to complain about the loss of their contract land (Chang 2004). The numbers of conflicts have risen constantly over the years, producing countless 'nail houses' (钉子户 *dingzihu*) across the country – that is, those who stand up against local governments and refuse to sell their houses for the low compensation offered.

Conclusion: reinterpreting Article 10 of the constitution

In order to stop land grabs, China needs to reinterpret Article 10 of its constitution, so as to return to the people both the urban 'state-owned' and the rural collectively owned land.

With respect to the state ownership of urban land, China could learn from the system practised in the United Kingdom, Canada and other former British colonies, where land is nominally owned by the Crown, but the people retain full rights to its use. Even in socialist countries where land is declared public or state owned, the right to use the land should be left predominantly to the people. Here it is necessary to distinguish between strictly defined state-owned land that is actually used or managed by the state, and the nominally owned state-owned land. The latter should be constitutionally protected for the benefit of the people as the *de facto* owner and manager of the land on which they live and work. This approach is difficult in practice, however, because the government is not satisfied with formal ownership of urban land. Instead it wants to reap the full benefits derived from the substantive ownership of land so that it can pre-empt at will the infrastructure it builds.

With respect to the collective ownership of village land, it is imperative to reinterpret Article 10 so as to return the land to villagers and to de-link urbanization from government land taking. Before any land is taken, the constitutional principles requiring public interest and just compensation need to be observed and made consistent with the objective of building a 'socialist market economy' as laid down in Article 15 of the constitution. These principles will be taken seriously only with effective public participation in the land taking process.

First, the Chinese government must realize that the market principle is respected only if voluntary exchange is the rule and the first recourse. State confiscation should be a rare exception used only in the public interest, e.g. for railway and highway construction. In other words, the state should be obligated to prove the presence of a public interest before it can take any land, and it should attempt voluntary private exchanges first by negotiating with the landowners, as is the situation in the UK. The state may only initiate the compulsory taking process when all efforts to secure a voluntary exchange have failed.

Second, land taking should offer the original landowner just compensation based on the market value of the land. This has been a long-standing universal standard, to which China is moving. As Professor Lye Lin Heng pointed out in his comment on this paper, Singapore's Land Acquisition Act did not originally follow the just compensation rule since the government felt that the increase in land value was often due to the adjacent publically built infrastructure. Yet in 2007, Singapore returned to the international standard by amending the act to give full market value to the owner whose land is taken. It is noteworthy that governments committed to the rule of law, as in Singapore, use the revenue derived from a below-market value compensation scheme in the public interest, whereas in China such public resources may simply be a target for official misappropriation or corruption.

Measuring just compensation may be difficult for countries like China, where rural land is separated from the national land market, and thus technically has no market value. Yet solutions to this problem can be found – for example, rural land in a city suburb could use the price of urban land in its vicinity as a reference. In any case, the first step is to eliminate the invidious division of urban and rural land markets, and establish a uniform land market nationwide. The Decisions of the Third Plenum of the 18th Congress of the CCP explicitly endorsed this idea and vowed to establish a system that will allow rural land to enter the market based on the 'same condition, same rights and same price' as that of urban land.

Finally, these principles will remain empty words without the support of adequate institutions. For example, if the court fails to exercise its fair and independent judgment for the market price of the land taken, it will be impossible to obtain just compensation as required by the relevant laws. The question in front of the Chinese public has always been the missing guardian of its constitution. If public officials pursue their own profits at the expense of the public interest as defined in the constitution, who will enforce the constitution? Since it is the people who need protection, they must stand up to guard their own interests as protected by the constitution (Zhang 2010).

Thus, it is particularly important to guarantee public participation in the land taking process. Sometimes village committees collude with developers and township or county officials, and sell the land without even informing the peasants to whom the land has been leased. Such was the case in Wukan village in Guangdong (Patience 2011; Li 2011). To prevent corrupt deals of this type, transparency, timely notices and full public knowledge, consultations and informed consent should be made the general principles that must be observed before the state may lawfully take the land. Some of these principles have already been adopted by the Regulation on Taking and Compensation for Houses on State-owned Land, and need to be expanded to rural land taking.

In the past two decades, popular movements have arisen where people try to protect their private property. As the case in Chongqing (*New Beijing Daily* 2007) illustrates, property owners may successfully use the constitution and the Property Law to obtain market-value compensation. So far, such successes are isolated, but they do give hope to popular initiatives and efforts in China. To protect their economic and property rights effectively, the people themselves must look beyond narrow economic benefits and make full use of their legal and political rights.

Notes

1 See Zhang 2012: Chapter 3.
2 See *New Beijing Daily* 2007.
3 For example, Article 3 of the new regulation requires that land taking and compensation should follow the principles of democratic policy making, due process and openness. Regulation on Taking of and Compensation for Houses on National Land, issued by the State Council in 2011.
4 See Zhang 2005.

References

163 News (2009) 'A Relocatee in Chengdu Died of Self-immolation after Resisting the Urban Demolition Team for 3 Hours', 2 December, news.163.com/09/1202/10/5PH8QC3K00011229.html.

Chang, H. (2004) 'Toughening the Law on Land Contract', *Finance* 14: 110–112.

Duan, H. (2004) 'Waiting for Supreme Court's Judicial Interpretation of Demolition', *Finance* 11: 104–109.

He, Y. and Chen, F. (2004) 'The Chaos of Tieben', *Caijing*, 20 May: 77–86.

Huang, F.X. (2004) 'The Path to Clarity: Development of Property Rights in China', *Columbia Journal of Asian Law* 17: 191–225.

Li, Q. (2011) 'Deputy Party Secretary of Guangdong Province Visited Wukan Village, Claimed to Resolve the Issues by Relying on the Mass', *Southern Daily*, 23 December.

Mao, Y. (2008) 'Ensuring the Red Line of 1.8 billion acre Farm Land Caused Housing Price to Rise Dramatically', *Daily Economy News*, 12 December.

New Beijing Daily (2007) 'The Strongest Holdout Sticks to the Isolated House', 23 March.

Patience, M. (2011) 'China's Wukan Village Stands Up for Land Rights', *BBC News Online*, 15 December, www.bbc.co.uk/news/world-asia-china-16205654.

Qiao, S. (2015) 'Small Property, Big Market: A Focal Point Explanation', *American Journal of Comparative Law* 63(1).

Tu, C. (2010) 'Many Provinces and Municipalities Forcibly Abolish Villages to Exchange for Construction Land and Expand Land Finance', *New Beijing Daily*, 2 November.

Xie, H. (2009) 'The Defence Battle for South Nanjing', *Southern Metropolitan Week*, 21 August.

Yu, F. (2012) 'On the Establishment of Constitutional Government and Rule of Law in China from the Prospective of Protection of Peasants' Land Benefits', *Consumer Fin. L.Q. Rep* 66: 328.

Yu, S. (2013) 'How May China Eliminate Land Finance?' *Financial Times*, 20 June.

Zhang, M. (2008) 'From Public to Private: The Newly Enacted Chinese Property Law and the Protection of Property Rights in China', *Berkeley Business Law Journal* 5: 317–363.

Zhang, Q. (2005) 'Just Compensation and the Constitutional Limitation on Takings Power', *Chinese Journal of Law* 2: 25–37.

Zhang, Q. (2010) 'A Constitution without Constitutionalism? The Paths of Constitutional Developments in China', *International Journal of Constitutional Law* 8: 950–976.

Zhang, Q. (2012) *The Constitution of China: A Contextual Analysis*, Oxford: Hart Publishing.

Zhao, X. (2004) 'Political Economy Behind the "Land New Deal"', *Finance* 21: 90–93.

4 Il-legality with Chinese characteristics

How administrative litigation addresses land grabs-related issues in China

Jing Qian[1]

Background and research questions

On the one hand, Article 50 of China's Administrative Litigation Law (ALL) states flatly: 'Mediation is not applicable to administrative litigations via the People's Courts.'[2] However, administrative litigation cases (ALGs) have been widely mediated by the courts, between defendants (government agencies) and plaintiffs (citizens), ever since the ALL came into force (Clarke 1997; Landry 2005; Palmer 2006: 165; He 2011). According to basic requirements of legality (Fuller 1964), mediations in ALGs remain unlawful until the ALL is amended accordingly by the National People's Congress; yet within legal practice, mediation seems to be acceptable, even desirable, to all parties in administrative litigation. Why is this so, and how does this 'illegal' practice function? How does such a gap between law in books and law in action reflect the nature of legality in China more generally?

On the other hand, house taking and site demolition in urban areas, and land taking in rural areas are the top two types among all ALG cases in recent years (He 2012),[3] primarily due to the urbanization-centred economic development model and the taxation system involving central-local relations. Issues of land/house expropriation, forced site demolition and related matters have become battlefields between the state and society, and are more frequently dealt with via administrative litigation.

Combining these two backgrounds, this study aims to analyse a case study of land/house taking-related administrative litigation with mediation 'illegally' applied, from three perspectives. First, based on ethnographic observations of court trials, the actual proceedings of judicial mediation, and extensive interviews with judges who preside over the trials and mediations, this study reveals how judicial mediation actually works in administrative litigation in China. A concrete acquisition/demolition-related ALG case was observed during empirical study in Zhejiang in spring 2013, together with some additional illustrations of relevant cases from secondary sources.[4]

Second, besides presenting the internal operations of judicial mediation of ALG cases, this study evaluates the functional fulfilment of the (il)legal mediation within ALG cases, as well as its effects on the grand mission achievement put forward by the central leadership. With depiction of the incentives of all players in the ALG case who choose to mediate, this study terms this (il)legal phenomenon a 'legal collusion' (He 2004) among the involved local governmental agencies (the defendants), the judicial institutions and the plaintiffs. In turn, it is also the aim of this chapter to develop the conceptual framework of (il)legal collusion.

Third, to put this questionable practice of mediation in administrative litigation, which is also an interesting legal phenomenon, into the general picture of gap problems between law in books and law in action, this study sheds some light on the evolving nature of legality in China, along with the changing official guiding philosophy of judicial mediation.[5] The analytical focus will be on the 'autonomy of law' as a core element of legality, particularly in regard to two key aspects: the mechanism to check governmental power and formal/procedural values of the legal system (Shen 2000).

Outline

Via a three-layer examination of the legal phenomenon of 'illegal' mediation practice within ALG cases in Zhejiang province, this chapter argues that the functioning of mediation within the ALG cases is a result of legal collusion among local governmental agencies, judicial institutions and the plaintiffs, based on their respectively calculated best interests, which will not only undermine the projected functions of this legal mechanism but also sacrifice the formal rationality (procedural values for social planning) which is critical to the autonomous existence and sustainable operation of a legal system.

The argument is made via three interrelated perspectives. First, to illustrate the internal logic and operational patterns of ALG mediation, with an all-round analysis of the incentives of different players within the process, so as to capture such gap problems as a process of (il)legal collusion, with comprehensive backgrounds of: 1 political pressure and power structure; 2 economic interests and rational calculation; and 3 cultural norms and legal tradition.

Second, to depict and demonstrate the fundamental limits of such legal mechanism on the dispute resolution of land/house takings, and consequences of this gap problem (reflected as an (il)legal collusion) from both functional fulfilment and mission achievement perspectives.

Third, with both the logic and consequences of this gap problem demonstrated, this chapter aims to shed light on the theoretical implications of the nature of legality in China via the Weberian formal rationality and procedural justice value and Shapiro's social planning value of legality (Shen 2000; Shapiro 2011).

This chapter concludes that the informal approach of mediation contributes to neither the check on administrative misconduct nor the alleviation of social discontent, both of which are core functions designed into the mechanism of ALG. It also argues that formal rationality and procedural values, both of which are key elements of legality, are required to fulfil the designated functions of certain legal mechanisms within a legal system. In other words, a functioning legal system essentially requires an environment of legality to sustain itself.

Moreover, this article argues that the system of laws in China has not yet developed into an independent system with autonomous values, but rather it is a policy arrangement (and a tool) of political control and economic development. Under this type of legality, the legislation in China has a strong statist tendency within a fragmented authoritarian state, which to a limited extent incorporates the interests of both the fragmented state and the pluralizing society. Judicial behaviours are result oriented and pressure sensitive, and by their nature are inconsistent and unpredictable in the medium and long terms. With limited participation and predictability, the stakeholders of the laws and regulations tend to display a great deal of un-legal, extra-legal and anti-legal behaviour patterns when dealing with legal matters. This involves a substantial degree of political struggle, economic calculation and human discretion, instead of autonomous legal reasoning.

The administrative litigation cases

General data of the ALG cases: 'litigation without a ruling'

He Haibo's insightful studies on the legal institution of withdrawal of administrative litigation reveal an interesting legal phenomenon, namely that ALG cases are largely concluded without judicial rulings but instead with plaintiffs' withdrawals. The percentage of withdrawals, according to national statistical data from 1987 to 2010 collected by He, varies between 30 percent and 57 percent.[6] This displays an increasing trend in recent years under the official directives promoting judicial coordination, also known as the movement of 'grand mediation' and the doctrine of 'three supremes' which made the Chinese legal development a 'u-turn against law' (He 2011; Minzner 2011). He's observation echoes my own observations at the intermediate court H, where cases concluded by withdrawal as a result of mediation/coordination reached an average of 31 percent from 2008 to 2012, while province-wide the average annual rate reached 34 percent.[7]

Since the law clearly forbids mediation in these cases, it is worth noting that other terms such as 'coordination', 'reconciliation', 'settlement' and so on, are creatively adopted to make the illegality less obvious. However, as Hu and Tang comprehensively analysed, all these terms are used to describe more or less the same judicial practice (Hu and Tang 2011). Therefore, to simplify, 'mediation' will solely be used hereinafter to describe this (il)legal phenomenon.

So how is the legally inapplicable mediation applied in the process of administrative litigation?

The process of a mediation-applied ALG case

Legislators of the ALL and the ALG mechanism projected two core functions: to check administrative misconduct and alleviate social discontent.[8] Moreover, in the process of judicialization of administrative governance in China, the ALL was the first law that empowered people to challenge any misconduct of the executive via the judiciary. This opens a door, not only for citizens to sue the government and for judicial institutions to expand territory, but also for observers of China and Chinese law to evaluate the promises of 'administration in accordance with law' made by the central leadership.[9] The ALG mechanism (and mediation illegally applied), like other imported political/legal institutions, has not simply been transplanted, but completely localized to fulfil the purposes of the party-state, while also being utilized by the courts, the people and society as a whole, according to specific cultural, political and legal contexts.[10]

The following is a set of related questions to ask in regard to the case study. First, have the projected functions of the ALG mechanism been fulfilled? Has administrative misconduct been modified after the ALG? Has the related social discontent been alleviated? Second, is the application of the ALG mechanism enhancing the overall legality of the system? Does it enhance administration in accordance with the laws? Does it increase the legal awareness of the general public?

Case study: the tale of a pigeon house[11]

Sun v. Y District Housing and Urban & Rural Construction Bureau

1 The procedural history and a brief summary of facts

Sun, the plaintiff, aged 55, retired from the state sector and currently runs a pigeon business. He possessed a condo of 92m^2 in Y district of H city, located in a building in a newly planned construction zone approved to become the new city on 19 July 2010. However, negotiations for compensation and site demolition between Sun and the developer (Y Corp) did not go well, due to the historical ambiguity of the ownership of the condo and other matters.[12] With no terms agreed, on 25 August 2011, Y Corp submitted the dispute for a ruling to the Construction Bureau of Y district (CBY), which had authority over disputes of this sort. CBY accepted the case, and on 23 September 2011, it ruled in favour of Y Corp and forced Sun to move out of the condo so that the site demolition could proceed and construction could start as soon as possible. This ruling (hereafter [2011] No. 8) was the key controversial issue in the following litigation and mediation processes.

Sun, dissatisfied with the ruling by the CBY, filed immediately for administrative reconsideration to the Y district government, but on 15 February 2012 the district government confirmed the previous ruling. These seemingly unfair administrative rulings eventually led Sun to file for administrative litigation on 26 March 2012, to the Y district court which had territorial jurisdiction over the case.

Considering the complicated nature of this case, in which both the Y district government and the Y District Housing and Urban & Rural Construction Bureau (HCB)[13] were involved, a senior judge in the administrative branch of the Y district court reported to the intermediate court of H city for recommendations.

The H city intermediate court intervened as requested, and decided to decrease political influence by transferring the case to another jurisdiction in the G district of H city. The G district court agreed to take the case, and on 16 May 2012, the case was officially moved to G district court for trial.

In the following months, with comprehensive investigation and two rounds of trials,[14] the G district court recognized the legal authority of the newly founded HCB to uphold the administrative decision of site demolition, but the court found tremendous maladministration and procedural flaws in both the ruling of [2011] No. 8 and Y Corp's dealings with the site demolition and with compensation negotiations, according to the relevant rules and regulations.[15] The two most apparent examples are: first, Article 14(3) of the Regulation on the Administrative Rulings of the Dismantlement of Urban Houses allows 15 days for the resident to vacate the residence for site demolition, but in [2011] No. 8 it gave Sun only seven days – a clear violation of the regulation; second, the official address of Sun as printed on his identification card was Unit 2, Room 204, but in [2011] No. 8 the address was Unit 2, Room 202 – a clear mistake due either to historical ambiguity or simply a careless administrative error. As a consequence, the administrative decision of [2011] No. 8 was revoked and the G district court demanded that HCB re-issue another administrative decision with all factors and laws taken into consideration.

2 The appeal: the official trial and the unofficial mediation process

Not surprisingly, right after the ruling was made by the G district court in November 2012, both the defendant and the plaintiff appealed to the intermediate court of H city, on 27 and 28 November, respectively.

On the one hand, the HCB, along with Y district government and Y Corp, wanted to get rid of the Sun 'nail household', push forward the site demolition and carry out the construction plan as soon as possible. On the other hand, Sun and his family did not appreciate such a win over the government. As became clear later, what they really wanted was substantial compensation.

The intermediate court of city H was not unfamiliar with this case and the real intentions of both parties, so they accepted both appeals on 10 December 2012, and scheduled a trial for 9 January 2013.

As expected, there was not very much new in the appeal trial. The facts found and laws applied in the first trial were re-examined and re-affirmed.

The only difference was that Sun and the HCB, Y Corp and B Corp, as third parties, agreed to a court-led mediation in private.[16]

The first round of mediation was quickly set for 16 January 2013, one week after the appeal trial. Sun and his wife, and Liu, a staff member of the HCB, as a representative of the government, joined the mediation.

Sun came well prepared. He accused the HCB and Y Corp of many instances of illegal conduct in the site demolition planning and negotiations,[17] and demanded compensation of 1.3 million RMB, which was three times the average equivalent compensation rate in the region. Liu clearly had no final say in the situation, so under constant pressure from the judge, he kept calling back to ask for direction and only responded vaguely to Sun's accusations and requests.

The first round of mediation did not yield any fruitful agreement. The leading judge, Wu, was unhappy about the absence of those who were in charge of the matter from the government side and deemed the mediation a waste of time. After Judge Wu demanded that the HCB send senior officials to mediate towards an authoritative agreement, the second round of mediation was set for 23 January 2013. However, due to a last-minute occurrence, the head of the HCB did not show up; instead, the head of B Corp was sent to deal with the outstanding issues.[18]

Although over one hour was spent again arguing the historical dispute, the mediation session actually went well, with a mutually agreed two-option solution reached: B Corp would either compensate the Sun family 900,000 RMB[19] or provide a condo of similar size and condition at another location in town as a replacement for Sun and his family. Sun seemed satisfied with the offer but insisted on inspecting the condo that B Corp was offering before signing the deal and withdrawing the case. Judge Wu agreed and demanded that both parties sign the agreement and file for withdrawal of the case as soon as possible.

However, by the end of that week, the case had not been withdrawn. Sun was probably dissatisfied with the replacement condo, but he did not take the monetary compensation either. Instead, Sun demanded a further round of mediation.

A relevant factor was that this case was cited as an example in a report on social unfairness/unrest invoked by land acquisition and site demolition, in which other potential issues of this project and the like were exposed, such as starting construction before final permissions were granted, and taking more land units than the licence actually permitted.

Sun said he was contacted for an interview about further reports on this matter. Apparently, neither B Corp (and the HCB) nor the court wanted any more controversy added to this already overdue case, so the third round of mediation was agreed and set for 30 January 2013.

Finally the head of the HCB, Wang, who should have shown up at the trial and at the earlier round of mediation, came to save the day. Wang opened the mediation by saying he was there to solve the problem and to reach a win-win-win solution for Sun, Y Corp and the court (a typical local official's attitude).

Sun followed strongly (probably because of the potential media support), and insisted that the original compensation demand of 1.3 million RMB was a fair deal.

The head of B Corp replied angrily that he had sincerely offered 900,000 RMB, which could buy a brand new condo of the same condition, and it was more than double the average compensation rate to other residents.

Then Sun produced his 'joker': a wooden pigeon house of nearly 40m^2 which he had built on the roof of the condo (it was illegally built, with no licence or permission, as we found out later), which would justify the extra 400,000 RMB.

This sounded almost like a joke, as B Corp responded. This shaky wooden pigeon cage would be worth no more than 10,000 RMB, and one could not treat this as of real estate value. It is notable here that neither Wang of the HCB nor B Corp argued the illegality of this construction. The focus was always on the unfair value evaluation of the pigeon house/cage, which to some extent shows people's indifference to the formal laws of China.

However, Sun was determined and insisted that the original compensation rate was the only way out; otherwise, he would keep on suing, petitioning to various governments and reporting to the mass media. He knew he was in an advantageous position; as time passed, he would have more leverage. The mediation was halted by Sun's threats. Wang said he would have to discuss it carefully within the HCB, so the three-hour third round of mediation reached no consensus.

However, out of the blue, on the evening of 30 January, Judge Wu received a call from Wang saying that B Corp would compensate Sun 1.3 million RMB, but Sun would need to sign a document of confidentiality and a letter of assurance of no further action, and then file for withdrawal of the administrative litigation. Sun happily agreed. So after almost two years, this case was concluded with both parties withdrawing from the intermediate court on 31 January 2013.

3 Outcomes and consequences

There were certain consequences to this outcome. First, illegalities in this case were reinforced and encouraged, instead of punished and deterred, which creates an internal contraction for sustaining an autonomous legal system. On the one hand, the massive amount of administrative misconduct and historical illegality was buried with a mediated confidential agreement; on the other hand, the plaintiff's illegally built unit was rewarded instead of being removed according to the HCB's own regulations. Moreover, the mediation conducted by the H city intermediate court was in itself an illegal practice.

Second, the mediation also reveals an external contradiction: both projected functions of the mechanism of ALG were unfulfilled: maladministration was not only left uncorrected but also reinforced, while social discontent was invoked rather than discouraged. Ideally, this case could have ended in a formal ruling by the G district court which: 1 demanded the HCB correct its administrative misconduct; 2 demanded Y Corp correct its flaws in site demolition; and 3 clarified the historical ambiguity to solve Sun's problem and to establish a precedent-like ruling to provide guidance for similar situations. However, it was all wrapped up in an informal, extra-legal, result-oriented way, which neither formally checked the incidents of administrative misconduct, nor sustainably alleviated social unrest. As the Supreme People's Court reported, 'the failures of administrative litigation (to be completed in a formal way) have resulted in an increased number of petitions and irrational behaviours, which severely undermine social stability'.[20]

Furthermore, this informal, extra-legal and result-oriented form of dispute resolution reveals two other critical characteristics of the Chinese legal system. First, a vicious cycle of stability-seeking/instability-causing behaviour is created (Lee 2014). The utilization of both the market nexus and the mass line nexus by the government to address social discontent was by nature unsustainable and was merely postponing the crisis to a later point in time at a greater scale and level. Second, the overall extra-legal logic employed by all relevant players of the supposedly legal process is alarming and illustrative. This will be further demonstrated in the next section under the theoretical generalization of an '(il)legal collusion' with a stakeholder's analysis of the mediation within the ALG case.

Il-legal collusions, gap problems and their implications

With a stakeholder analysis of the incentives of the involved parties' extra-legal logics of action during the legal and illegal processes of the ALG case, this section first provides a picture of (il)legal collusion among the local governmental agencies, the judicial institutions and the plaintiffs. It then locates this interesting legal phenomenon into the general picture of gap problems with the Chinese legal system so as to shed some light on the evolving nature of legality in China.

An il-legal collusion with a stakeholder analysis

1 THE DEFENDANTS: THE POWERFUL GOVERNMENT AGENCIES

The government agencies, particularly at local levels, have been the main target of social discontent and public distrust, and the overall governance capacity faces tremendous challenges from the rapidly changing state-society interactions. The ALG mechanism makes local governments even more uptight, and there are a number of reasons why government entities, as the defendants, favour the illegal practice of mediation to solve the ALG cases against them.

First, to save face (*mainzi*). *Mainzi*, like *guanxi* (connections), is a widely acknowledged value (and sometimes commodity) in the Chinese culture. In addition, the paternalistic views of the government are still deeply rooted in the mindset of a great number of local cadres. So when their (mis)conduct is challenged in the court, it would be more acceptable for them to cover it up without publicly being found wrong. However, the obvious dilemma here is, while the government officials' mainzi is temporarily saved with this illegal practice, the legal system's *mianzi* is eternally lost because legality is sacrificed.

Second, to maintain stability (weiwen). Economic development in the past decades has been accompanied by maladministration, corruption, inequality and injustice, all of which cause mounting social unrest. Therefore, the preservation of stability has, in recent years, become as important as economic development in the job descriptions of local government agencies. As a working mechanism, there is also a more rationally created governance performance evaluation system, within which a loss in an ALG suit would be a minus, and thus cannot be overlooked. So the government agencies need not secure a win, but merely avoid losing and thus gain full marks in that section of 'administration in accordance with laws'.[21] Mediation, which leads to withdrawal of the ALG suits, would serve this purpose well.

Furthermore, a new operating mode under local government bureaucrats is called to 'buy peace with money' (*chuqian mai taiping*). It is a combination of the market nexus enabled by uncontrolled fiscal capacity and the mass-line mechanism enabled by the party's organizational penetration into society. It is applied to absorb social discontent, which weakens the formal status of the ALG.[22] However, this newly formed mechanism is clearly unsustainable and actually creates a vicious cycle of maintaining stability while creating instability. Local government organs have clear incentives to maintain the instability at a certain level so as to ensure continuous budgetary support and personal career advancement. The widely circulated popular maxim in regards to maintaining stability – namely, 'big disturbance big resolution, small disturbance small resolution, no disturbance no resolution' – also encourages the protesters to go for a bigger disturbance so as to gain better compensation.[23]

In conclusion, this systematic politicization of legal issues brutally bypasses the formal legal mechanisms in dealing with disputes between the government and society, and undermines the authority of the legal system by creating an informal set of rules that are actually much better implemented or followed than the formal ones.

2 THE COURTS: AN AWKWARD INTERMEDIARY?

An autonomous and independent judiciary apparently maximizes the interests of the judges as part of the legal profession and for the court as an active institutional actor seeking authority in the power structure. However, the current institutional arrangements put the judges and the courts in an awkward position and force them to choose and pursue solutions other than judicial independence and autonomy. The ALG mechanism is one of the illustrative examples.

The establishment of the ALG mechanism can expand the courts' power, particularly in balancing the power of the government via the grievances voiced by the people to fight against maladministration. However, a number of reasons incentivize the judges individually, and the courts as institutions, to collude with the government agencies via the 'illegal' mediation.

First, the courts' dependence on the corresponding levels of government for both personnel and finance capacities suffocate the rational functioning of the court as an independent institutional player in the long run. Moreover, multiple party units also exercise organizational leadership over the courts from both within (dangzu) and above (*zhengfawei*).

Second, besides the existing power structure, the Party also actively interferes with the guiding principles for judicial work. As stated above, the most recent movements are 'grand mediation' and 'three supremes', which encourage and, to a degree, force judges to solve disputes informally and often extra-legally.

Third, against the above-mentioned political background, judges gradually formulate incentives to apply mediation in ALG cases. For one, the pressure of appeal is neutralized when an ALG case is mediated. For another, via discretionary manipulation within mediation, judges can gain personal favours from government officials informally.[24]

Last, but not least, both judges and plaintiffs must consider the enforcement in action after the ruling on paper is made. A mediated outcome, accepted by government agencies, will ensure voluntary enforcement, and often agreements reached informally provide better compensation to the plaintiffs than those achieved formally, as illustrated in the next section.

3 THE PLAINTIFFS: RIGHTFUL RESISTANCE VIA EXTRA-LEGAL STRATEGIES

First we must ask, who are the plaintiffs in ALG cases? They are normally the weak, with limited guanxi and resources to sort out a dispute. To seek remedy via the judicial system is often not the first choice in dispute resolution in Chinese culture and legal tradition, and to sue the government via the ALG mechanism is surely one of the last straws that people grasp.[25]

Second, although the ALG is considered one of the last straws, most plaintiffs have limited faith regarding relying solely on this legal mechanism to restore justice. They tend to mobilize all available resources and exhaust all possible channels, official and unofficial, formal and informal, legal and extra-legal. Prior to, or at the same time as, using the ALG mechanism, the plaintiffs normally have been filing for administrative reconsideration, for petitions via letters or visits, organizing and participating in collective actions of protest, and reaching out to the mass media. Chinese people are sophisticated enough to understand that judicial redress is neither final nor binding in terms of effective enforcement. More often than not, an ALG case and even a winning ruling is just one more bargaining chip in their political game with the government.

Chinese people are also sophisticated enough to know where the boundaries of resistance are. According to Lee, Chinese citizens' '"rights consciousness" is very much shaped by the transformative and malleable process of engagement with officials', and they do seriously fear any retaliation from the government, as administrative penetration is still so widespread, enhanced but not replaced by the force of marketization in the past decades. So, their guiding principle of seeking justice is not only to know how to keep pressing until it hurts, but also when to stop pressing when it hurts too much.

Third, in a certain sense, we can deem the nature of the ALG-involved mobilization of resources as a political process with extra-legal strategies, aiming for economic pursuits following non-legal logics. Based on the interestingly useful term 'rightful resistance' coined by O'Brien and Li, I tend to modify the term to better describe such a process as 'rightful but extra-legal resistance', in which there are basic logics of rightfully fighting for one's lawful rights as a citizen, but the essential drive, based on ALG cases I have observed, is politically formed, aiming for materialistic gains in the name of justice and legality,[26] which I also tend to term 'rights consciousness without legal awareness'.

4 AN IL-LEGAL COLLUSION

The overall analysis of all stakeholders' motivation and conception of the legal process of mediation within the ALG case depicts this interesting legal phenomenon as an '(il)legal collusion' (He 2004) among the involved local governmental agencies (defendants), the plaintiffs and the legal institutions. In turn, this case of the illegal practice of ALG mediation also expands the conceptual framework of (il)legal collusion.

Traditional studies on legal enforcement basically rely on a dichotomy between the regulatory agencies and regulated subjects, which limits understanding of the issue by excluding interactions among different subgroups of the regulated. Law and society scholar He Xin, via a particular case study of how rural–urban internal migrants collaborate with local residents to bypass a series of discriminatory regulations against migrants in business licence applications with the purpose of protecting local businesses, coins a concept of '(il)legal collusion' to describe the 'subtle cooperation' between the regulated subjects (migrants and locals) to evade the regulation and reach a win-win situation that 'flounders the intended goal of law', which expands the traditional approach of legal enforcement (He 2009).[27]

The case of mediation in the ALG cases pushes this conceptual endeavour a bit further, with the involvement of the legal institutions (as well as the legal profession). It also reveals more complexities under a more general context of the current Chinese unitary system, with a triangular state-society relationship among the central state, the local state and society.

The concept of (il)legal collusion can be extended from 'interactions among subgroups of the regulated' to the interactions among the protected (the plaintiffs), the regulated (the government agencies, particularly those at local levels), and the supposedly neutral court. This case is different from the case He Xin used to form the conceptual descriptions, in terms of: 1 the legal institution is actively involved in the 'subtle cooperation'; and 2 the dynamics of the triangular central state-local state-society relationship is also put into context. Both add substantially to the sophistication of the conceptual framework.

However, it also shares certain basic elements: if we see the plaintiffs as the protected, and the local government agencies as the regulated, a similar line of logic would be: a number of the protected (Beijing locals in He Xin's case and the plaintiffs in the ALG mediation) by certain laws, with aims of short-term, self-interested gains, collude with the regulated, at the cost of the protected as a whole, and also the overall authority of the legal system. To be more specific, both '(il)legal collusions' will not only undermine the projected functions of this legal mechanism, but also sacrifice the formal rationality (procedural values for social planning) that is critical to the autonomous existence and sustainable operation of a legal system.

Nonetheless, the dynamics of the mediation of the ALG, compared with He Xin's regulatory case, reveal more complexities of the illegal collusion, reflected in the authoritarian regime's central-local relationship, the state-society relationship, and the judiciary-executive relationship.

In terms of the central-local relationship, this illegal collusion via the mediation of the ALG case reveals once again the basic 'measures and countermeasures' logic between local governments and central government, which is so commonly seen in the literature (He 2009; Ginsburg and Moustafa 2008). In terms of the state-society relationship, there is collusion between the state and society to erode the authority and sustainability of the legal system, which implies a lack of long-term commitment to formality, regularity and predictability in the environment of legality. In terms of the judiciary-executive relationship, this legal phenomenon is clearly uneasy, and without centralized administration of the judicial system, behaviours in favour of local protectionism would be a rational choice for both the court as an institution and the judges as individuals.

All in all, the conceptual framework of (il)legal collusion offers unique explanatory insights into the law and policy enforcement and implementation issues within the Chinese legal system, and surely has the potential to be expanded and developed to be more inclusively and illustratively useful.

Gap problems and il-legality with Chinese characteristics

Furthermore, as reflected by this study via the case of mediation of ALG, this gap problem between law in books and law in action (which is only one of thousands within the Chinese legal system) entailed in the (il)legal collusion can be attributed to a combination of reasons: 1 the fundamentally policy-oriented tendency of legislation in China precludes adequate representation of the interests of both the fragmented state and the pluralizing society; 2 the lack of institutional design of an independent judiciary makes judicial behaviour pressure sensitive and result oriented, which are inconsistent and unpredictable in the medium and long terms; and 3 with such limited participation and predictability, and people's constant failures at communicating formally via the law, the stakeholders of the law and regulation gradually adopt un-legal, extra-legal and anti-legal behaviour patterns when dealing with legal matters, and this involves a substantial degree of political struggle, economic calculation and human discretion, instead of autonomous legal reasoning.

All of these factors reveal the nature of legality in China, for which both the rule of law and the rule of man are indispensable but which have to date proven impossible to capture. On the one hand, laws and men are inseparable from the very beginning: the legislation, interpretation and implementation are all made by humans. On the other hand, it is unfair to say China does not rule by law, given the tremendous outcomes of the three-decade legalization movement. However, it is also unrealistic to say China has a rule of law system like that of the USA, as the fundamental environment of legality is yet to be formed.

The concept of rule by law is of limited explanatory power as well, as it fails to capture the extra-legal strategies adopted by the general public to bypass formal laws and maximize their interests during state-society interactions. Also it cannot display the dynamics of all contradictions among national and local laws, regulations, rules and other policy directives that result from the complicated central-local interactions.

Without a more appropriate term to describe the nature of the legality of the current legal system in China, the author tends to label it tentatively as 'il-legality with Chinese characteristics', and intends to generalize the core characteristics it contains as follows. First, formal legal rationality is weak, if not totally absent. Under the current regime of a party-state, the autonomous values and procedural justice are inferior compared with other substantive values and policy goals incorporated into the legal system.

Second, the legislative processes bear a strong statist tendency. Without a democratic formulation of public opinion and a systematically functioning interest representation platform, the elites in power determine the priorities of legislation on behalf of all people, but eventually in their own interests.

Third, gap problems such as inconsistencies between law in books and law in action are widespread within the system. Internal contradictions among national and local laws, regulations and other forms of rules are commonly detected but remain unfixed.

Fourth, massive gap problems invoke the uncontrollable exercise of discretionary power. Especially in the realm of public law (constitutional and administrative law), the Chinese legal system is turning against the rule of law, and is bearing stronger and stronger features of 'rule of men'.

Fifth, laws are often not obeyed by government officials, even those made by themselves. Under the current institutional arrangements and power structure, the costs of maladministration remain very low, while gains are very high. This situation is now changing, due to an anti-corruption campaign, but it still has a limited effect on improved legality.

Sixth, related to the fifth point, laws are often utilized by both the state and society in extra-legal ways. For government officials, anti-corruption is often used as 'a method of political assassination' to sideline political opponents (Yang 2004: 14). For the general public, in their 'rightful resistance' via laws, strategies are often invoked by the people, mobilizing them when laws help, bypassing them when laws might harm, and generating more suitable alternatives when laws are inadequate.[28] Such rightful but extra-legal resistance shows an interesting phenomenon of people's rights consciousness without legal awareness.

Seventh, 'politicization of the judiciary' describes the status quo in the courts in China. What makes the tensions between legal development and extra-legal strategies adopted by state-society interactions even more intriguing is the awkward role of legal institutions – in particular, the extra-legal uses of the legal institutions by both the people and the local governmental agencies to reach informal, case-by-case, result-oriented dispute resolutions, most of which involve deviated applications of the formal laws and regulations.[29]

A preliminary conclusion

This chapter analyses a case study of mediation within administrative litigation, first, to present why and how self-interested local government agencies, local judicial institutions and plaintiffs collaborate to form an (il)legal collusion to bypass the formal laws and invalidate the legislative intents set by the central leadership, which in turn expands the application of this conceptual framework.

Second, this case study reveals that with informal dispute resolution via mediation prevailing over formal judicial review via adjudication, administrative misconduct is largely left unchecked and thus uncorrected, which allows further maladministration to degrade the already uneasy state-society interactions, and eventually fails the projected functions/mission of this particular legal mechanism (such as administrative misconduct checks and social unrest alleviation).

Third, the study argues that this gap problem created by (il)legal collusion decreases regularity and predictability of formal rules, and encourages utilization of extra-legal strategies by both the state (maladministration at low cost) and society (rightful but extra-legal resistance) to reach informal dispute resolutions, leading to a vicious circle which not only puts the court's autonomy awkwardly between populist and political influence, but also undermines the overall legality of the regime. In other words, without autonomous and formalistic values of legality realized, the legal system's instrumental and substantive values would eventually be undermined.

Finally, the author calls for more studies to understand better the evolving nature of legality in China via the lens of the widespread gap problems within the Chinese legal system.

Notes

1 My deepest gratitude to Professor William P. Alford and Professor Andrew J. Harding for their delightful enlightenment and invaluable mentorship all the time, to Professor Connie Carter and Professor Zhang Qianfan for thoughtful encouragement and constant inspiration, and to the Faculty of Law of the University of Victoria, the Center for Asian Legal Studies at National University of Singapore, and the Harvard Law School Summer Academic Fellowship Program for their generosity and overall support. For a fuller version of this chapter, see: 'Il-legality with Chinese Characteristics: A Socio-legal Study of "Illegal" Judicial Mediation in Land/housing Taking-related Administrative Litigation', Harvard Law School, graduation thesis (May 2014).

2 Administrative Litigation Law of China, 1989.

3 19.3 percent and 18.7 percent, respectively.

4 This study is based on ethnographic observations of more than 20 administrative litigation trials, and a number of associated mediations that I attended at an intermediate court in city H in Zhejiang province from January to March 2013. The intermediate court of city H was selected as the empirical setting of this research based on two considerations. First, as Jiang Ming'an has advocated, making the intermediate court the default court of first trial for ALG is wise because of more professional personnel and less local protectionism, therefore the quality of ALG cases at this level are normally comparatively higher and thus more illustrative; second, city H and the province in which it is located have one of the most liberalized and pluralistic state-society relationships, thanks to the developed private economy, which provides a tolerant environment for administrative litigation (Jiang 2006, 2011). Research data come mainly from three sources. The first is direct observations of over 20 ALG trials and a number of mediations conducted for three cases out of the 20. Gaining access to the court through personal connections, I was allowed to sit and listen to the whole trial process, which typically took two to three hours, with normally one court session in the morning and/or one in the afternoon. Since tape recording of proceedings is prohibited in the courts, the fieldwork relied mostly on written notes and copies of a number of official court transcripts. Pseudonyms were used to protect the parties' identities. The second source involved interviews with the judges who presided over the trials, normally at lunch after the morning session or a brief talk on the bus home after the afternoon session. There was not a fixed set of questions as the interviews were conducted mostly in informal settings, but certain common questions were used in the interviews/talks with judges with regard to their perspectives on the cases, and their rationale of decision making for both trials and mediations. The third source was data collected via informal talks with some of the lawyers, plaintiffs and defendants before and after court sessions, mostly about their willingness to mediate or not, as well as their motivations behind their actions. Secondary sources included the series of publications titled 'ALG Manuscripts' (*ban'an shouji*), by

Yuan Yulai, known as the first and best (or at least the most well-known) lawyer who has specialized in ALG cases for nearly two decades.

5 The judicial capacity of local courts is largely shaped by: 1 political pressure from local governments; and 2 varying guiding principles of higher courts (which are normally translated as the central leadership's intentions), as well as the quality of personnel (both the court leadership and judges' capabilities) (He 2011).

6 According to He's investigations, in the past couple of decades, increasingly withdrawal by the plaintiff has been the most popular way to conclude ALG cases. It was 21.3 percent in 1987, rising to 57.3 percent in 1997, and after a series of ups and downs due to various judicial considerations, the rate of withdrawal is now around 30 percent.

7 Internal annual reports made by intermediate court H from 2008–12.

8 For a detailed discussion, see Ginsburg and Moustafa (2008: 67). He (2009: 143, 161) illustrates the changing socio-economic conditions, such as the local corporatist arrangements and the decline of the 'win-win' economic development model in the development of administrative litigation, and disputes Ohnesorge's conclusion, emphasizing the positive correlation between the changes in the socio-economic and political-constitutional conditions in China.

9 Hard evidence of the state's promotion of 'administration in accordance with law' (*yi fa zhizheng*) includes three monumental directives issued by the State Council: 1 the 'Decision to Comprehensively Implement Administration in Accordance with the Law', in November 1999; 2 the 'Outline for Comprehensively Implementing Further Administration in Accordance with the Law', in March 2004; and 3 'The Decision to Enhance City and County Level Governments' Administration in Accordance with Law'. See Peerenboom 1999; Zheng 2010).

10 See the examination of People's Congresses in this regard and Qian (n.d.). Also, China's legal development should not only be viewed as a simple imposition of Western models, but as a more complex process of adaptation and institutional transformation.

11 Observations and interviews, at the intermediate court of city H (January and February 2013).

12 Y Corp, with government background in the Y district to implement the site demolition – a common practice in the urbanization process in China. Here is some background information regarding Sun's possession of the condo: Sun has worked since 1979 as a staff member at the Bureau of Township and Village Enterprises Management of Y county (later on, the Y district), and as a benefit for state sector employees, Sun and his family were entitled to a public residence. In 1984, when Sun got married, the Bureau of Township and Village Enterprises Management allocated a condo owned by the 2nd Construction Company of Y district (a township enterprise under the management of the bureau) to Sun and his family to fulfil the initial promise of housing benefits. At that time the public housing policy was lifetime occupation for one's family, but the state owned the condo. Sun duly settled with his family in the assigned condo. However, following reforms, the situation changed dramatically during the next decades. For instance, following a wave of privatization some public properties of the 2nd Construction Company, including Sun's condo, were transferred to a new private company named Beili Company, which later became Beili Construction Corporation (B Corp hereinafter). The Bureau of Township and Village Enterprises Management where Sun worked was also incorporated into other government departments, and Sun chose to go into business (*xia hai*). Over the years, Sun tried and failed to have his previous employers and B Corp transfer ownership of the condo to him or his family, as many of his colleagues had done. However, Sun and his family remained in the condo until the recent city centre construction and demolition plans were approved.

During the trial, both sides acknowledged that illegal transactions were made in the privatization of the properties, and in the administrative streamlining of Sun's previous employer. These were referred to as historically left issues (*lishi yiliu wenit*). Under such circumstances, Sun has been allowed to live in the condo, despite the fact that the owner on paper is B Corp.

13 In early 2012, the Y District Construction Bureau was incorporated into the Housing, Urban & Rural Construction Bureau of the Y district.

14 According to interviews with judges in the intermediate court of city H, there is usually just one trial for these cases.

15 These include: the Regulation on the Dismantlement of Urban Houses adopted in 2001 and repealed in 2009 by the State Council; the Regulation on the Administrative Rulings of the Dismantlement of Urban Houses adopted in 2003 by the Department of Construction; the Zhejiang Provincial Regulation on the Dismantlement of Urban Houses adopted in 2011 and revised in 2007 by the Standing Committees of the Provincial People's Congress of Zhejiang.

16 This mediation appeared in the official court documents as 'coordination towards settlement'.

17 Such as the deceitful information provided for the actual price of the new properties and the different rates of compensation the Y Corp gave to different households depending on their *guanxi*. He also mentioned the wrongs done during the privatization of properties of the 2nd Construction Company, including the condo he resided in and other public properties. He further accused B Corp of being irresponsible since it enjoyed all the benefits of taking over the public assets, while doing nothing to solve the historical problems. Sun made a comparison with another similarly privatized state-owned enterprise in the Y district which built new apartments in which to place all previous employees.

18 It is understandable that the head of the HCB, a newly incorporated bureau, hesitated to take over old disputes from the previous Construction Bureau. The same applied to the head of B Corp, who had very limited knowledge about the old agreements between Sun, his previous employer and the second construction company. Nonetheless, the head of B Corp came with a political task assigned to him by the head of the HCB, and he had the authority to make a decision.

19 This was twice the package given to many other residents in the zone and equalled the current market value of a brand new condo of the same size in the region.

20 The Opinion of the Supreme People's Court on Protecting the Parties' Right to Sue in Administrative Litigation According to the Law (*Zuigao Renmin Fayuan Guanyu Yifa Baohu Xingzheng Susong Dangshiren Suquan De Yijian*), 2009.

21 Interviews at the intermediate court of city H (January and February 2013).

22 For a discussion, see Lee 2014; Hook 2011.

23 For a discussion, see Tan and Yates 2002.

24 For example, occasionally certain judges are invited to give lectures as part of legal education at government agencies, and some can be invited to provide consulting services on issues such as how to plan and implement land acquisitions and site demolitions at low legal risk. Sometimes, when the judge-consulted site demolition causes social unrest and results in an ALG case, the consulting judge will try his/her best to rule in favour of the government. This was also confirmed during interviews at the intermediate courts.

25 With empirical studies of 2,724 documents of decisions from Shanghai courts, He and Su found that the stronger parties not only win more often, but also do so by a large margin (He and Su 2013).

26 From interviews with plaintiffs at the intermediate court of city H, the author realizes the age of Qiu Ju has long gone, and current Chinese plaintiffs are calculating very rationally how to maximize their interests, in the name of 'seeking justice' (*tao ge shuofa*).

27 To prevent migrants from pouring into the city, the Beijing municipal government promulgated a series of discriminatory regulations against migrants in business licence applications. Since it is far more difficult for migrants than locals to apply for an individual business operator (*getihu*) licence, many migrant entrepreneurs decided to rent licences from locals, or use locals as a cover while migrants actually conducted their own business. Based on this, He Xin uses the term 'legal collusion'.

28 See similar reflections in Marshall and Barclay 2003.

29 With the mediation processes, the judicial process becomes more and more 'result oriented' instead of rule oriented, and law becomes an arbitrary tool of the state. On 'result-oriented' judicial behaviours, see Zhao 2005. On criticisms of the retreat in legal reforms in China in recent years, see Jiang 2010; Zhang 2010.

References

Clarke, D. (1997) 'Dispute Resolution in China', in T.V. Lee (ed.) *Contract, Guanxi, and Dispute Resolution in China*, New York: Routledge.

Fuller, L. (1964) *The Morality of Law*, New Haven, CT: Yale University Press.

Ginsburg, T. and Moustafa, T., eds (2008) *Rule By Law: The Politics of Courts in Authoritarian Regimes*, Cambridge: Cambridge University Press.

He, H. (2011) 'Litigations without a Ruling: The Predicaments of Administrative Law in China', *Tsinghua China Law Review* 3: 257–281.

He, H. (2012) 'Trapped Administrative Litigation', *Journal of East China University of Political Science and Law* 2, article.chinalawinfo.com/Article_Detail.asp?ArticleID=68848&Type=mod.

He, X. (2004) 'The Stickiness of Legal Collusion: A Difficulty of Legal Enforcement', *International Journal of the Sociology of Law* 32: 103.

He, X. (2009) 'Administrative Law as a Mechanism for Political Control in Contemporary China', in S. Balme and M.W. Dowdle (eds) *Building Constitutionalism in China*, Basingstoke: Palgrave Macmillan.

He, X. and Yang, S. (2013) 'Do the "Haves" Come Out Ahead in Shanghai Courts?' *Journal of Empirical Legal Studies* 10: 120.

Hook, L. (2011) 'Beijing Raises Spending on Internal Security', *Financial Times*, www.ft.com/intl/cms/s/0/f70936b0-4811-11e0-b323-00144feab49a.html#axzz1Ohfwyzsk.

Hu, J. and Tang, Z. (2011) 'Administrative Mediation, Reconciliation or …' (Xingzheng susong tiaojie, hejie, yihuo xietiaohjie), *Tribune of Political Science and Law* (*zhengfa luntan*) 4, hetong.cnki.net/law/detail/detail.aspx?filename=ZFLT201104006&dbcode=CLKJ&dbname=CLKJ.

Jiang, M. (2006) *Jurisprudence of Administrative Litigation Law* (*Xingzheng Susongfaxue*), 2nd edn, Beijing: Law Press.

Jiang, M. (2011) 'Six Issues in the Revision of the ALL' (Xingzheng susong zhong de liuda nanti), *Jurisprudence Daily*, article.chinalawinfo.com/Article_Detail.asp?ArticleId=65850.

Jiang, P. (2010) *Chen fu yu ku rong: ba shi zi shu*, Beijing: Law Press.

Landry, P.F. (2005) 'Administrative Conflicts in China: Initiation, Escalation and Resolution', Hong Kong Baptist University, GIS Working Paper No. 7.

Lee, C.K. (2014) 'State and Social Protests', *Dædalus* 143: 124.

Marshall, A. and Barclay, S. (2003) 'In their Own Words: How Ordinary People Construct the Legal World', *Law & Soc. Inquiry* 28: 617.

Minzner, C.F. (2011) 'China's Turn against Law', *American Journal of Comparative Law* 59: 935.

Palmer, M. (2006) 'Controlling the State? Mediation in Administrative Litigation in the People's Republic of China', *Transnational Law & Contemporary Problems* 16: 1.

Peerenboom, R. (1999) 'Ruling the Country in Accordance with Law: Reflections on the Rule and Role of Law in Contemporary China', *Cultural Dynamics* 11(3): 315.

Qian, J. (2014) '"Il-legality with Chinese Characteristics?" A Socio-legal Study on the "Illegal" Judicial Mediation in Land/Housing Taking Related Administrative Litigation', Harvard Law School, Graduation thesis.

Qian, J. (n.d., forthcoming) 'Corporatist Representation via People's Congress – An Aspect of the State-society Relationship in Contemporary China', in H. Cao and J. Paltiel (eds) *China in the 21st Century: Domestic and International Dynamics from a Multidisciplinary Angle*, China in the 21st Century Series, Ottawa: University of Ottawa Press.

Shapiro, S. (2011) *Legality*, Cambridge, MA: Belknap Press of Harvard University Press.

Shen, Y.Y. (2000) 'Conceptions and Receptions of Legality: Understanding the Complexity of Law Reform in Modern China', in K.G. Turner, J.V. Feinerman and R.K. Guy (eds) *Limits of Rule of Law in China*, Seattle: University of Washington Press.

Supreme People's Court of the People's Republic of China (2009) 'The Opinion of the Supreme People's Court on Protecting the Parties' Right to Sue in Administrative Litigation According to the Law' (Zuigao renmin fayuan guanyu yifa baohu xingzheng susong dangshiren suquan de yijian), news.xinhuanet.com/legal/2009-11/16/content_12464614.htm.

Tan, H.-T. and Yates, J.F. (2002) 'Financial Budgets and Escalation Effects', *Organizational Behavior and Human Decision Processes* 87: 300.

Yang, D. (2004) *Remaking the Chinese Leviathan: Market Transition and the Politics of Governance in China*, Stanford, CA: Stanford University Press.

Zhang, Q. (2010) 'Why is the Reform Decaying?' (Weishenme gaige yuegai yuezao?), www.aisixiang.com/data/detail.php?id=35976.

Zhao, X. (2005) 'Anti-judicial Theories from Grassroots Judiciary' (Jiceng sifa de fansifa lilun?), *Journal of the Study of Sociology* (*Shehuixue yanjiu*) 2.

Zheng, G. (2010) 'Towards Regulatory Neutrality in a Party-State: A Review of Administrative Law Reforms in China', in J. Gillespie and A. Chen (eds) *Legal Reforms in China and Vietnam: A Comparison of Asian Communist Regimes*, London: Routledge.

5 The legal design of land grabs

Possession and the state in post-conflict Cambodia

Daniel Fitzpatrick

Introduction

In Cambodia the determination of private ownership of land has relied on a rule of special acquisitive possession: as of 2001 citizens may claim ownership of land on the basis of five years' continuous possession of land. At its face, this rule of possession is a simple, low-cost mechanism for securing private ownership of land. It establishes a link between possession and property that should offer safeguards against arbitrary evictions from land. Yet in Cambodia widespread land grabbing has occurred as a result of circumstances of war and population displacement, demand for land from transnational capital, and elite political control over the allocation of rights to land. This chapter argues that the design of Cambodia's 2001 Land Law – including, in particular, the process for determining state title to land – provides pathways for land grabbing by the political elite notwithstanding the potential for private property security arising from the rule of possession.

In property terms principles of respect for possession are said to provide an easily understood response to the potential for conflict over rights to resources. A common example is that of the first car to enter a one-way bridge: it has the right of way as any other rule would be highly productive of social disorder (see McDowell 2004: 774; Sugden 1989: 88–90; Sugden 1986: 70–71). Most animals appear to resolve territorial conflicts through principles of respect for prior possession.[1] There seems to be a basic human understanding that first possession is connected to entitlement.[2] In legal terms, a principle of respect for possession is manifest in the 'finders keepers' rule in both civil and common law systems, under which the first person to gain possession of an abandoned or unowned object acquires rights of ownership.[3] Most legal systems also have rules on acquisition of ownership of land through adverse possession (common law) or prescription (civil law).[4] For both common and civil law systems, a core purpose of the rule is to put an end to litigation over land at the expiry of a term of years.

Why has the legal rule of special acquisitive possession failed to secure private rights to land for large numbers of people affected by land grabs in Cambodia? Part of the answer lies in another part of the Land Law: the provisions governing state title to land. Article 12 provides that land is deemed to belong to the state unless private claimants establish special acquisitive possession of land. Article 16 prevents the acquisition of state property through acts of private possession. The intent is clear: to establish a default rule of state title to land. Land that belongs to no one (*res nullius*) belongs to the state. Yet the design of the law helps to create Kafka-esque obstacles for private claimants of land – a private claimant cannot obtain possessory title because it is state land, and it is state land because a private claimant may not obtain possessory title. This circular logic lies at the heart of most contemporary cases of state-sanctioned land grabs in Cambodia.

International legal advisers supported the drafting of Cambodia's 2001 Land Law. In post-conflict circumstances such as Cambodia there are incentives for international legal advisers to formulate laws by reference to presumptive views of state viability, projected into the future, and not necessarily as context-specific responses to risks of land grabbing by state-connected actors. Land laws that strengthen the state are consistent with donor objectives relating to international security and development.[5] Land law can be central to the territorialization of state power as it includes certain projections and assumptions of state sovereign authority (Peluso 2009: 49–78). In James Scott's (1998) well-known expression, government officials 'see like a state' and interpret complex social relations with land through a legal lens of abstraction from local social relations. In similar vein, international legal advisers may also 'look for a state' to facilitate strategies of programme exit and the achievement of programme outputs.[6]

Default presumptions of state ownership of land lie within orthodox common and civil law conceptual frameworks. Yet in post-conflict cases the capacity to prove private land claims, so as to carve out entitlements from the state domain, is complicated by circumstances of population displacement, destruction of records, and undocumented forms of landholding. There are also incentives and opportunities for government officials to claim large areas as unowned land to facilitate private benefits from the grant of rights to state land. These rent-seeking incentives arise from investor interest in agribusiness developments, and political pressures to generate private benefits from control over the state in order to entrench political power. In all these circumstances, a default rule favouring state land may provide a pathway for government actors to obtain private benefits from the grant of land concessions to investors, who would otherwise face uncertain negotiations with purported groups of private landowners. Cambodia's Land Law allows this result as state officials may place the burden to establish ownership of land on private claimants simply by declaring that an area of land has not been occupied in accordance with the rule of special acquisitive possession, and is therefore available for grant to an outside investor.

Background

During the Khmer Rouge period from 1975 to 1979, between 1.4 and 2 million Cambodians died as a result of purges, famine, forced urban evacuations and war with Vietnam. Around 2 million were forced to evacuate from the cities to collectivized farms. There was almost total destruction of pre-Khmer Rouge land and cadastral records. By the time the Vietnamese-backed Kampuchean People's Revolution Party (KPRP) expelled the Khmer Rouge in 1979, almost all the population had been displaced, with large numbers of refugees in the neighbouring countries of Thailand, Laos and Vietnam.[7]

Khmer Rouge forces re-grouped in the Western provinces, with a political base in Thailand, and fought a civil war against the KPRP until the Paris Peace Accord of 1991. The 1991 Agreement on a Comprehensive Political Settlement of the Cambodia Conflict provided for disarmament of the warring parties, and the return and integration of Cambodian refugees and displaced persons (Art. 19, 20) At the time of the Paris Peace Accord there were approximately 353,000 Cambodian refugees in Thailand, with another 180,000 displaced persons in Cambodia itself (UNHCR 2000: Chapter 6). From March 1992 to May 1993 the United Nations High Commissioner for Refugees (UNHCR) organized the repatriation of around 360,000 Cambodian refugees. While the scale of return was a notable success, the repatriation process did not involve an organized process of return to specified land. Around 87 percent of returnees chose to accept cash from UNHCR rather than the alternative offer of 2 hectares (ha) of resettlement land (Bernander *et al.* 1995: 104). Most returnees settled either in north-west Cambodia, near the border with Thailand, or in urban areas such as the Phnom Penh.[8] Very few returned to their pre-1975 land.

In the early 1980s the KPRP undertook a process of distribution of land to households which, as a general rule, did not account for the possibility of return of refugees or internally displaced persons (Chanthy and Watson 2001). In rural areas the lead actors were village (commune) government officials who entrenched a substantial *de facto* role in land administration. Subsequently, these officials exhibited antagonism to the resettlement of returnees originally from other parts of Cambodia. For example, Bernander *et al.* describe a case where local village officials forced returnees to accept land distant from the village despite an agreement with UNHCR to provide land closer to employment and services (Bernander *et al.* 1995: 107). This type of land is now far more likely to be classified as state land. Un and So (2011) also describe the role of local government authorities in the occupation of urban areas classified as state land by returnees and other displaced groups. The role of local commune officials is important to land grabs as they have the authority, along with provincial and national levels of government, to grant economic land concessions over state private property (Sub-Decree on State Land, Chapter 8, Article 20).

From 1992 to 1995 the UN Transitional Administration in Cambodia (UNTAC) oversaw implementation of the peace agreement. In 1993, UNTAC organized national elections for the Constituent Assembly. The party with the largest share of the vote (45.5 percent) was the royalist Funcinpec Party, led by Prince Norodom Ranariddh. The second party – the Cambodian People's Party (CPP) – received 38.2 percent of the vote (Nohlen *et al.* 2001: 70). However, the CPP threatened a return to civil conflict unless they were included in a power-sharing arrangement. The CPP had absorbed large numbers of Khmer Rouge fighters and was able to make credible threats of armed conflict. To salvage its peace-building efforts, UNTAC created the office of 'second prime minister' for Hun Sen, the CPP leader (Maguire 2005: 82). The CPP went on to win the 1988 election and all subsequent elections to date. The undemocratic circumstances of the CPP's ascent to power, combined with the recent history of armed conflict, provides important context to the contemporary phenomenon of land grabbing, as it illustrates the imperatives for the CPP to extract private benefits from control of the state in order to entrench its political power.

The 2001 Land Law: possession as the basis of title

The key elements of the 2001 Land Law reflect Cambodia's post-conflict circumstances of population return and resettlement. The law bases the determination of title on acquisitive possession rather than restoration of pre-Khmer Rouge rights to land (Art. 7, 30, 38). Even for those who sought rights to their original lands, there were few prospects of restoration of pre-1979 titles given the context of governmental weakness, almost total destruction of land records, and land distribution by the KPRP to *in situ* households in the early 1980s. Some scholars have argued that Cambodia should have adopted a programme of restitution of original lands to displaced persons, consistent with restitution programmes in places such as former Yugoslavia, as well as the provisions of soft international law instruments on the rights of displaced persons.[9] However, the alternative adopted in Cambodia – that possession provides the basis for original acquisition of title – is a long-standing principle of property law in both common and civil law systems. A rule of possession fits well with post-conflict circumstances as physical control rather than documentary title is more likely to be the local determinant of entitlements to land.

Establishing a link between possession and property tends to accord with local norms of respect for household possession, while also minimizing the potential for chronic conflict over rights to resources. In Hayekian analysis, property rules favouring possession provide competing parties with a mechanism to avoid Hobbesian conflict, particularly when there is uncertainty as to respective prospects of success in a game of resource competition.[10] Once both parties expect the other to follow a possessory rule, there is a natural tendency towards cooperation as it is costly to break the cooperative pattern.[11] All else being equal, those who have incurred costs to obtain possession may be expected to assert their possessory relationship with a resource more fiercely than those who simply wish to obtain possession.[12] This leads to mutually reinforcing expectations of relative success, with possessors more likely to defend their claims with confidence and aggression, and other claimants more likely to forego their own claims in order to search for possessory claims elsewhere. In these circumstances, social order may emerge autonomously from spreading patterns of respect for possessory claims, unless there is intervention by third-party authority, or a change of circumstances so that the net benefits of violent acts of dispossession outweigh the costs.[13]

The development of the common law illustrates the relationship between rules of possession and concerns to maintain social order. The traditional focus of the common law of property was on physical control rather than documentary title.[14] Possession provided a basic means of proving title. For example, possession without challenge was sufficient to establish a freehold estate in land. The delivery of possession was necessary to complete transfer of title as under the feudal doctrine of tenure the feudal tenants did not obtain a proprietary interest in land without a delivery of seisin, which was actual or *de facto* possession of land. Commonly, the delivery of seisin required the symbolic transfer of a twig or a clod of earth to the transferee. Finally, possession provided the basis for remedies in trespass as the action in trespass vindicated rights to possession rather than title. A wrongful possessor of land could thus sue in trespass to recover land against a subsequent wrongful possessor (Gray and Gray 2006: 106; Dukeminier and Krier 1993: 103–21).

Even though Cambodia inherited a civil law system from the French, there are elements of the 2001 Land Law that reflect common rather than civil law principles of property. In Roman law, possession may be a basis for the original acquisition of title either to unowned things (*res nullius*), or to the property of another through the acquisitive possession process known as *usu capio* (prescription). However, unlike the common law, possession of itself did not provide a basis for (*in rem*) actions for the recovery of land. Only an owner could bring the Roman action known as *rei vindicatio* (vindication of property) to recover possession of property (Hausmaninger and Gamauf 2012: 1–3). As a general rule, a possessor who was not an owner could sue either for monetary damages or injunctive relief through *in personam* actions under the law of *delicts* or *interdicts*, respectively. In contrast, and consistent with the common law, Cambodia's Land Law provides that possession alone may constitute a right *in rem* over land.[15] The Land Law also provides that *in rem* rights of possession may be the subject of exchange, transfers of rights and transactions (Art. 39).

The rule of possession and state title to land

While Cambodia's Land Law provides that possession since 1989 constitutes a proprietary interest in land, it establishes a default rule of state rights to land that is more similar in character to civil than common law notions of sovereign title. Article 12 states that the state is the owner of property in Cambodia that has not been the subject of due and proper private appropriation, or that is not presently being privately occupied in accordance with Chapter 4 of the law, which sets out the provisions on special acquisitive possession. Article 15 lists areas of land that fall within the public property of the state (e.g. areas on the banks of lakes or rivers). Article 16 provides that state public property cannot be acquired by means of special acquisitive possession, but may be subject to temporary authorization to occupy or use. It also states that state public properties may be converted to the private property of the state once they 'lose their public interest use'. From the date the Land Law becomes effective, no more encroachment of state private land may take place, even if it complies with the provisions on special acquisitive possession (Art. 39). The private property of the state may also be the subject of sale, exchange, distribution or transfer of rights as determined by law (Art. 17).

In the civil law, the Roman law principle is that title to the public lands of the state could not be acquired through acquisitive possession (*usucapio*). In the non-Italian provinces of the Roman Empire, a legal status as conquered territory meant that title to all land vested as the public property of the Roman state (*ager publicus*). The native inhabitants held proprietary interests under charter or revocable grant from the state (Stephenson 2004: Sections 3, 4). For the colonies of European civil law sovereigns, the status of possessory interests arising before the acquisition of sovereignty required legislation to clarify the extent of public property of the state. For example, in the Dutch East Indies, the 1870 Agrarische Besluit (Royal Agrarian Decree) stated in Article 1 that all land not held under ownership (*eigendom*) rights fell within the domain of the state. Eigendom was interpreted in terms of Civil Code rights of ownership rather than 'native' rights of a possessory or customary nature. The effect was to extend the notion of state domain over very large parts of the Dutch East Indies (and modern-day Indonesia).[16]

In the common law the capacity to extend sovereign authority through acts of annexation forms part of the prerogative power of the crown. The prerogative act is not justiciable.[17] At the time of acquisition of sovereignty, the reception of the common law brings with it English laws of land tenure, including the radical or ultimate title of the crown.[18] However, modern jurisprudence establishes that the ultimate or radical title of the crown is not a form of absolute beneficial ownership that extinguishes without more prior possessory interests, but is an incident of sovereignty that provides public authority to grant interests in the land and to declare unalienated land part of the royal demesne.[19] In a colonial context, while there is authority for the crown to extinguish prior usufructuary interests through inconsistent acts, such as the grant of a freehold estate in the land,[20] there are Privy Council cases upholding usufructuary interests in land arising before the acquisition of sovereignty without the need for subsequent grant or recognition by the sovereign.[21]

A key difference between Cambodia's Land Law and the common law of property lies in the burden of proof of possessory title. In the common law, possession 'generates its own title'. It creates both a proprietary interest and a presumption of a freehold estate in land. While the onus of proof lies on the applicant in a claim for adverse possession, the onus of proof in a claim to recover land from a possessor lies on those claiming a better title than the possessor. The burden of proof on claimants other than the possessor applies to crown land as well as privately held land. The state must bring an action to recover crown land from a possessor *inter alia* by disproving the right to a freehold estate. Even in a colonial context, the state must prove a better title than those in occupation of land at the time of receiving the common law, because of the principle that possession creates a freehold estate in land unless proven otherwise.[22] In this event, the proprietary right recognized does not take the form of a usufructuary interest that survives the acquisition of sovereignty, but a possessory interest recognized by the common law that creates a presumption of freehold estate. Moreover, the mere fact of acquisition of sovereignty does not vest a better title in the state as, without more, the state acquires a radical title only and not a freehold right to possession of occupied land.[23]

In Cambodia, as in other civil law systems, there is no presumption that possession alone provides evidence of a freehold estate in land. Satisfaction of the criteria for special acquisitive possession grants only a right to request rather than receive title. Ownership arises from the administrative act of registration of ownership rather than through automatic implication of law upon satisfaction of the criteria of special acquisitive possession. Moreover, the possessory applicant must provide evidence of possession to the Cadastral Commission in order to register an ownership title acquired through special acquisitive possession. Under the 1992 Land Law (Art. 66), the evidence of possession included a letter of support from the chief of the local commune as well as payment of land taxes. In doctrinal terms, the design of the law subordinates possessory interests to the principle that ownership rights stem only from the (discretionary) sovereign authority of the state.

A critical failing of legal design in Cambodia is the absence of mandatory, verifiable and enforceable procedures for the testing of assertions of state title to land. Article 47 of the Land Law provides that '[d]isputes over an immovable property between possessors shall be submitted for investigation and resolution' to the Cadastral Commission. As Adler *et al.* note, it is not clear whether this provision vests jurisdiction in the commission to determine disputes between a possessor and the state.[24] As a practical matter, however, these types of disputes generally have not been referred to the commission (or the courts). Government agencies have few incentives to refer disputed classifications of state land because of the involvement of government actors in the initial determination of the legal status of the land and, in some cases, the subsequent commercial development of the land. Moreover, individual claimants rarely refer disputed classifications of state land because it requires money, knowledge of the law, and a willingness to pursue legal claims before an agency established by the state itself. Even in circumstances where disputes were referred to adjudicatory agencies, the absence of public maps of state property, or precise legal criteria for its determination, reduces the likelihood of findings adverse to the interests of powerful state-connected actors.

The interpretation of state title to land: the politics of possession

The default rule of state title to land in the civil law did not lead to excessive land grabbing by the state in continental Europe. Why has it allowed the state to claim up to 80 percent of all land as state property in Cambodia?[25] While the design of the law provides pathways for state claims to land, there must also be incentives for state officials to interpret the law in an expansive manner. The issue of political incentives raises questions of legal design in post-conflict circumstances. Should legal advisers adapt basic provisions of land law to take into account risks of land grabbing by state actors? What is the appropriate balance between constraining and strengthening the state? To what extent will the trappings of legal democratic order, including multi-party democratic elections and the constitutional protection of private property, constrain incentives for state actors to use their discretionary powers over land to facilitate widespread acts of land grabbing?

In public choice terms, political actors have incentives to generate rents, votes or tax revenues from the grant of proprietary rights to resources. Legislators may 'sell' property legislation not only for votes, but for campaign contributions, or even bribes. They may receive private benefits from legislation to create property for a constituency or interest group without necessarily incurring the costs of compensating those who do not receive property.[26] Stuart Banner provides the example of property rights allocation in British colonial systems. Minoritarian control over coercive political structures minimized the costs of property formation through state action by avoiding distributional compensation to less powerful members of society such as indigenous groups.[27]

Public choice orthodoxy holds that democratic order may offset political incentives to create minoritarian forms of property. In a multi-party democratic system there are incentives for political parties to propose platforms that maximize chances of voters across interest groups. Voter preferences filter through mechanisms such as media monitoring, electoral surveys, public demonstrations, lobbying and campaign contributions. While a legislator or regulator may prefer one group, where the marginal gains in votes are offset by any loss in votes from another adversely affected interest group, the incentives for majority vote increase the likelihood of promises to make compensating side payments to the adversely affected group.[28]

The Cambodian case challenges orthodox prescriptions for the design of land law that rely on constitutional democratic order to constrain the state. After armed conflicts, in particular, circumstances of new regime formation provide incentives for land grabbing that may outweigh majoritarian incentives established by public law devices such as multi-party democratic elections and constitutional rights to private property. Armed conflicts that cause regime change and large-scale population flight create conditions that favour violent competition for both rights and authority over resources.[29] The opportunity to obtain possession and the incentive to claim property may create struggles for possession and violent conflicts over acts of possession. The opportunities created by regime change will also encourage competition for public authority relating to land, particularly as control over the machinery of the state will allow privileged access to rents from land and natural resources. The risks of a return to conflict remain high as weak enforcement circumstances mean that groups and individuals with access to means of violence, through non-state patrimonial networks, are more likely to calculate that the net pay-offs of political violence outweigh the net benefits of non-violent forms of competition for public authority.[30] Violent races for political authority may then interact with disputes over the possession of land to cause further outbreaks of armed conflict and state instability (Brinkerhoff 2005: 1, 4).

There are incentives for domestic political actors to respond to the threat of group violence by co-opting individuals and groups with access to means of violence.[31] These incentives extend to UN transitional administrations. The imperative to stabilize the state leads to co-option of actors who could otherwise destabilize or de-legitimize the state. North, Wallis and Weingast (2009a: 108) argue that the co-option process is facilitated by inducements based on privileged access to rents, which are benefits above ordinary returns from control of an asset. Privileged access to rents for members of the new political elite is not 'simply a method of lining the pockets of the dominant coalition … [but] the essential means of controlling violence' (ibid.: 59). The elite formation process that North *et al.* identify as essential to state stabilization includes incentives to control the development and application of new laws on land. These incentives encompass the interpretation of default rules of state title to land. A legal baseline of state title to sovereign state territory suits elites seeking to extract rents from state control over resources. In particular, a rule that the state holds title to land without an owner places the burden of proving private title on private claimants, and creates opportunities for extraction of rents from the grants of rights to public land, including grants of licences and concessions to commercial interests. In a post-conflict state where determinations of contested title are likely to be slow, a default rule of state title to land increases the likelihood that investment funds will flow through (rapid) personalized grant of state titles rather than impersonal exchange of (uncertain) private rights.

The Boeung Kak Lake case

The well-known Boeung Kak Lake case illustrates the way in which possessory claims are subordinated to government claims of state property in

Cambodia.[32] Boeung Kak Lake is a 74-ha lake near Phnom Penh, historically used for recreational purposes. Households began to settle on the shores of the lake in the 1980s. Most settlers have documents of purchase or lease executed by government officials that purported to have title to the land. During the course of their residence, the settlers received other symbolic items of ownership, such as house numbers, minor infrastructure improvements and witnessing by local government officials of land sale contracts. By 2006 there were approximately 4,000 households with 20,000 members living in an area of 43 ha around the lake.

In 2005 the government of Cambodia provided in principle agreement to a corporation, Shukaku Inc., to develop land around the lake. The principal of Shukaku was a senator from the ruling CPP. In 2006 Sras Chok Commune, which formed part of the land surrounding Boeung Kak Lake, was designated as an adjudication area by Cambodia's Land Management Administration Project (LMAP). LMAP included a systematic land titling component. The project was funded and coordinated by the World Bank. LMAP adjudication teams collected survey data on village and land parcel boundaries until February 2007. At this time, the adjudication teams were informed by local authorities that the Boeung Kak Lake area was state public property. The adjudication teams recorded 'unknown ownership' of land parcels in the Sras Chok Commune, which indicated the existence of a dispute over ownership. Yet neither the registration teams nor the individual claimants referred the dispute to the Cadastral Commission (Bekhechi and Lund 2009).

In February 2007 the municipality of Phnom Penh executed a 99-year lease with Shukaku over the Boeung Kak Lake area. In August 2008, the government of Cambodia issued a sub-decree converting the area from state public property to state private property. These events breached the Land Law in a number of respects. First, state public property may not be the subject of a lease. The lease was issued before the land was converted to state private property. Second, state public property may only be converted to state private property once its public use is exhausted. The public utility of the lake shore remains as a result of its continued recreational use. Third, the maximum term of a lease over private property is 15 years (not 99 years). At its face, therefore, the Boeung Kak Lake case is simply an example of unlawful land grabbing by the state. However, the core legal design problem was the fact that the mere assertion of state ownership of the land was sufficient to halt the determination of private ownership of the land.

As a result of the Boeung Kak Lake case, LMAP conducted a desk study of land disputes reported in Cambodian media and nongovernmental organization (NGO) reports (World Bank 2009). The review covered approximately 8,448 households that fell into the broad category of reported evictions, pending evictions or other multi-party land disputes in areas where LMAP land titling was active. These cases were in addition to the approximately 4,000 households affected in the Boeung Kak Lake area. The desk study reached conclusions that were already widely known (and should have been known by LMAP) – namely, that 'a significant proportion' of land disputes in Cambodia concerned state claims over currently occupied land, and that 'in a number of these cases' the residents had good faith claims to recognition as lawful possessors.[33] The desk review then states: 'Similarly to the [Boeung Kak Lake] case households' claims in these areas were not registered as part of the titling prices on the basis of assertions that they were unlawful occupiers of state land' (Bekhechi and Lund 2009).

A 2009 survey of 39 Phnom Penh communes titled under LMAP reached a similar conclusion. In these areas, approximately ten communities with 2,000 families received land titles while 100 communities housing more than 10,000 families did not receive titles. The success rate for households claiming title was a strikingly low 20 percent. A sample of 12 communities that did not receive titles concluded that eight had not been subject to titling simply because government officials had asserted that the land was state property. Yet in no case had the claim to state property been tested before the Administrative Commission or the National Cadastral Commission (Bekhechi and Lund 2009). A World Bank research report into a number of land disputes in Cambodia reaches a similar conclusion: 'The fact that none of the disputes was submitted to the Cadastral Commission indicates a preference for more coercive forms of dispute resolution than that offered by the Commission' (Adler *et al.* 2006: 69).

Both the Boeung Kak Lake case, and the findings of land conflict surveys, illustrate the legal dimension of land grabs in Cambodia. Land grabs often have elements of non-compliance with law. Yet in the majority of cases they also involve assertions of lawful title by the state itself. It is not so much that the law fails to act as a safeguard against arbitrary deprivation of rights to property, but rather that the law provides the basis for a broad regime of state-sanctioned land grabs.[34] Land grabbing is not limited to the widespread grant of economic land concessions over agricultural land. It extends to the grant of state concessions for the logging of state forests, the construction of mines and hydroelectric dams, the establishment of special economic zones, and the development of tourist resorts and other commercial projects. In each case, the primary technique is to declare that the land is the public or private property of the state, which means that it may not be the subject of claims to private title on the basis of lawful possession.

Conclusion

The term 'land grabs' has connotations of illegal behaviour. Some studies identify land grabs as a violation of the right not to be arbitrarily deprived of property.[35] Yet, in many cases, land grabs involve *ab initio* denial of rights rather than arbitrary deprivation of rights recognized by law. Those in occupation of land are classified as illegal occupiers with no *de jure* property rights for arbitrary deprivation. In these circumstances, land grabs are not a violation of law, as law provides a legal basis for the act of land grabbing itself. National law is the primary mechanism for land grabs as it controls the classification of land and the allocation of rights to land. While the legal literature on land grabs tends to focus on rights in international law to food security and adequate housing,[36] there are basic questions of property law – most notably the interaction between private possession and state title to land – that deserve more attention in policy efforts to protect long-term occupiers of land from arbitrary dispossession.

Notes

1 See John Maynard Smith 1982, as cited in Krier 2009: 151–52.
2 Krier 2009: 154–55, discussing Sugden's application to the human context of evolutionary explanations for the relationship between first possession and expectations of entitlement.
3 For a discussion, see Lueck 1995.
4 See Sugden 1986: 88–9: 'The maxim that possession is nine points of the law is more than a description of a particular legal system; it describes a pervasive tendency in human affairs.'
5 See McAuslan 1998: 525–7, discussing the seminal importance of land reform to donors and from within recipient countries, wherein the reform of land law cohabitates seamlessly with 'good governance'.
6 See for example, Braithwaite *et al.* 2010: 6: '[The] focus has been on rebuilding the core pillars of the central state to the comparative neglect of the specific factors that fuelled conflict.'
7 For overviews see Kiernan 1997; Jackson 1997; Tyner 2008.
8 Approximately 58 percent of returnees settled in the provinces of Banteay Meanchey and Battambang, close to the Thai border, and 8 percent settled in Phnom Penh (Bernander *et al.* 1995: 106).
9 See, for example, Williams 2009: 19–20: 'In light of subsequent peace-building practice, one of the most obvious criticisms relates to the fact that UNTAC countenanced a ... Land Law that extinguished all pre-1979 claims to property. In doing so, this law locked in earlier land re-allocation measures that included a good deal of official self-enrichment and denied a remedy to dispossessed victims of the Khmer Rouge and those who fled in the wake of the 1979 Vietnamese invasion.' The primary international law instrument recommending restitution of land and property as the preferred response to displacement is the Pinheiro Principles, which are set out in the UN Principles on Housing and Property Restitution for Refugees and Displaced Persons, UN doc. E/CN.4/Sub.2/2005/17 (2005), Principles 2.1, 2.2.
10 Zerbe and Anderson 2001: 134, analysing the first possession rule in the Californian goldfields.
11 See Epstein 1980: 672–3, discussing rule of deference to possession as an evolutionarily stable strategy. See also McAdams 2000.
12 See Gintis 2007: 1.
13 For further discussion, see Krier 2009: 154–5.
14 For an overview see Gray and Gray 2006: 90–95. See also Pollock and Wright 1888; Tay 1964: 476–97.
15 Art. 29. This provision limits the recognition of proprietary aspects of possession to possession since 1989. The implication is that possessors may bring actions 'against the world' to recover possession of land.

16 For a discussion, see Fitzpatrick 1997.

17 See, for example, *Post Office v. Estuary Radio Ltd* (1968) 2 Q.B. 740, at 753 per Diplock J: 'it still lies within the prerogative power of the Crown to extend its sovereignty and jurisdiction to areas of land or sea … For such extension the authority of Parliament is not required.'

18 See *New South Wales v. Commonwealth* 1975 5 CLR 337, at 438–39 per Stephen J: 'the prerogatives of the Crown were a part of the common law which the settlers brought with them on settlement.'

19 *In Amodu Tijani* (98) (1921) 2 AC, at p. 403 Viscount Haldane; *Mabo v. Queensland (No. 2)* (1992) 175 CLR 1 per Brennan J. (para. 51). For further discussion see Gray and Gray 2004: 67: '["Radical title"] denoted the political authority of the Crown both to grant interests in the land to be held of the Crown and also to prescribe the residue of unalienated land as the sovereign's beneficial demesne.'

20 *Johnson v. McIntosh* (1823) 21 US 240, at 259; *St Catherine's Milling and Lumber Company v. The Queen* (1888) 14 AC 46; *Tee-Hit-Ton Indians v. United States* (1955) 348 US, at 279; *Hamlet of Baker Lake* (1979) 107 DLR (3d), at 549.

21 *Amodu Tijani* (1921) 2 AC; *In re-Southern Rhodesia* (1999) AC, at 233: 'upon a conquest it is to be presumed, in the absence of express confiscation or of subsequent expropriatory legislation, that the conqueror has respected [rights of private property] and forborne to diminish or modify that.'

22 *Mabo v. Queensland (No. 2)* (1992) 175 CLR 1 per Toohey J. (para. 95): 'According to common law then, as now, possession of land gives rise to a title which is good against all the world except a person with a better claim. Such a possessor is "seised" of the land so that he or she acquires an estate in the land which is an estate in fee simple. It is a fee simple because the interest acquired is presumed to be such until shown otherwise.'

23 *Mabo v. Queensland (No. 2)* (1992) 175 CLR 1 per Toohey J. (para. 111): 'There is no foundation for the conclusion that by annexation the Crown acquired a proprietary title or freehold possession of occupied land. It acquired a radical title only.' Toohey J. further suggests that the legal fiction that all possession of land was vested in the crown after the Norman Conquest, thereby allowing the grant of land in return for feudal services, applies to the special purposes of feudal tenure only, and does not necessarily govern the status of possessory interests through common law reception at the time of acquisition of sovereignty (ibid.: paras 112–13).

24 Adler *et al.* (2006) reach the tentative conclusion that the Cadastral Commission does have jurisdiction over disputes between a possessory claim and the state based on the legal status of the land in question. The authors cite the Sub-Decree on Organization and Functioning of the Cadastral Commission, which states that it 'applies to disputes over unregistered immovable property', and that '[t]he Cadastral Commission has a preliminary right to decide the recognition of the lawful possessor' (Art. 2).

25 While there is no publicly available official figure on the extent of state land in Cambodia, the estimate of 80 percent is widely stated (see COHRE 2009).

26 See for example, Haddock 2003: 186: 'In the absence of effective limits, government actors are at least as apt to extract property rights as to protect them.'

27 See Banner 2002: 368.

28 For a general discussion, see Mueller 2003: 344.

29 See Fitzpatrick and Barnes 2010: 205–38.

30 Zartman 1995: 5: 'As the authoritative political institution, [the state] has lost its legitimacy, which is therefore up for grabs …'

31 North *et al.* 2009b: 55, 59: 'Individuals and groups with access to violence form a dominant coalition, granting one another special privileges. These privileges – including limited access to organizations, valuable activities, and assets – create

rents. By limiting access to these privileges, members of the dominant coalition create credible incentives to cooperate rather than fight among themselves.'

32 Details of the case are drawn from: Bridges Across Borders Cambodia 2010; Cambodian Human Rights Action Committee 2009: 65; Bugalski 2008: 1.

33 The Boeung Kak Lake case led to a World Bank review of LMAP in 2009. See Bekhechi and Lund 2009. The review panel concluded: '[S]upervision of the Project for several years overlooked the critical issue of adjudicating private claims on land claimed by [the] State. This failure of Management, in the Panels view, contributed to the events in the [Boeung Kak Lake] area.' As a result of the review the World Bank did not renew funding for LMAP. Other donors, most notably the German government, now provide funding for a systematic land titling successor to LMAP.

34 For further discussion and example, see Mgbako *et al.* 2010: 39, 52; Hughes 2008: 69, 70; Amnesty International 2008: 4; Cambodian Human Rights Action Committee 2009: 65; Bugalski 2008: 1.

35 The Universal Declaration of Human Rights (Art. 17).

36 See for example, De Schutter 2009.

References

Adler, D., Chhim, K., Heang, P., Hak, S., Sou, K. and Heng, K. (2006) 'Justice for the Poor? An Exploratory Study of Collective Grievances Over Land and Local Governance in Cambodia', ssrn.com/abstract=983317.

Amnesty International (2008) 'Rights Razed: Forced Evictions in Cambodia', 11 February (ASA 23/002/2008), www.amnesty.org/en/library/info/ASA23/002/2008/en.

Banner, S. (2002) 'Transitions between Property Regimes', *The Journal of Legal Studies* 31(2): S329–S371.

Bekhechi, M.A. and Lund, L. (2009) 'Cambodia Land Management and Administration Project: Enhanced Review Report', go.worldbank.org/IUTVJ7CXG0.

Bernander, B., Charny, J., Eastmond, M., Lindahl, C. and Ojendal, J. (1995) 'Facing a Complex Emergency: An Evaluation of Swedish Support to Emergency Aid to Cambodia', Swedish International Development Cooperation Agency Evaluation Report No. 4.

Braithwaite, J. *et al.* (2010) *Pillars and Shadows: Statebuilding as Peacebuilding in Solomon Islands*, Canberra: ANU E Press.

Bridges Across Borders Cambodia (2010) 'Boeung Kak', 23 September, babcambodia.org/stopevictions/Boeung_Kak.htm.

Brinkerhoff, D. (2005) 'Rebuilding Governance in Failed States and Post-conflict Societies: Core Concepts and Cross-cutting Themes', *Public Administration and Development* 25(1): 3–14.

Bugalski, N. (2008) 'Housing Rights Litigation in Cambodia: The Boeung Kak Lake Case', *Housing and ESC Rights Law Quarterly* 5(4): 1–4.

Cambodian Human Rights Action Committee (2009) 'Losing Ground: Forced Evictions and Intimidation in Cambodia', September, www.chrac.org/eng/CHRAC%20Statement%20in%202009/Losing%20Ground%20FINAL.compressed.pdf.

Chanthy, S. and Watson, G. (2001) 'Cambodia: Revisiting the Land Law', in D. Cohen, R. de la Vega and G. Watson (eds) *Advocacy for Social Justice: A Global Action and Reflection Guide*, Bloomfield, CT: Kumarian Press, pp. 173–185.

Center on Housing Rights and Evictions (COHRE) (2009) 'Cambodia Land Management and Administration Project: Request for Inspection by World Bank Inspection Panel', letter, 4 September, go.worldbank.org/IUTVJ7CXG0.

De Schutter, O. (2009) 'Addendum, Large-scale Land Acquisitions and Leases: A Set of Minimum Principles and Measures to Address the Human Rights Challenge', A/HRC/13/33/Add.2, 28 December, www2.ohchr.org/english/bodies/hrcouncil/docs/13session/A-HRC-13-33-Add2.pdf.

Dukeminier, J. and Krier, J.E. (1993) *Property*, 3rd edn, New York: Aspen Publishers.

Epstein, R.A. (1980) 'A Taste for Privacy? Evolution and the Emergence of a Naturalistic Ethic', *J. Legal Stud.* 9(4): 665–681.

Fitzpatrick, D. (1997) 'Disputes and Pluralism in Modern Indonesian Land Law', *Yale Journal of International Law* 22(1): 171–212.

Fitzpatrick, D. and Barnes, S. (2010) 'The Relative Resilience of Property: First Possession and Order without Law in East Timor', *Law & Society Review* 44(2): 205–238.

Gintis, H. (2007) 'The Evolution of Private Property', *J. Econ. Behav. & Org.* 64 (1): 1–16.

Gray, K. and Gray, S.F. (2004) *Elements of Land Law*, 4th edn, Oxford: Oxford University Press.

Gray, K. and Gray, S.F. (2006) *Land Law*, Oxford: Oxford University Press.

Haddock, D. (2003) 'Force, Threat, Negotiation', in T.L. Anderson and F.S. McChesney (eds) *Property Rights: Cooperation, Conflict and Law*, Princeton, NJ: Princeton University Press, pp. 168–195.

Hausmaninger, H. and Gamauf, R. (2012) *A Casebook on Roman Property Law*, Oxford: Oxford University Press.

Hughes, C. (2008) 'Cambodia in 2007: Development and Dispossession', *Asian Survey* 48(1): 69–74.

Jackson, K.D. (1997) *Cambodia 1975–1978: Rendezvous with Death*, Princeton, NJ: Princeton University Press.

Kiernan, B. (1997) *The Pol Pot Regime: Race, Power, and Genocide in Cambodia under the Khmer Rouge 1975–79*, New Haven, CT: Yale University Press.

Krier, J.E. (2009) 'Evolutionary Theory and the Origin of Property Rights', *Cornell L. Rev.* 95: 139–159.

Lueck, D. (1995) 'The Rule of First Possession and the Design of the Law', *J. Law & Econ.* 38(2): 393–436.

Maguire, P. (2005) *Facing Death in Cambodia*, New York: Columbia University Press.

McAdams, R.A. (2000) 'Focal Point Theory of Expressive Law', *Virginia Law Review* 86(8): 1649–1729.

McAuslan, P. (1998) 'Making Law Work: Restructuring Land Relations in Africa', *Development and Change* 29(3): 525–552.

McDowell, A. (2004) 'Real Property, Spontaneous Order, and Norms in the Gold Mines', *Law & Soc. Inquiry* 29(4): 771–819.

Mgbako, C., Gao, R.E., Joynes, E., Cave, A. and Mikhailevich, J. (2010) 'Forced Evictions and Resettlement in Cambodia: Case Studies from Phnom Penh', *Washington University Global Studies Law Review* 9(1): 39–76.

Mueller, D. (2003) *Public Choice III*, Cambridge: Cambridge University Press.

Nohlen, D., Grotz, F. and Hartmann, C., eds (2001) *Elections in Asia and the Pacific: A Data Handbook: Volume II: South East Asia, East Asia, and the South Pacific*, Oxford: Oxford University Press.

North, D., Wallis, J. and Weingast, B. (2009a) *Violence and Social Orders: A Conceptual Framework for Interpreting Recorded Human History*, Cambridge: Cambridge University Press.

North, D., Wallis, J. and Weingast, B. (2009b) 'Violence and the Rise of Open-access Orders', *Journal of Democracy* 20(1): 55–68.

Peluso, N. (2009) 'Rubber Erasures, Rubber Producing Rights: Making Racialised Territories in West Kalimantan, Indonesia', in T. Sikor and C. Lund (eds) *The Politics of Possession: Property, Authority and Access to Natural Resources*, Malden, MA: Wiley-Blackwell, pp. 49–78.

Pollock, F. and Wright, R.S. (1888) *An Essay on Possession in the Common Law*, Oxford: Clarendon Press.

Scott, J. (1998) *Seeing Like a State: How Certain Schemes to Improve the Human Condition have Failed*, New Haven, CT: Yale University Press.

Stephenson, A. (2004) *Public Lands and Agrarian Laws of the Roman Republic*, Baltimore: The Johns Hopkins Press.

Sugden, R. (1986) *The Economics of Rights, Cooperation, and Welfare*, Oxford: B. Blackwell.

Sugden, R. (1989) 'Spontaneous Order', *Journal of Economic Perspectives* 3(4): 85–97.

Tay, A. (1964) 'The Concept of Possession in the Common Law: Foundations for a New Approach', *Melb. Univ. Law Rev.* 4(4): 476–498.

Tyner, J.A. (2008) *The Killing of Cambodia: Geography, Genocide and the Unmaking of Space*, Aldershot: Ashgate Publishing.

Un, K. and So, S. (2011) 'Land Rights in Cambodia: How Neopatrimonial Politics Restricts Land Policy Reform', *Pacific Affairs* 84(2): 289–309.

United Nations High Commissioner for Refugees (UNHCR) (2000) 'The State of the World's Refugees in 2000: Fifty Years of Humanitarian Action', www.unhcr.org/4a4c754a9.html.

United Nations, Department of Public Information (1991) 'Agreements on a Comprehensive Political Settlement of the Cambodia Conflict', 23 October, Paris.

Williams, R. (2009) 'Stability, Justice and Rights in the Wake of the Cold War: The Housing, Land and Property Rights Legacy of the UN Transitional Authority in Cambodia', in S. Leckie (ed.) *Housing, Land, and Property Rights in Post-conflict United Nations and Other Peace Operations: A Comparative Survey and Proposal for Reform*, Cambridge: Cambridge University Press, pp. 19–61.

World Bank (2009) 'Cambodia Land Management and Administration Project: Management Response to the Request for an Inspection Panel Review of the Cambodia Land Management and Administration Project', go.worldbank.org/IUTVJ7CXG0.

Zartman, W. (1995) 'Introduction: Posing the Problem of State Collapse', in W. Zartman (ed.) *Collapsed States: The Disintegration and Restoration of Legitimate Authority*, Boulder, CO: L. Rienner Publishers, pp. 1–15.

Zerbe, R.O. and Anderson, C.L. (2001) 'Culture and Fairness in the Development of Institutions in the California Gold Fields', *Journal of Economic History* 61(1): 114–143.

6 Indonesia's land acquisition law

Towards effective prevention of land grabbing?

Laurens Bakker and Gustaaf Reerink[1]

In recent years, Indonesia has taken its place in the global economy with a vengeance. The nation experienced an annual economic growth of around 6 percent and became a member of the G-20. One of the main drivers of this growth are the extractive industries, for which huge amounts of land are required. In striving to maintain growth, the Indonesian government is working hard on improving the country's business climate. Important measures include addressing such elements as widespread corruption in government and bureaucracy, the unpredictability of the regulatory environment, but also simplifying access to land for business and industrial needs. Such measures fit in a longer, broader series of political, economic and judicial reforms aimed at improving democracy, transparency and the rule of law in order to benefit development of the economy, sustainability, as well as society at large.[2] The 2011 Master Plan for the Acceleration and Expansion of Indonesia's Economic Development (MP3EI), which sets out economic development for the period 2011–25, states:

> The role of Government in the implementation of MP3EI is to provide a set of rules and regulations that provide incentives for investors to build sectoral industries and infrastructure. Incentives can be conducive policies on tariff, taxes, import duties, labour regulations, licensing and permits, land procurements, etc.
>
> (Coordinating Ministry for Economic Affairs *et al.* 2011: 21)

In this chapter, we focus on government incentives for land acquisition as facilitated by the 2012 Law on Land Acquisition for Development in the Public Interest. We examine the changes that the 2012 Law intends to facilitate and the currently perceived effects it will have on the land acquisition process. After an overview of the changes, we explore the reception of the law, and discuss a number of recent cases to illustrate the effects of the law in practice. To conclude, we consider the law's main problematic points, including its ability to facilitate land grabs.

In Indonesia, land governance is divided among various official and unofficial authorities. Roughly 30 percent of the country's territory is controlled by the National Land Agency (*Badan Pertanahan Nasional*, hereafter NLA), which can register a variety of rights to this land. The remaining approximately 70 percent is designated forest land and is governed by the Ministry of Forestry. 'Forest land' is an administrative generalization. Such land can be developed and contain farms, houses, whole villages, plantations and even open pit mining rather than forests. However, for such usage no ownership rights can be registered. Furthermore, throughout the nation and disregarding the official division of forest and non-forest areas (*kawasan*), people hold land on the basis of custom (*adat*). Individual *adat* rights on non-forest land can be converted into individual land rights that can be registered by the NLA. Communal (*ulayat*) rights can only be registered if research has established that custom is still a valid source of rules in the lives of the local community and that an active system of communal land usage still exists (see Bakker and Moniaga 2010). In addition, the population in urban areas, notably in the large cities of Java, contains numerous squatters who have no other claim to the land they use than the fact of that usage. The regulation of land rights thus includes official and informal claims and has, as we shall see, a strong reputation for the interests of small landholders and urban poor being overridden by those of politically connected business elites.

Land rights and land usage indeed have a history of being applied to further the interests of the elite rather than protect the rights of the weak and are socially sensitive issues in Indonesia.[3] Government measures aimed at stimulating growth attract considerable criticism from nongovernmental organizations (NGOs) and analysts for putting business interests before those of the population. The current debate on Indonesia's development thus contains a strong focus on a more equal division of revenues in the face of potential land grabs by power holders, elites and (international) businesses that is strongly driven by current affairs (e.g. Rachman *et al.* 2009; Susanti and Budidarsono 2014).

Overview of changes under the 2012 Law

Until enactment of the 2012 Law, Indonesian law offered two options for land acquisition: compulsory land expropriation and voluntary land release. Compulsory land expropriation finds its legal basis in the 1960 Basic Agrarian Law. Article 18 of this law allows for land expropriation (*pencabutan hak atas tanah*) if this is in the public interest (*kepentingan umum*), including the interests of the nation, the state and the people as a whole, provided that appropriate compensation is paid and in accordance with a procedure laid down by an act of parliament.

In accordance with Article 18 of the 1960 Basic Agrarian Law, Law No. 20 of 1961 on the Revocation of Rights on Land and the Buildings Erected on It sets out an intricate procedure for compulsory land expropriation. The procedure is to be followed when all efforts to obtain the land voluntarily on the basis of *musyawarah*, the traditional process of discussion and deliberation, have failed. The Law also provides an alternative, accelerated procedure, but it can only be applied in case of emergency, such as an epidemic or a natural disaster.

In practice these procedures have seldom been used. This can largely be explained by the nature of the procedure, which requires involvement of various high-level authorities, including the president. The government institution requiring land for development in the public interest must file a motivated expropriation request to the president. It does so through the head of the NLA, who prior to the president's decision, must consult the head of the region where the land is located, an Appraisal Committee (*Panitia Penaksir*), the minister of justice and the minister competent in the field of the institution requesting the land expropriation. Landholders can appeal the proposed compensation to the Court of Appeal (*Pengadilan Tinggi*) with jurisdiction in the region where the land is located.

Rather than applying this complex and time-consuming procedure, authorities commonly reverted to the procedure for voluntary land release. During the New Order several presidential decrees on voluntary land release (through sale, exchange or otherwise) were enacted. In practice, voluntary release was often involuntary as land owners and land users were frequently pressured through the army, police or hired thugs to accept low compensation and release their land. Such instances of land grabbing contained a major role for the mayor or the district head of the area, who were appointed rather than elected, so their loyalty lay with government and the regime rather than with the population. Civil society groups or other non-state actors potentially able to influence the process on behalf of individuals pressured into land release were virtually non-existent, as the state kept a tight rein on the development of such groups (see Lucas and Warren 2003).

Post-New Order democratization allowed for a politicization of land appropriation processes. Article 18(4) of the second amendment to the 1945 Constitution and Article 24(5) of Law No. 32 of 2004 on Regional Autonomy require the direct election of mayors and district heads, who therefore stand to lose societal support if they are insufficiently engaged. For opposition parties and party-related legal aid institutions, land appropriation cases are occasions to manifest their presence and dedication. The rise of NGOs and independent media further provides a platform to people under threat of losing their lands. Although this rarely prevents the lands from being lost, by delaying the land acquisition process, landholders who stood their ground in the face of pressure to release the land, succeeded in negotiating relatively high compensation. Presidential decrees required that compensation be based on the real and actual value of the land, with attention being paid to its sale value as a tax object (*nilai jual obyek pajak*). However, the authorities were commonly forced to pay more, also to landholders who did not hold formal land titles (see Reerink 2011). Other delaying factors included land speculation, administrative chaos at regional NLA offices which allowed plots of land to be registered by multiple parties, refusals to sell, unwillingness of regional administrations to enforce existing legislation in support of construction projects, and late payments of government financial support to private partner companies (see Widhiarto 2011).

Faced with difficulties to make land available for development in the public interest, two new presidential decrees on voluntary land release were promulgated: Presidential Decree No. 36 of 2005 on Land Acquisition for Development in the Public Interest, as amended by Presidential Decree No. 65 of 2006 concerning the Amendment of Presidential Decree No. 36 of 2005.[4] The 2005 Presidential Decree put a 90-day time limit on negotiations between the government institution wishing to clear the land and titleholders. The 2006 Presidential Decree extended this term to 120 days. If after several meetings 75 percent of the titleholders still refused to accept and the project could be realized at another location, an alternative location should be proposed. If the development activities could not be realized elsewhere, the procedure elaborated in Law No. 21 of 1961 had to be applied, which, as discussed above, was not an attractive alternative. Until recently, the government thus still depended on the willingness of landholders to release their land voluntarily.

Law No. 51 of 1960 concerning the Prohibition to Use Land without Permission of the Title Holder applies to those who use land without permission from the state or rights holders, making such use a criminal offence. It also grants the regional heads discretionary power to evict these landholders. However, it appears that for the above reasons, regional heads are increasingly reluctant to evict these landholders without any form of compensation.

The delays in land acquisition in recent years triggered the government to introduce a new bill on land acquisition for development in the public interest. In January 2012, the bill was enacted as Law No. 2 of 2012. Several implementing regulations were enacted during 2012, 2013 and 2014 (Presidential Decree No. 71 of 2012, as amended by Presidential Decree No. 40 of 2014 and Presidential Decree No. 99 of 2014; Decree of the Minister of Home Affairs No. 72 of 2012; Decree of the Minister of Finance No.13/PMK.02/2013).

Law No. 2 of 2012 provides three important changes, which are designed to limit the duration of the land acquisition process. First, there is no longer a distinction between compulsory land expropriation and voluntary land release. Article 5 of Law No. 2 of 2012 provides for negotiations with landholders, which, upon failure after a predetermined period, allows for an obligatory release of the land rights after payment of compensation or the ruling of a court in relation to this compensation which is final and decisive. Second, Law No. 2 of 2012 transfers the authorities relating to land acquisition from the elected regional heads to appointed officials of the NLA. Third, Law No. 2 of 2012 basically limits the discretionary powers of the authorities to determine for what purpose and against which compensation land may be acquired. This should lead to a de-politicization of the land acquisition process.

Law No. 2 of 2012 also limits government institutions that may follow the land acquisition procedure. It clarifies that such institutions are state bodies (*lembaga negara*), ministries, non-ministerial agencies (*lembaga pemerintah nonkementerian*), provincial and district/municipal governments and state-owned legal entities (*Badan Hukum Milik Negara*, or BHMN) and state-owned enterprises (*Badan Usaha Milik Negara*, or BUMN), with a special government-assigned task (Art. 1(1) Law No. 2 of 2012). Notably, state-owned companies qualify as such as long as at least 51 percent of the shares are held by the state (Art. 1(2) Law No. 19 of 2003 on Government-owned Companies). The remaining 49 percent of the shares may be held by private parties, which may thus have considerable influence in such companies. There are many state-owned companies, including in agriculture, industry and the services sector: plantations, mining, construction and real-estate companies, telecommunication companies, etc. Contrary to other institutions that may follow the land acquisition procedure, following completion of the procedure, not the central or regional government but the state-owned company will become the owner of the land (Art. 11(2) Law No. 2 of 2012).

The land acquisition procedure may be followed if there is substantive justification to do so. According to Article 10 of the 2012 Law, the procedure may be used for:

- national defence and security;
- public road, toll road, tunnel, railroad, rail station and rail operation facility;
- dam, reservoir, irrigation, potable waterway, drains, and sanitation and other irrigation building;
- seaport, airport and terminals;
- oil, gas and geothermal infrastructure;
- generator, transmission, grid, network and distribution of electricity;
- government telecommunications and information network;
- waste and landfill processing;
- government/district government hospital;
- public safety facility;
- government/district government public cemetery;
- social facility, public facility and green open public space;
- natural and cultural heritage;
- government/district government/village offices;
- restructuring of urban slums and/or land consolidation, and housing for low-income people with rent status;
- education infrastructure or government/district government school;
- government/district government sports infrastructure; or
- public market and public parking space.

The land acquisition procedure is implemented by the government. However, in doing so, it may collaborate with national state-owned companies, regional state-owned companies or private companies (Article 12(1) Law No. 2 of 2012). Given the list of activities for which the procedure may be used, it is quite plausible, for instance, that the 2012 Law would allow a regional government to evict urban slum dwellers for restructuring purposes, after which the land would be made available to a developer to build residential or commercial real estate. However, this would arguably be contrary to Indonesia's obligations under the International Covenant on Economic, Social and Cultural Rights, which requires that it may subject land rights solely for the purpose of promoting the general welfare in a democratic society (General Comment by UN CESCR No. 7, 1997; General Comment by UN CESCR No. 3, 1990).[5]

Law No. 2 of 2012 gives a broad definition of 'right holder' (*pihak yang berhak*), which is the person who should be paid compensation if the land is acquired. A right holder is someone who has control over or has a recognized right to land, buildings, plants and other assets connected to land that may be valued (Art. 1(3–4) Law No. 2 of 2012). The elucidation to Article 40 of Law No. 2 of 2012 states that such right holders include:

- holders of a recognized land right;
- holders of land on which previously *adat* (customary) ownership rights were established;
- *adat* law communities;
- parties controlling state land in good faith;
- landholders basically controlling the land; or
- owners of buildings, plants and other assets that are connected with the land.

In view of the above, the law appears to acknowledge the broad range of land tenure that exists in Indonesia. However, implementing legislation puts several restrictions on the definition of the term 'right holder'. For instance, an *adat* law community may only be acknowledged as such, provided that:

- there is a group of people that is still bound by its *adat* law as one *adat* law community, which acknowledges and applies these community rules in daily life;
- there is *ulayat* (community) land that forms the environment of the *adat* law community and the place that provides its daily needs; or
- there are certain *adat* rules regarding the organization, control and use of *ulayat* land that are applicable and abided to by the *adat* law community.

Whether or not the adat law community meets these requirements should be based on research and be confirmed by a local regulation, thus putting an *adat* law community's fate in the hands of the regional head and regional council (Art. 22 Presidential Decree No. 71 of 2012).

It appears that many communities that call themselves adat law communities do not meet the above criteria, which means that on the basis of the law, they are not entitled to any form of compensation. It is unlikely that these communities will accept this. They will probably do all they can to prevent having to give up their land, which may effectively lead to further delays.

Furthermore, Law No. 2 of 2012 states that in order to receive compensation, parties must show evidence of their control or ownership over the land that is being acquired. The responsibility to provide this evidence rests with the right holder who is eligible for compensation. The law also requires that the right holder guarantees the validity and integrity of the evidence. The right holder will be liable for any third-party claims relating to the released land (Art. 41 Law No. 2 of 2012). Evidence consists of such documents as are defined as such in national land law, which means that multiple registrations to the same plot by the NLA and different types of overlapping or conflicting rights remain valid issues.[6]

It seems that Law 51 of 1960 will continue to apply to landholders whose rights are not acknowledged under the new law's definition of rights.[7] This means that these landholders may be evicted without any form of compensation.

Those who are acknowledged as right holders are entitled to adequate and just compensation. The compensation is calculated by an independent land valuer who has a permit from the Ministry of Finance and a licence from the NLA (Art. 1(11) Law No. 2 of 2012).[8] The valuer should assess the value of land, buildings, plants, other assets connected to the land and other damages that can be valued, for instance damages caused by loss of business opportunities or work, moving costs and costs to change profession (Art. 33 Law No. 2 of 2012). Although land valuers should be independent, it is likely that conflicts of interest arise, as they are appointed by the head of the NLA following a public procurement process organized by the institution that needs the land, which may want the assessed value of the land to be as low as possible.[9]

Compensation may consist of money, replacement land, other buildings, shares, or any other form agreed between the parties. Compensation for *ulayat* land shall be replacement land, other buildings or in any other form agreed with the *adat* community. The national or regional governments must guarantee the availability of funds to finance land acquisition (Art. 36 Law No. 2 of 2012).

Law No. 2 of 2012 creates several procedural protections for right holders who are affected by the land acquisition procedure. The institution that needs the land must prepare an acquisition plan in accordance with the regional spatial plan and development priorities (Art. 14 Law No. 2 of 2012). The land acquisition plan must be publicized and those affected are to be consulted (Art. 16, 17, 19 Law No. 2 of 2012). Public consultation should initially take a maximum of 60 working days. If there are parties who still object to the plan, there will be another 30-day public consultation (Art. 20 Law No. 2 of 2012). If after this second public consultation, there are still objections, the institution must inform the governor, who shall form a team to assess the objections. The team must issue a recommendation within 14 days of receiving the governor's request. Based on the recommendation, the governor will issue a letter rejecting or accepting the objections (Art. 21 Law No. 2 of 2012). If the objections are rejected, the governor will determine the location for land acquisition (Art. 22 Law No. 2 of 2012). Right holders may file a claim to the Administrative Court, asking it to review the governor's decision within 30 days after the determination of the location. The Administrative Court will issue its ruling within 30 days after having received the claim. The party who does not agree with the ruling may appeal to the Supreme Court within 14 days. The Supreme Court must issue a ruling within 30 days of the appeal (Art. 23 Law No. 2 of 2012).

Although the law stipulates that local populations and other parties involved must be consulted before governments engage in any public interest development, it does not state whether the results of such consultations must be heeded in any way. Furthermore, Law No. 2 of 2012 arguably again fails to fulfil Indonesia's obligations under the ICESCR, in that it does not explicitly require government institutions that wish to use the land acquisition procedure to explore feasible alternatives in consultation with right holders and affected persons (General Comment by UN CESCR No. 4, 1991; General Comment by UN CESCR No. 7, 1997; General Comment by the UN CESCR No. 3, 1990).

The NLA will negotiate with the right holder about the form and amount of compensation to be paid within a maximum of 30 working days after the land valuer has issued its report (Art. 37 Law No. 2 of 2012). If no agreement is reached, the right holder may submit an objection to the District Court within 14 working days after the negotiations have ended. The District Court will determine the form and amount of compensation within 30 days of receiving the objection. The party who does not agree with the ruling may appeal to the Supreme Court within 14 days of the ruling. The Supreme Court is required to issue a ruling within 30 days of receiving the appeal (Art. 38 Law No. 2 of 2012). If the right holder rejects the form and amount of compensation following negotiations or a ruling of the court, the amount of compensation will be stored at the local District Court. This procedure will also be followed if the right holder cannot be located or the land is in dispute, has been attached or is mortgaged to a bank (Art. 42 Law No. 2 of 2012).

Although on paper the above creates sufficient protections for right holders against arbitrary evictions and unjust compensation, there is no guarantee that court procedures will lead to a favourable outcome. On the basis of a quick search in the Supreme Court's database of court rulings (kepaniteraan.mahkamahagung.go.id/perkara/), we conclude that claims of individual right holders are rarely awarded.

Based on implementing legislation, a government institution that is in need of less than 5 hectares (ha) of land for development in the public interest may conduct a direct sale and purchase or exchange or otherwise of land with the right holder.[10] In other words, for smaller acquisitions, such as are common in urban areas, there is no obligation to follow the land acquisition procedure set out in Law No. 2 of 2012.

The above land acquisition procedure does not apply when the land that is needed for public interest development is located in so-called forest areas. Forest areas are administered by the Ministry of Forestry. Unfortunately, it is unclear which areas qualify as forest areas. The Ministry of Forestry deems that currently, 68.4 percent of Indonesia's landmass constitutes forest area, over which it has management control. However, as a result of a 2012 ruling of the Constitutional Court, it is unclear whether this position can be upheld.[11] Another ruling by the Constitutional Court in May 2013 adds to the uncertainty. Based on this ruling, customary forest (*hutan adat*) should no longer be considered part of state-owned forest, which means that people using forest according to *adat* (*masyarakat hutan adat*) now have gained control over the land located in customary forest.[12]

At present there is no mechanism for the clearance of land in (adat) forest areas. However, in a recent ruling, the Constitutional Court determined that the state is required to protect *adat* law communities.[13]

Reception of the new land acquisition law

Unsurprisingly, business analysts and government officials affirm that they expect that the 2012 Law will speed up the land acquisition process,[14] although a common critique is that since the law is not implemented retrospectively, it does not solve ongoing land acquisition conflicts based on the old legislation which the 2012 Law replaces. Only if these issues remain unresolved by 31 December 2014 will the 2012 Law become applicable to them.[15] However, the announcement of the law attracted considerable critical attention from NGOs and opinion makers, fearing that this law would further harm the position of landholders (see Harahap 2012; Saturi 2012).

In June 2012 a coalition of 14 NGOs jointly using the name *Karam Tanah* (*Koalisi Rakyat Anti Perampasan Tanah Rakyat* – Coalition of People Against Land Grabbing) filed a judicial review with the Constitutional Court. They requested annulment of Articles 9(1) and 10 for lack of clarity and for going against the public interest, and of Articles 14(1), 21(1), 23(1), 40, 42(1) and 42(2) for contravening the constitution or otherwise being in contradiction with the law.[16] *Karam Tanah* argued that Law No. 2 of 2012 did not serve the public interest but rather allowed the government to seize land in the interest of wealthier population groups who can afford, for instance, to use toll roads, buy on luxury housing estates or invest in mines. The poor who lacked these means lost access and were hence being disadvantaged. In February 2013 the Constitutional Court rejected the request. The judges found, inter alia, that all of society would eventually benefit from the developments brought about by the law, and that ambiguous definitions could be overcome in supporting legislation that would guarantee beneficial effects for all.[17] The plaintiffs found the court's findings unsatisfactory in that no explanation of the balance between public interests and those of local communities was offered.

In July 2014 another judicial review was filed by a group of eight individuals who maintained that the formulation of Article 1(10), which defines compensation as 'adequate and fair compensation to the entitled party in the process of land acquisition', is a step back from the security provided in Presidential Decree 36 of 2005.[18] The plaintiffs maintained that this presidential decree states that those who stand to lose their land must be compensated so as to achieve a higher living standard on the socio-economic level of the local community, while the formulation in Law No. 2 of 2012 is open to multiple interpretations of what 'adequate' and 'fair' entail.[19] The Constitutional Court's findings in this case were still forthcoming at the time of writing.

Interestingly, no judicial review has been submitted in relation to implementing legislation such as Presidential Decree No. 71 of 2012. It is possible to submit such a request to the Supreme Court, which would then review the relevant legislation against laws enacted by parliament (in this case Law No. 2 of 2012 and Law No. 11 of 2005).[20] Given that Presidential Decree No. 71 of 2012 contains some controversial provisions (as discussed above), it may well be worth a try to get parts of this decree annulled.

First experiences with Law No. 2 of 2012

An immediate reason for the formulation and implementation of Law No. 2 of 2012 was the delays that conflicts and settlement in acquisition procedures caused in infrastructure projects. Throughout Indonesia, numerous toll road construction projects had been brought to a standstill by such issues. The 2011, MP3EI called for the construction of 70 roads and 28 toll roads throughout the country. Some of these were continuations or implementations preceding Law No. 2 of 2012, which meant that they had to be settled according to the previous legislation discussed above. By April 2014, 32 toll road projects were behind schedule, including many listed in the MP3EI. According to the Ministry of Public Works, the delays were not so much caused by problems with the availability of land, but with the matter of reaching consensus over fair compensation (Piri 2014). The delays are a growing concern to investors, as problems in acquiring a small plot of land can delay the opening of entire toll roads. In order to prevent lack of capital adding to further delays and to ensure investor trust in Indonesia's capacity, all or most financing of land acquisition for toll roads may hence come from the state budget in 2015 (Suryowati 2014). At the same time, successes are given considerable attention. The Gempol–Pandaan toll road was opened for temporary free usage in July 2014 in time to relieve the heavy congestion of Lebaran traffic around the Javanese city of Malang (Faizal 2014).

Yet events on other stretches indicated that Law No. 2 of 2012 still left projects vulnerable to delays. The Cikampek–Palimanan road, the longest (116 kilometres) of nine stretches of the Trans-Java Toll Road, was initially celebrated as a success story because virtually all of the required land had been acquired and construction had moved ahead of schedule. The stretch was expected to be finalized before Lebaran 2014. Only small groups of families proved unwilling to agree with the compensation they were offered, since they felt it did not come close to the value of the land and houses they were to give up (Ichsan 2014). The authorities applied Article 47 of Law No. 2 of 2012, which states that if no relinquishment of the land is obtained within 60 days, the land will be considered as delivered and therefore as state land, and may be used directly for development. In February 2014 a blockade by families and their lawyers resisting relinquishment was cleared and their 12 houses demolished. The lawyers reported the regional chief of police who assisted in the clearing to the investigation division of the national police, maintaining that the proper administrative procedure was not followed and that the eviction was therefore illegal (Wiguna 2014).

Shortly after the demolition of the 12 houses, 11 other families who also stood to lose their land and houses before a satisfactory settlement was reached, brought a lawsuit against the government authorities. They argued that the sums for compensation determined by the land valuer were based on a 2005 district head decision (*keputusan bupati*) on the basic prices of buildings (*harga dasar bangunan*). Sums indicated here were much lower than market values in 2011. This 2005 decision, however, had been revoked in August 2011, four months before the valuer's report was delivered. The plaintiffs maintained that because of this, the valuer's report had no legal validity and requested that the regional head as well as the provincial governor annul the valuer's report (see Prayoga and Tandri 2013). As the regional head's written reply in September 2013 did not revoke the report and continued to be based on the 2005 decision, the plaintiffs' legal team sent a request to the national ombudsman to examine the process and establish whether, as the team suspected, maladministration had taken place (Prayoga and Tandri 2013). At the time of writing the various procedures were delaying construction of the road and completion was not envisioned before 2015. Sustained opposition and inventive usage of legal options other than those specified by Law No. 2 of 2012 – here the investigation division of the national police and the national ombudsman – thus presently still allow delays to take place.

Another project, a major new toll road connecting the business city of Balikpapan with East Kalimantan's provincial capital Samarinda, illustrates the problem of the acquisition of forest land. A new and more direct road of 99 kilometres had been planned for some time, but no land had been acquired as two stretches of the trajectory would need to go through two Protected

Forest Areas (*Kawasan Hutan Lindung*) under the authority of the Ministry of Forestry. Furthermore, the province suffers from its own economic success and high prices. The Provincial Department of Public Works in 2011 expected that total reimbursement costs for land to be acquired would reach 1.23 trillion rupiah, against a yearly available provincial budget of 149 billion rupiah (Rahmad 2011). These conditions were not conducive to attracting outside investors. Inclusion of the road in the MP3EI brought new life to the project.

Initially the project had a difficult start. Environmental NGOs objected to road construction in the forest areas and the Ministry of Forestry rejected the project on the grounds of the damage it would do. On the other hand, local government and the local population were collaborating quite effectively and the stipulations of Law No. 2 of 2012 were mostly used to establish compensation, with very few cases being brought before the district court. A government official involved in the negotiations believed that this was because most of the land was not in use for farming or housing as most of the area's population lived along the road already in existence, while the compensation being offered was fair and according to current market prices.[21] The main issue was obtaining the cooperation of the Ministry of Forestry as well as sufficient funding to finish the project before the 2016 deadline given in the MP3EI master plan (see Coordinating Ministry for Economic Affairs *et al.* 2011: 200). With neither forthcoming, the head of East Kalimantan's provincial planning agency publicly expressed his doubts as to the viability of the project in August 2013. He pointed out that it was unclear why the Ministry of Forestry refused to give permission: the land in question was already being used by local farmers and, as such, of little conservation value (Wibisono 2013). The minister of forestry granted permission in the same month and requested that the national parliament alter the forest's status from protected conservation area to land available for construction.[22] Parliamentary permission was given in July 2014. Whether the deadline of 2016 would be met remained uncertain. About half of the road was completed at time of writing. Furthermore, it was expected that the farmers illegally using the forest land would demand compensation as well. This situation – the removal of illegal farmers from land recently redefined from protected forest to state land available for the development of projects of general interest – is likely to be a legal first, with which Law No. 2 of 2012 is equipped to deal, but which will cause further delays (Dwinanto 2014).

A final example of problematic issues concerns the development of a new state technical university in Balikpapan. The city obtained this institution by promising the Ministry of Education that the Institut Teknologi Kalimantan would be operating by 2012 as it would use the Institut Teknologi 10 Nopember (ITS) in Surabaya as an up-and-running first base, as well as by promising a huge campus. Whereas local governments are required to facilitate 30 ha for new state universities, Balikpapan's mayor promised to make 300 ha available so as really to create possibilities for the institute to develop into a prominent, state-of-the-art research institution. The new development suited the city well as the campus would be located in the north of the city – an area that was somewhat neglected as most investors preferred the city centre and coastal districts.

Part of the land was made available by moving the National Electrics Agency PLN (*Perusahan Listrik Negara*), which was using 120 ha of municipal and provincial government land, to a new location. A further 50 ha was bought from the owners (*Kaltim Post* 2014). However, most of the rest of the land was owned by third parties who demanded extremely high compensation, while the municipal government was under great pressure from the ministry to obtain NLA certification of all the land before the end of August 2013 in order to ensure permission to accept new students in the academic year 2013/14 (*Balikpapan Post* 2013). Many of these plots were owned by various government officials and employees who had been aware of the plans and had acquired the land in order to obtain high compensation (Rumengan 2013). The fact that these were chefs, members of city parliament and colleagues made the civil servants tasked with acquiring the land unwilling to drive too hard a bargain. Land acquisition thus allows for misuse of public funds as well.[23]

Conclusion

Although at first sight the 2012 Law and its implementing legislation seem to create new possibilities for not only quick but also just land acquisition for development in the public interest, thus preventing historically common instances of land grabbing, upon closer inspection it becomes clear that the law contains some serious weaknesses. The law allows for a broad range of institutions to follow the procedure, including state companies in which private shareholders have an important say. The possibility for these institutions to collaborate with private companies may make the distinction between public and commercial interest even more blurred. Although the definition of 'right holders' is broad, it may be difficult for some landholders to qualify as such. Particularly *adat* law communities are in a weak position: they depend on the willingness of the regional head and the regional council to acknowledge them as right holders. Those landholders who do not qualify as right holders in the meaning of Law No. 2 of 2012 can still be evicted without any form of compensation. Although land is valued by an independent valuer, it remains to be seen whether right holders will indeed receive adequate and just compensation. Law No. 2 of 2012 creates procedural protections for right holders who are affected by the land acquisition procedure. They should be consulted on a land acquisition plan and may submit a claim to the court if they do not agree with the location of land acquisition or with the compensation offered. However, it is unclear where these consultations should lead. The institution in need of the land is not obliged to explore feasible alternatives in consultation with affected persons. Furthermore, courts generally do not rule in favour of individual right holders. In any event, Law No. 2 of

2012 only applies to land in non-forest areas. At present there is no mechanism for the clearance of land in (*adat*) forest areas.

The first experiences with Law No. 2 of 2012 confirm that the goal of speeding up land acquisition for development in the public interest may not be reached. Opposition remains fierce and procedures other than those specified by Law No. 2 of 2012 still allow for delays to take place. Indonesia's intricate system of formal and informal land rights, with a related complexity of administrative authorities at the national and regional levels, will likely lead to additional setbacks. The widespread problem of corruption further complicates the practice of land acquisition. Broader series of governmental, economic and judicial reforms aimed at improving democracy, transparency and the rule of law will be needed to tackle these issues.

Notes

1 The authors would like to thank Santy Kouwagam for her critical input on an earlier version of this paper. Laurens Bakker's contribution to this work was supported by WOTRO [grant number W 01.65.334.00] as part of the research project '(Trans)national Land Investments in Indonesia and the Philippines: Contested Control of Farm Land and Cash Crops'.

2 Examples of laws aimed to promote economic development include Law 22 of 2001 on Oil and Gas, Law 18 of 2004 on Plantations, Law 4 of 2009 on Mining and Law 25 of 2007 on Investment. Laws promulgated to promote development for the general interest include Law 26 of 2007 on Spatial Management and Law 14 of 2008 on Public Information Transparency.

3 For recent discussions on social aspects of land law in Indonesia, see Lucas and Warren 2013; McCarthy *et al.* 2012; Brockhaus *et al.* 2012; Peluso 2011.

4 Decree No. 36 of 2005 was amended following a firestorm of criticism from various organizations and individuals for failing to protect the rights of landholders.

5 Indonesia became party to the International Covenant on Economic, Social and Cultural Rights (ICESCR) on the basis of Law No. 11 of 2005 on the Ratification of the ICESCR.

6 The elucidation to Article 40 does, however, go a long way in detailing the types of rights eligible for compensation and includes customary as well as religious rights, and individual rights as well as communal ones.

7 Art. 58(c) Law No. 2 of 2012 states that existing legislation will remain applicable as long as it does not contradict or has not yet been replaced by the provisions of Law No. 2 of 2012.

8 Notably, according to Presidential Decree No. 71 of 2012, the land can also be valued by a so-called 'public valuer', who only holds a permit from the Ministry of Finance. This seems to be in contradiction with Law No. 2 of 2012, which explicitly states that land should be valued by a valuer who holds both a permit from the Ministry of Finance and a licence from the NLA.

9 Article 63(3) Presidential Decree No. 99 of 2014.

10 Art. 121 Presidential Decree No. 40 of 2014. Prior to the amendment of Presidential Decree No. 71 of 2012, only a government institution in need of less than 1 ha of land for development in the public interest could conduct a direct sale and purchase or exchange or otherwise of land with the right holder. This limit was extended 'in the framework of efficiency and effectiveness'.

11 Ruling of the Constitutional Court No. 45/PUU-IX/2011, dated 21 February 2012.

12 Ruling of the Constitutional Court No. 35/PUU-X/2012, dated 16 May 2013.

13 Ruling of the Constitutional Court No. 34/PUU-IX/2011, dated 16 July 2012.
14 See, for instance, the keynote speech on the law by the head of the NLA, in which he emphasizes that the process can go quickly if parties are in agreement, but allows more time in case of conflicts (Supandji 2013; also Antana 2012).
15 According to Article 123A(1) of Presidential Decree No. 99 of 2014, the deadline can be extended to 31 December 2015 if on 31 December 2014 the land acquisition process has not been completed, but at least 75 percent of the needed land has already been acquired.
16 Article 9(1) states that a balance must be sought between public interest and development interest without, however, defining what development interest is. The other articles are discussed earlier in the chapter. *Karam Tanah* feared that this lacuna provided a legal possibility for all sorts of projects to overrule (local) public interest (see Istman 2012). The other articles for which a judicial review was requested were discussed earlier in this chapter.
17 Ruling of the Constitutional Court No. 50/PUU-X/2012, 13 February 2013.
18 Authors' translation of '*Ganti kerugian adalah penggantian yang layak dan adil kepada pihak yang berhak dalam proses pengadaan tanah*'.
19 Constitutional Court Summary of hearing No. 42/PUU-XII/2014, 14 July 2014. See also Triyono 2014.
20 Regulation of the Supreme Court No. 1 of 2011 on the Right to Substantive Review in conjunction with art. 79 Law No. 14 of 1985 on the Supreme Court and art. 20 Law No. 48 of 2009 on Judicial Power. On Law 11 of 2005, see note 5.
21 Personal communication in Balikpapan, 22 July 2014.
22 According to government officials to whom Bakker spoke in Balikpapan, the stalling was just to negotiate as good a deal as the ministry could get out of giving its permission. Part of the final agreement was that the provincial government would refrain from criticizing mining being allowed by the ministry in the same forest areas. The same officials also suggested that pressure from within parliament in Jakarta got the ministry to approve the request.
23 Officials involved, personal communication in Balikpapan, July 2014.

References

Antana, L. (2012) 'Terbuka Peluang Investasi di 4,500 km Jalan Tol', 30 August, swa co.id (accessed 18 July 2014).

Bakker, L. and Moniaga, S. (2010) 'The Space Between: Land Claims and the Law in Indonesia', *Asian Journal of Social Science* 28(2): 187–203.

Balikpapan Post (2013) 'Pemprov Yakin Sertifikasi ITK Segara Selesai', 7 August, www.balikpapanpos.co.id (accessed 24 July 2014).

Brockhaus, M., Obidzinski, K., Dermawan, A., Laumonier, Y. and Luttrell, C. (2012) 'An Overview of Forest and Land Allocation Policies in Indonesia: Is the Current Framework Sufficient to Meet the Needs of REDD+?' *Forest Policy and Economics* 18: 30–37.

Coordinating Ministry for Economic Affairs, Ministry of National Development Planning/National Development Planning Agency (2011) *Master Plan for Acceleration and Expansion of Indonesia Economic Development 2011–2025*, Jakarta: Coordinating Ministry for Economic Affairs.

Dwinanto, R. (2014) 'Lahan Masih Menjadi Kendala Tol Balikpapan-Samarinda,' *Tribun Kaltim*, 18 July, www.tribunnews.com (accessed 24 July 2014).

Faizal, A. (2014) 'Proyek Tol Gempol-Pandaan Dibuka Gratis untuk Jalur Mudik', 24 July, www.kompas.com (accessed 25 July 2014).

Harahap, A.S. (2012) ‘Ahli: UU Pengadaan Tanah Berorientasi Penggusuran’, 31 August, www.hukumonline.com (accessed 18 July 2014).

Ichsan, N. (2014) ‘Sejumlah Warga Tetap Menolak Tanahnya Dipakai Tol Cikapali’, 17 February, www.tribunnews.com (accessed 24 July 2014).

Istman (2012) ‘UU Pengadaan Tanah Dinilai Tak Berpihak Masyarakat’, 11 June, www.tempo.com (accessed 18 July 2014)

Kaltim Post (2014) ‘Setahun Mangkrak, ITK Dilelang’, 24 January, kaltimpost.co.id (accessed 24 July 2014).

Lucas, A. and Warren, C. (2003) ‘The State, the People and their Mediators: The Struggle Over Agrarian Law Reform in Post-New Order Indonesia’, *Indonesia* 76: 87–126.

Lucas, A. and Warren, C., eds (2013) *Land for the People: The State and Agrarian Conflict in Indonesia*, Athens: Ohio University Press/Swallow Press.

McCarthy, J., Vel, J. and Afiff, S. (2012) ‘Trajectories of Land Acquisition and Enclosure: Development Schemes, Virtual Land Grabs, and Green Acquisitions in Indonesia’s Outer Islands’, *Journal of Peasant Studies* 39(2): 521–549.

Peluso, N. (2011) ‘Emergent Forest and Private Land Regimes in Java’, *Journal of Peasant Studies* 38(4): 811–836.

Piri, E. (2014) ‘Pembangunan 32 Ruas Tol Mangkrak’, *Sinar Harapan*, 1 April, sinarharapan.co (accessed 24 July 2014).

Prayoga, A. and Tandri, L.D. (2013) *Laporan Maladministrasi Penyelenggaraan Pelayanan Publik Bupati Cirebon*, Cirebon: Kantor Hukum Agus Prayoga dan Rekan.

Rachman, N.F., Savitri, L. and Shohibuddin, M. (2009) ‘Questioning Pathways Out of Poverty: Indonesia as an Illustrative Case for the World Bank’s Transforming Countries’, *Journal of Peasant Studies* 36(3): 621–627.

Rahmad (2011) ‘Ganti Rugi Tanah Untuk Tol Rp1.230 triliun’, 24 October, kaltim.antaranews.com (accessed 24 July 2014).

Reerink, G. (2011) *Tenure Security for Indonesia’s Urban Poor, A Socio-legal Study on Land, Decentralisation and the Rule of Law in Bandung*, Leiden: Leiden University Press.

Rumengan, J. (2013) ‘Pejabat Pemkot Balikpapan Dituding Hambat Proses Pembebasan Lahan’, 17 October, m.portalkbr.com (accessed 24 July 2014).

Saturi, S. (2012) ‘Konflik Agraria 2012, Ratusan Petani Ditahan dan 25 Tertembak’, *Mongabay Indonesia*, 28 December, www.mongabay.co.id (accessed 18 July 2014).

Supandji, H. (2013) ‘Pidato Kepala BPN RI’, *Badan Pertanahan Nasional*, 10 April, www.bpn.go.id (accessed 18 July 2014).

Suryowati, E. (2014) ‘Pembebasan Tanah untuk Jalan Tol Bakal Didanai APBN’, 25 March, www.kompas.com (accessed 24 July 2014).

Susanti, A. and Budidarsono, S. (2014) ‘Land Governance and Oil Palm Development: Examples from Riau Province, Indonesia’, in M. Kaug and A. Zoomers (eds) *The Global Land Grab. Beyond the Hype*, London: Zed Books, pp. 119–134.

Triyono, A. (2014) ‘UU pengadaan tanah digugat ke MK’, 14 July, www.kontan.co.id (accessed 18 July 2014).

Wibisono (2013) ‘Proyek Jalan Tol Balikpapan-Samarinda Mandek’, 15 August, www.tempo.co (accessed 24 July 2014).

Widhiarto, H. (2011) ‘Land Acquisition Remains a Tough Nut to Crack’, *Jakarta Post*, 25 April, www.thejakartapost.com (accessed 18 July 2014).

Wiguna, A. (2014) 'Ayo Laporkan Kapolres ke Divpropam', *Radar Cirebon*, 2 May, www.radarcirebon.com (accessed 24 July 2014).

Cases

Ruling of the Constitutional Court No. 45/PUU-IX/2011, 21 February 2012.
Ruling of the Constitutional Court No. 34/PUU-IX/2011, 16 July 2012.
Ruling of the Constitutional Court No. 50/PUU-X/2012, 13 February 2013.
Ruling of the Constitutional Court No. 35/PUU-X/2012, 16 May 2013.
Constitutional Court Summary of Hearing No. 42/PUU-XII/2014, 14 July 2014.

Indonesian legislation

The amended 1945 Constitution.
Law No. 19 of 2003 on Government-owned Companies.
Law 32 of 2004 of Regional Government.
Law No. 2 of 2012 on Land Acquisition for Development in the Public Interest.
Presidential Decree No. 71 of 2012 on the Organization of Land Acquisition for Development in the Public Interest as amended by Presidential Decree No. 40 of 2014 and Presidential Decree No. 99 of 2014.
Decree of the Minister of Home Affairs No. 72 of 2012 on Operational Costs and Supporting Costs for the Organization of Land Acquisition for Development in the Public Interest that is Funded by the Regional Budget.
Decree of the Minister of Finance No. 13/PMK.02/2013 Concerning Operational Costs and Supporting Costs for the Organization of Land Acquisition for Development in the Public Interest that is Funded by the National Budget.

UN comments

General Comment by the UN Committee on Economic, Social and Cultural Rights (CESCR) No. 3 on the Nature of States Parties Obligations (adopted at the 5th session, 1990).
General Comment by the UN Committee on Economic, Social and Cultural Rights (CESCR) No. 4 on the Right to Adequate Housing (adopted at the 6th session, 1991).
General Comment by the UN Committee on Economic, Social and Cultural Rights (CESCR) No. 7 on Forced Evictions (adopted at the 16th session, 1997).

7 Winners and losers

Land grabbing in the new Myanmar

Connie Carter[1]

The terms 'land grab' and 'land grabbing' have become common currency in Myanmar, often making front page news in both the English- and Myanmar-language newspapers and journals. The articles do more than document the lived experiences of displaced victims. They also report and comment on the news from high places: 'Land grabbing investigations commence' (*Mizzima*, 20 November 2012); 'Military involved in massive land grabs: Parliamentary Report' (*The Irrawaddy*, 5 March 2013); 'Land-grab discussion blocked in the Union Parliament' *Mizzima*, 16 August 2013); 'MPs slam government for delaying on land grabs' (*Myanmar Times*, 17 July 2013). It is a refreshing change from attitudes in the West, where the terms are often taboo and considered devoid of any legal meaning. My experience among local, everyday people, smallholder farmers, parliamentarians, government officials, academics, business executives, journalists and civil society groups in Myanmar[2] helped me define land grabbing in Chapter 1 of this volume. The two-word phrase is opaque, and perhaps emotionally charged, but in Myanmar it is not novel. As Kevin Woods points out, its use among the Myanmar people 'reflects the more open political space available to talk about injustices, as well as the escalating severity and degree of land dispossession under the new government' (Woods 2014: 2).

In this chapter, a land grab is defined as the physical taking or capture for possession and control of land and homes, including the usurpation of the power to decide how and when these will be used and for what purposes – with no consent, little or no prior consultation, and little or no compensation to the displaced individuals. In short, a land grab is the appropriation or confiscation of land and homes without due process of law, or the unjust application of law, and sometimes even inappropriate, opaque and unjust laws. This analysis uncovers examples of how and why it is done in Myanmar.

In August 2012, the Myanmar parliament (Hluttaw) mandated the Farmland Investigation Commission to investigate alleged land confiscations going back to 1988. The commission published its first report in March 2013, in which it disclosed what confiscated land was used for: 1 urbanization; 2 industrial zones (also referred to as special economic zones, or SEZs); 3 expansion of army battalions and military units; 4 construction of state-owned factories;

5 implementation of state-run agricultural and husbandry projects; and 6 land allocation to private companies with links to the military. This confirms that Myanmar's experience comprises state- or government-led appropriation of land mostly for 'development' purposes and not, as the popular land grabs literature suggests,[3] appropriation just for large-scale land deals with foreign investors who wish to invest in food, feed and fuel for export.

Recognizing that 'various State and non-state armed actors have been responsible for land grabs in Myanmar during the past several decades' (Woods 2014: 2), this chapter posits that land grabs in the new Myanmar are facilitated and legitimized by the rules that govern the acquisition of land use rights mainly because they reside in a tangle of overlapping, opaque and often contradictory laws which allow huge, unbridled discretionary powers to decision makers, and create an environment conducive to coercion, corruption, cronyism, violence and graft.

In this environment, land tenure in Myanmar remains insecure for most of the population, and especially for smallholder farmers who comprise about 70 percent of the population. The reasons for insecure land tenure are wide ranging. Of the six main reasons confirmed by the Organisation for Economic Co-operation and Development (OECD), weak, unjust, opaque and unclear laws must take the lion's share of the blame. The six reasons are:

> (i) a complex and long registration process …; (ii) rigid land classifications …; (iii) lack of recognition of customary land use rights; (iv) weak protection of registered land use rights; (v) inefficient land administration; and (vi) active promotion of large-scale allocations without adequate safeguards.
>
> (OECD 2014: 295)

This chapter analyses the relevant legal framework and shows how the law directly and indirectly contributes to insecure land tenure and through that facilitates and legitimizes land grabs. The first part provides a brief introduction to Myanmar's legal system in an effort to encourage a deeper understanding of the current regulatory climate. The second part examines the bundle of laws that regulates land use rights and foreign investment as it relates to land, and shows how some provisions assist in and facilitate the unjust taking of occupied land. Drawing on empirical evidence from field research conducted among stakeholders in and around areas designated for three proposed SEZs, this part also presents some of the findings from Dawei, Thilawa and Kyuak Phyu SEZs, which indicate that many land takings involved little or no prior consultation, no consent, and little or no compensation to previous or current occupiers of land. This part also presents similar findings from villages near Kyuak Phyu township where the Chinese-owned oil and gas pipelines start their overland transit from the new deep-sea port in Rakhine state on Myanmar's west coast to Yunnan province in China. In some cases contractual agreements were formed but many provisions in the contracts were woefully inadequate. The chapter concludes with recommendations for policy makers that might help minimize future livelihood disruptions among villagers and smallholder farmers, as well as secure better conditions for investors who might be affected by state-driven development plans.

The current legal climate: confusion and distrust

Since 2011, Myanmar has been transitioning from a 'pariah state' ruled by generals to a quasi-civilian government set on turning the country into a democracy that respects the rule of law. Encouraged by the recent developments, the international community lifted economic sanctions in 2012 (Lowrey 2012), and both President Thein Sein and opposition leader Aung San Suu Kyi have vowed to ensure that the country's development is guided by the rule of law, sustainability and responsible investment. To this end, the government has reviewed, amended, abolished and enacted hundreds of laws within a very short time, thus attempting to transform society and rapidly change the legal landscape. This is reminiscent of what happened in China in 1979 and the early 1980s when Deng Xiaoping and his government rushed to launch four coastal SEZs and promulgate a raft of domestic and foreign investor-friendly laws in order to kick-start China's economic development (Carter 2003, 2011: 54; Gallagher 2005; Chan *et al.* 1986; Crane 1994; Litwack and Qian 1998; Sit 1985).

However, the legal system in Myanmar is very different from China's because, for one, as many legal scholars agree,[4] Myanmar's legal system is rooted in the English common law family. Burma,[5] as Myanmar was called in those days, inherited its legal system including many statutes and regulations from British colonial India and continued to observe common law practice after independence in 1948.[6] However, as discussed below, Myanmar's legal system also mirrors the recent historical period which has been marked by decades of military dictatorship and socialist authoritarianism.

According to the International Commission of Jurists (2012: 12), a Laws Revision Committee classified and published all the pre-independence laws that were still in force and laws enacted up to 1954 in the Burma Code, Volumes I to XIII. They included all the then in force Codes enacted in or transplanted to Burma from India by the British colonial authorities. All existing laws that were not repealed or found contrary to the 1947 Constitution remained in force. Some scholars claim that there are dozens of laws that relate directly or indirectly to land management, land use and land as property in Myanmar (Leckie and Simperingham 2009; Displacement Solutions 2012), but there is no certainty about which of these were still in force as of September 2013.[7]

Socialist laws and regulations were layered on top of the colonial statutes and regulations from 1962 when a military coup established the Union Revolutionary Council and launched its 'Burmese way to Socialism'. In reality, the new socialist laws existed side by side with pre-existing laws insofar as they were not repealed and did not conflict with the 1947 Constitution. The 1953 Land Nationalization Act had already nationalized former colonial-held land, and to implement the Burmese socialist path there was further confiscation of whatever had not been nationalized previously, including industry and the financial sector. Farmers were obliged to sell their produce to the government. Myanmar's decline must have started shortly after the launch of the Burmese way to Socialism, for as the OECD (2014: 23) reports:

> [I]n the early 1960s, Myanmar was one of Asia's leading economies, with a per capita income more than three times that of Indonesia and twice that of Thailand. Fifty years later, per capita income on a purchasing power parity basis is roughly ten times higher in Thailand.

The 1974 Constitution confirmed that all land was the property of the state. Therefore government authorities would allocate land use rights to all people and businesses in need of land. The way in which the allocation system operated is unclear. However, it would appear that both state ownership of land and some form of state allocation system remained intact even when the 1974 Constitution was suspended in 1988. As discussed below, the 2008 Constitution reconfirmed that all land is state property.

Following huge pro-democracy, student-led protests in 1988, a second military coup suspended the 1974 Constitution, established the State Law and Order Restoration Council (SLORC) and applied harsh, repressive emergency rules. In the wake of the protests, the government also attempted to attract foreign investment to kick-start economic development as witnessed by the 1988 Foreign Investment Law (FIL). However, the effort was not very successful as the SLORC failed to cede power to Aung San Suu Kyi and her National League for Democracy (NLD) after they won the 1990 national election. This triggered economic sanctions from the West. However, Myanmar remained open for business. It conducted trade with and received foreign investment from Asian countries, especially Thailand, Malaysia, and China and India, the two emerging economic powerhouses with which Myanmar shares borders. Mining and the extractive industries were the most popular investment targets, both of which required substantial appropriation of land. This was facilitated mainly by the 1991 Wasteland Law. However, there is abundant evidence that the military also rode roughshod over property rights of minority ethnic groups – especially in the north, east and borderland areas, where civil war and ethnic conflicts resulted in the mass displacement of villagers and forest people, many of whom fled to exile in Thailand (Kachin Development Networking Group 2010; Karen Human Rights Group 2012). The military-acquired land was often allocated to military-operated companies and crony-owned businesses (Buchanan *et al.* 2013).

The 1991 Wasteland Law allowed the authorities to declare nominally unoccupied land as wasteland, which the government then allocated to insiders who could then lease to or otherwise cooperate with foreign investors in joint ventures. Some interviewees confirm that the confiscation of their land dates back to this period. For example, they explained how the military closed several villages in the Tennaserim Hills north of Dawei in order to expand the operation of a tin and tungsten mine in 1994. More villages were affected by 1999, when the military formed a joint venture with Pongpipat, a Thai company, which also received foreign direct investment (FDI) incentives under the 1988 FIL. Villagers were neither consulted nor compensated. By 2006 the nearby Myaung Pyo creek had dried up or become clogged with sediment from the mine. During the rainy season in 2012 sediment rose four feet up the stilts on which local houses are built, causing water and mud to penetrate the floors. Today the mine is being sued by some villagers for environmental and other damages. It has been a long journey involving harassment and intimidation. However, to the surprise of civil society groups, in June 2014, the court agreed to accept the case for trial.

The Myanmar Citizens Investment Law, enacted in 1994, allowed local investors to benefit from incentives similar to those offered to foreign investors under the 1988 FIL.

The military government remained in power until 2011 – albeit with its 1997 name change to the State Peace and Development Council (SPDC). In 1997 Myanmar joined the Association of Southeast Asian Nations (ASEAN). Myanmar then became a party to a number of multilateral and bilateral investment treaties with countries in the region, including the ASEAN Comprehensive Investment Agreement (the ACIAA) and the ASEAN-Australia and New Zealand Free Trade Agreement (the ASEAN-ANZ FTA). Following the devastation of the southern half of the country by Cyclone Nargis in May 2008, the long-awaited new constitution was approved in a referendum. It set out, *inter alia*, provisions for national elections and the composition of the new bicameral parliament. Some of the provisions of the 2008 Constitution, as they relate to land and investment, are discussed below.

As is apparent from the foregoing, Myanmar has experienced almost 50 years when military governments introduced socialist law and dictatorships presided over its legal system. Therefore, although Myanmar's legal heritage might be rooted in the English common law system, common law practices such as relying on precedents and providing reasoned, written judgments were not commonplace during the socialist period and are not often used (International Commission of Jurists 2012: 3).

Interviews conducted in July and August 2013, and February and July 2014, reveal that Myanmar's current legal climate is characterized by distrust, and that the legal system as well as the legal profession are held in low esteem due to the history of political oppression, corruption and an erosion of respect for the rule of law. Indeed, judges, lawyers, law professors, law students, civil society and business executives who were interviewed all testified to the lack of judicial independence, low respect for the rule of law and an almost universal public expectation that bribery can be used to achieve desired results. In their report on the status of the legal profession in Myanmar, the International Commission of Jurists (2012: 3) confirmed that:

> … lawyers in Myanmar pointed out the pervasive and corrosive effect of corruption on the independence of individual lawyers and to the legal profession overall in Myanmar. It underlies and affects every aspect of a lawyer's career, and is thus never absent from lawyers' calculations vis-à-vis legal fees, jurisdictions, and overall strategy. Crucially, the public also generally assumes that corruption will play a part in any interaction involving the legal system …

Some lawyers also reported discrimination based on religion and ethnicity; this, in a country where ethnic groups comprise an estimated 30–40 percent of the total population, and ethnic states occupy some 57 percent of the total land area (TNI 2013). It is said that, with colonization, the British had brought together over 130 ethnic groups into a single administrative unit, the so-called Union of Burma. It was this 'union' that gained independence in 1948. However, many ethnic groups – especially the larger ones – still seek greater autonomy and demand some working form of federalism (Henley 2014; Brand 2015; Saffin 2015; Williams 2015).

The 2008 Constitution enshrines respect for human rights and the rule of law (Chapter VIII), property rights (Article 37), separation of powers (Article 11), and provides that existing laws, regulations, by-laws, notifications, orders, directives and procedures remain in operation insofar as they are not contrary to the constitution, and until or unless they are repealed or amended by parliament or the government (Articles 446–447). Interviews with high-ranking officials, including two legal advisers to the president, reveal that the government knows that many laws may in fact be in conflict with the constitution, but that the lack of legal capacity sets a limit to how and when this situation may be remedied. Quite simply, Myanmar does not have enough qualified lawyers who can analyse and pin-point the inconsistencies, let alone do anything about them. The government itself has also conceded to foreign observers that many currently applicable laws are in fact contrary to the new constitution. See, for example, the United Nations Development Programme (UNDP 2012: 7), and the International Bar Association Human Rights Institute (2012: 41).

Equally troubling is the fact that the 2008 Constitution provides immunity for human rights violations committed by officials before March 2011 (Article 445); affords the military *de facto* veto powers over ratification of any amendment to the constitution (Article 436); and confers upon the Defence Services the right independently to administer and adjudicate all affairs of the armed services (Article 20(b)); and to establish permanent military tribunals whose decisions can be appealed only to the commander-in-chief (Articles 293(b), 319).

In light of these findings it is easy to understand why the general legal and regulatory climate is characterized by distrust, confusion and lack of clarity. It is against this background that the following sections explore the legal provisions that apply to land tenure, and aim to uncover how law facilitates land grabs.

How domestic law facilitates and legalizes land grabs

In Chapter 1 of this volume, it was argued that four categories of law are generally applicable to the issue of land tenure and land grabs: 1 domestic law; 2 international investment contracts; 3 international investment agreements – especially bilateral treaties (BITs); and 4 international human rights law.

In this chapter, the focus is on domestic law, especially the constitution and new laws that seek to attract foreign investment and regulate land tenure, since it is these that can affect the unjust or illegal taking of occupied land, and ought to provide safeguards against land grabs.[8] The next section therefore examines:

1 provisions of the 2008 Constitution as they relate to land;
2 the 2012 Vacant, Fallow, and Virgin Lands Management Law (VFV Law), which reclassifies land in Myanmar;
3 the 2012 Farmland Law, which governs land registration;
4 the 2012 Foreign Investment Law (FIL), which governs foreign investment in land-related projects, and creates the Myanmar Investment Commission (MIC), which is responsible for approving all investment proposals, issuing investor permits, and suspending them when an investor fails to comply with the law's provisions. The FIL also provides substantial tax and other incentives to attract FDI including a five-year tax holiday to businesses that manufacture and export goods or services, and those that are deemed 'beneficial to the Union';
5 the 2012 Special Economic Zone (SEZ) Law, which governs the establishment and operation of SEZs including tax and other incentives for attracting FDI and domestic investments into zones anywhere in Myanmar; this law repealed the 2011 SEZ Law and the 2011 Dawei SEZ Law; and
6 the 1894 Land Acquisition Act, which is still the primary instrument that governs expropriation of land for public and business purposes in Myanmar.

The constitution, capitalism and the commodification of land

Myanmar's 2008 Constitution, which came into force in 2010, sets the tone for developing Myanmar into a capitalist nation in which land becomes a commodity almost in line with Western notions of individual private property rights (this is discussed below). It also reaffirms the position that the state owns all land and all its natural resources, leaving it to bureaucrats' discretion to allocate land use rights.

First, the constitution provides that 'the economic system of the Union is [a] market economy system …' (Article 35), while Article 36 stipulates that:

> [T]he Union shall (a) permit all economic forces such as the State, regional organizations, co-operatives, joint-ventures, private individual [sic] so forth, to take part in economic activities for the development of [the] national economy; … (c) strive to improve the living standards of the people and development of investments …

Article 35, confirming that Myanmar is – or, perhaps better, will – strive to become a market economy is phenomenal for a country that was still deeply rooted in socialism at the time of its drafting. Article 36 firmly asserts that the purpose of the reform is development of the country. Article 37 declares that:

> [T]he Union: (a) is the ultimate owner of all lands and all natural resources above and below the ground, above and beneath the water and in the atmosphere in the Union; [and] (b) shall enact necessary law to supervise extraction and utilization of State-owned natural resources by economic forces.

Article 37 is problematic in light of the claims and armed conflicts that still exist between Myanmar's ethnic groups or more specifically between the majority Burmans, who reside predominantly in the country's south and centre, and ethnic groups who reside in the north, east and west, such as the Shan, Chin, Karen, Kachin, Rakhine (or Arakan), Mon and so on – ironically, also the places where nearly all of the coveted resources 'below the ground' can be found. Interviewees related many cases of violent resource-instigated land takings in Rakhine, Shan, Dawei, Karen and other resource-rich areas. For instance, in 2012, there was widespread land taking and displacement of four villages in the Sagaing region, as the military-owned company Union of Myanmar Economic Holdings Ltd confiscated 7,800 acres of land to support expansion of the Monywa copper mine by a subsidiary of the China North Industries Corporation. The land taking here must be characterized as a land grab as it was conducted without prior consultation, without consent or compensation and resulted in the forced displacement of four villages. Riot police suppressed the ensuing protests, and dozens were injured (USAID 2013: 20).

To support its move towards a market economy and 'development', the central government moved quickly to enact the 2012 VFV Land Management Law (see below), which provides for reclassification and reallocation of land all over the country; and the 2012 Farmland Law, which governs registration of Land Use Certificates (LUCs) for *all* farmers and users of farm land. Both laws are examined in detail below, and relevant provisions of the FIL and SEZ Law are also discussed.

The Vacant, Fallow and Virgin Land Management Law 2012 reclassifies land

There are two ways in which the VFV Law effectively puts land use rights up for grabs and then legitimizes those land grabs: one is by arbitrarily reclassifying occupied and notionally unoccupied land as 'vacant, fallow' and abandoned, and making it available as farmland. The other is by declaring 'reserved forests, grazing ground and fishery pond land' and 'uncultivated land' as 'virgin land' and making it available for farming or other uses. Under the Farmland Law (discussed below) use rights must be registered, giving any owner an LUC which represents tenured title. Reclassification cannot be appealed in the courts as the administrative decision is final.

The system works in the following way. Under the 2012 VFV Law, the Ministry of Agriculture and Irrigation (MoAI), and the Central Committee for the management of cultivatable land, fallow land and wasteland (the Central Committee), which the minister chairs, can declare certain lands vacant, fallow or virgin (all defined in Chapter 1 of the Law). Once declared, the Central Committee can then (re)allocate such lands for use in large-scale agriculture, livestock and poultry farming, mining and any other purposes permitted by the government (Article 4). Other government-permitted purposes can include SEZs and infrastructure.

Vacant and fallow land is defined as land that was 'abandoned by the tenant [for] any reason' and includes 'not only State designated land but also [land used] for agriculture or livestock breeding …' (Article 2(e)). The interpretation of these articles has been the ruin of many farmers' livelihoods in several places in and around the areas designated for SEZs. For example, farmers who practise crop rotation or shifting cultivation ('swidden') deliberately leave parts of their land uncultivated for a period. Many such farmers have lost their land use rights as their land was declared 'vacant' since bureaucrats implementing the law decided that the land had been 'abandoned by the tenant'. Ecological nurturing of the land is not recognized as a good reason for leaving it uncultivated for a while.

Virgin land is defined as land that has not been cultivated before, and land that 'has been cancelled legally from reserved forest, grazing ground and fishery pond land' and can be made available for large-scale agriculture, livestock and poultry farming, mining and any other purpose permitted by the government (Article 2(f)). The interpretation of this Article caused many locals in the forest areas near to the Dawei and Kyuak Phyu SEZs to lament that they are no longer allowed to forage in the forests or collect plants, roots and berries for food and traditional medicines. Some interviewed farmers have lost their lands to other purposes such as plans for building infrastructure to support the SEZs.[9] However, the 80-year-old Ka Lone Htar Buddhist monastery and the Ka Lone Htar village in the hills above Dawei

SEZ seem to have been reprieved as the planned hydro-electric dam and reservoir were cancelled following sustained protests by, *inter alia*, the Ka Lone Htar Social Committee headed by the abbot, Sayadaw U Pyinnya Wuntha, and the Dawei Development Association (DDA).[10] Lack of funding and general uncertainty around the plans for Dawei SEZ also seem to have assisted.

Article 7 of the VFV Law provides that the Central Committee in agreement with the Myanmar Investment Commission (MIC, formed under the 2012 FIL) can allocate to foreign investors, the right to use vacant, fallow or virgin land of up to 50,000 acres for agribusiness and other projects. However, while the VFV Law proposes 30-year leases, the FIL and the SEZ Law contemplate up to 70 years. A security fee must be deposited (Article 9) and the amount is assessed according to the 'type of enterprise' and decided at the sole discretion of the Central Committee (Article 13). There are no guidelines about how this fee is assessed or the relevance of the type of enterprise. The conditions of land use are set out in Article 16, and *any* breach will result in revocation of the land use right (Article 21). What constitutes a breach is also interpreted by the Central Committee, whose decision is final. Naturally, once the land use right is revoked, the tenant is evicted and the land becomes available for reallocation. No compensation seems to be contemplated as the land has been 'dealt with in accordance with the law'.

Article 16(g) of the VFV Law stipulates that:

> [I]f natural resources are found in the authorized [allocated] land and the Government being desirous of extracting the same on a commercial basis resumes [presumably 'reclaims'] the area required therefrom, it shall be surrendered as directed by the Union government.

This provision also renders land tenure insecure as it means that allocated land use rights can be withdrawn at any time subject to the government requiring it for mining and other extractive industries. The law is silent about the expropriation procedure or compensation. Furthermore, Article 19 reiterates that the government may withdraw authorized land use rights under several circumstances, including 19(b), 'If [an] infrastructure project or special project are [sic] desired to be constructed on the authorized land, in the interest of the State'. Article 20 contemplates compensation for Article 19 expropriations, but not Article 16 ones, leaving some lawyers to wonder whether Article 16 is aimed at domestic situations while articles 19 and 20 cover foreign enterprises – or at least those with formal contractual agreements with a state entity. In any event, under Article 20 compensation will be calculated 'by current value to cover the actual investment cost of the legitimate owner, with the agreement of the *Cabinet of the Union Government*' (emphasis added).

Article 22 provides that persons and organizations that have held land use rights prior to the coming into force of the 2012 VFV Law shall prove their land use rights by producing the registration date and serial number, together with photographs and other evidence of land use; any land that remains 'uncultivated' shall be relinquished to the state. Customary or traditional land use is not provided for.

Astonishingly, Chapter IX provides for criminal sanctions for persons who destroy 'the benefit' of land occupied by the new rights holders (Article 26); for trespassers, that is 'anyone who encroach[es] on the authorized land without the permission of the legitimate owner, or his representative …' (Article 27), or those who 'obstruct' the working of the land by the legitimate owner or his agent (Article 28). Such sanctions were already in force prior to enactment of the VFV Law. According to the Asian Human Rights Commission (2014), 65 farmers are languishing in Kanbalu prison in the Shwebo district of Sagaing Division for ploughing their own land which had previously been grabbed by the military. An additional 350 farmers in the region await a similar fate (ibid.).

Finally, Article 29 provides that anyone who fails to comply with an eviction order 'shall be sentenced with imprisonment for a term not exceeding one year or a fine', or both.

The Farmland Law creates a land market and opportunities for land grabbing

Three features set the 2012 Farmland Law apart and create a potential for land grabbing:

1 the law creates a market for land, and anyone without an LUC no longer possesses legal rights to use the land, and can be evicted;
2 it creates the Farmland Administration Body (FAB), chaired by the minister of agriculture and irrigation, which has sole power to allocate land use rights; and
3 the FAB is outside the reach of the judiciary, which means that FAB's decisions are final and cannot be appealed.

In general, the new law governs conditions under which farmers can retain and *must* register their land use rights, the state's power to revoke such rights, dispute settlement procedure and compensation in case of government land expropriation for public purposes. It repeals the 1953 Land Nationalization Act, the 1963 Tenant Farming Law, the 1963 Protection of Peasants' Rights Law, the Agriculturalists' Rights Protection Law, and the Disposal of Tenancies Law.

By creating an administrative hierarchy, the FAB (Article 16), which supervises the *compulsory* registration of *all* farmland (Article 8), gains a monopoly over land rights allocation which leaves it open to manipulation and abuse. The law provides that anyone who holds land use rights, whether through occupancy or title, *must* obtain an LUC (Article 4), and pay a registration fee. The LUC allows the rights holder to transfer, sell, pawn [mortgage], exchange, lease or donate [gift] their rights (Chapter 3). In short, through registration and possession of LUCs, this law creates a new market for land.

However, the registration provisions (Chapter 2 of the law) are so complex and restrictive that they essentially exclude many rural occupiers of land and de facto land right holders from obtaining the coveted LUCs. The burdensome application procedure is further elaborated in the Ward & Village Tract Administration Law 2012. Proof of occupancy among many villagers is the land tax receipt from the local township land office but not many can produce such receipts. Several interviewees reported cases where the township land office deliberately exploited their 'loss' and recommended revocation of their land use rights. Without the LUC, land use rights are revoked, tenants evicted and the land reverts to the state, which reallocates it following approval by the district FAB (Article 7).

In practice, this procedure legitimizes land grabbing by the state, which then allows administrators to reallocate land to others, typically insiders and cronies. The lack of qualified staff and overall administrative inefficiency also hamper implementation of this national land registration system.

Like the Central Committee under the VFV Law (discussed above), the FAB is chaired by the minister of agriculture and irrigation, and its decisions cannot be appealed in the courts. The only exception is decisions regarding inherited land.

The categories of person who are defined as 'farmers' also provide opportunities for land grabbing. According to Articles 6(a), (b) and 7(a), (b), farmland can be allocated to any person, over 18 years old, who has the right to farm in agricultural households; members, heads or guardians of such households who legally hold land rights and who worked the land under the existing law prior to the coming into force of the Farmland Law; legal beneficiaries deriving from this law; and citizens or residents in a relevant ward or village tract. These categories are clear. However, interviewees in Thilawa and Dawei provided evidence of wealthy city folks hiring people to burn plots of land and create hillside farms on which they plant crops in an attempt to prove that they had worked the land before the new law came into force.

Another loophole is provided by articles 6(c) and 7(c) which stipulate that government departments, nongovernmental organizations (NGOs) and companies are also 'farmers' to whom the FAB can issue LUCs.

Article 9(f) refers to the FIL and allows 'a foreigner or an organization containing a foreigner' the right to carry out farming 'in a joint venture'. However, rights holders can only transfer their rights to a foreigner or foreign joint venture with the state government's permission (Article 14), leaving the way open for influence peddling, abuse of power and corruption.

Another area in which interviewees provided early evidence of corruption and abuse that led to land grabbing, are the conditions for use that are set out in Article 12. Breach of *any* of the conditions results in revocation of land use rights. Article 12(f) declares that farmland shall not be worked without permission from the FAB; (g) that farmland shall not be used for non-agricultural purposes without permission; (h) that only prescribed crops may be grown; and (i) that farmland shall not be left fallow without 'a sound reason'. The latter three conditions are particularly divisive. Why should the government prescribe which crops are grown? Will this make it easier for the government to move to large-scale industrial farming of cash crops as it promises in its 2020 Plan? What is a 'sound reason' for leaving newly acquired land fallow? Is crop rotation or shifting cultivation a sound reason, or is this a loophole that will facilitate the large-scale taking of land by speculators who will invest for their portfolios on the expectation of reaping profits when the price of land in areas earmarked for development increases? Villagers in and around the Kyuak Phyu and Thilawa SEZs provided evidence which suggests that 'a sound reason' is a loophole that facilitates land grabbing for speculation in land. What constitutes a sound reason is at FAB's discretion, as is the Article 12(g) permit to use farmland for non-agricultural purposes. Even before the SEZ plans were announced officially, insiders and the well connected had grabbed large tracts of land near to the designated areas, and many of these acres remained uncultivated in summer 2014, probably waiting to be turned into lucrative residential and commercial buildings.

Chapter 8 of the law sets out the dispute resolution process when land rights and the right to farming are contested. As already noted, this power rests with FAB hierarchy, and under Article 25(c) the decision of the regional or state-level FAB is final.

Article 33 provides that 'pasture land and village common land' are to remain unchanged unless required by the union government or its representatives. This is the closest one gets to recognition of community-based land, but customary or traditional use rights are not mentioned and therefore not recognized. They do not fit into the rigid classifications created by the new laws. The laws do not reflect the reality of the majority of existing land users, who are characterized by family and community-based farming. However, by including government departments, NGOs, Myanmar-registered companies and foreign joint ventures in the definition of 'farmers', and allowing them to register and transfer LUCs to any entity, the government has created a commercialized property market. It has commoditized land and its associated natural resources, signalling the acceptance of a Western-style, private individual property market, as opposed to a more human rights-based approach to use, management and governance of land and natural resources (TNI 2013: 3). By placing classification and allocation decisions in the hands of unaccountable officials equipped with huge discretionary powers, the laws create an environment conducive to abuse, corruption and bribery. Villagers interviewed in Dawei, Thilawa and Kyuak Phyu provide ample evidence of such abuse.

Finally, the law *reaffirms* the state's power to confiscate tenured land for a 'public purpose' or 'public business', and compensation is contemplated. Field research uncovered an interesting example, namely land confiscation for a 'public business' on Made Island near Kyuak Phyu, where agents of the state-owned Myanmar Oil and Gas Enterprise (MOGE) contracted with local farmers to relinquish their land rights and their crops in exchange for 'compassionate compensation'. Contracts on file with the author show the woefully inadequate compensation that was given, and interviewees reveal that the confiscation procedure did not reflect any of the provisions of the Land Acquisition Act, which was their only hope. In practice, there was no consultation, bullying and intimidation accompanied the 'contract signing' where right holders were forced to accept predetermined 'compassionate compensation' whose evaluation procedure was not disclosed.

Conclusion: what it means on the ground and what can be done

Arguing that Myanmar's legal framework facilitates and legitimates land grabs, this chapter has analysed salient provisions in the constitution, two 2012 land laws and land-related provisions in the SEZ Law and FIL to illustrate two points: first, how the operation of the laws themselves create land insecurity, which fosters and has facilitated land grabs; and second, how the laws create an environment conducive to abuse of power and corruption. Field research supported the operation of the law in facilitating land grabs in the following ways: local smallholders lose their land rights and are evicted, first when their actual land use does not match the (new) legal classification of land, second when they fail to register their land rights and obtain the new prescribed LUCs, and third when they breach *any* of the use conditions set out in the 2012 Farmland Law – including a failure to grow the crop designated by the government. Once a farmer is evicted, the land is reallocated to another. Failure to obey an eviction order results in imprisonment, without appeal to the court. Field research uncovered many instances in which decision makers abused their power and used their discretion to allocate land to well-connected elites and their companies, to the detriment of smallholders. These are land grabs by unjust taking and the legal operation of inappropriate and unjust laws. Weak protection of registered land use rights also encourages insecure tenure and land grabs. Field research also revealed military and government agents confiscating land for 'a public purpose' or 'a public business' but without prior consultation, consent or compensation. Although the Land Acquisition Act 1894 requires notice, consultation, negotiation and compensation, Myanmar has yet to develop a system that implements and enforces this law.

To help prevent land grabs and safeguard landholders' rights, the government should, at a minimum:

- Provide and implement a land acquisition plan that incorporates the principles of FPIC: free, prior and informed consent for *all* stakeholders in *all* projects involving land use, recognizing that transparency and accountability are key to the projects' success.

- Provide a system of land use planning that encourages rational, consistent and democratically valid land use laws relating to classification, allocation and registration, and weed out the inconsistencies and contradictions in the system. This process must be informed by wide public consultations among stakeholders including domestic and foreign NGOs and civil society groups.
- Ensure that members of committees and commissions such as the Land Acquisition Security Commission, and the Rule of Law & Stabilization Committee are trained, and that their mandates are clearly communicated internally and to the public.
- Provide a plan that will create balance between large-scale and small-small farming, and ensure proper funding for small-scale farmers so that they can improve their methods and practise sustainable farming.
- Ensure that, faced with a weak regulatory system, companies – especially foreign investors – are encouraged to exercise good corporate citizenship, by adhering to the UN Guiding Principles on Business and Human Rights. This will include ensuring that local people, not imported labourers, are employed, and that their human rights and the environment are safeguarded.

Notes

1 This chapter benefits from field research conducted in Myanmar by Connie Carter, with assistance from Zaw Aung, a Burmese researcher who holds an MA in Development Studies from Chulalongkorn University, Thailand, and Sai Nyi Nyi Soe, an interpreter and director in Myanmar; and with financial support from the International Development Research Centre (IDRC) of the Government of Canada, and the Centre for Asian Legal Studies (CALS), National University of Singapore.

2 Field research was conducted among a wide range of stakeholders who are involved in the establishment of three government-mandated special economic zones (SEZs) in Myanmar, and among stakeholders involved with the oil and gas pipelines that transit overland from a deep-sea port near Kyuak Phyu on Myanmar's west coast to Yunnan province in China. Qualitative research methods were applied: collecting primary data through semi-structured, individual in-depth interviews and focus groups with stakeholder-informants in villages in and around the SEZ locations; and in Yangon, Nay Pyi Taw, Bangkok and Singapore to capture opinions from parliamentarians, government ministers, politicians, non-governmental organizations (NGOs), civil society groups, journalists, lawyers, entrepreneurs, educators, chambers of commerce and embassy staff, and business executives in Thai, Japanese and Myanmar corporations. The opinions of women and various minority ethnic groups were canvassed specifically in Dawei and Kyuak Phyu. The research team undertook field research over a period of 14 months. Data collection in and around the three SEZs and in Nay Pyi Taw and Yangon was conducted in July, August and October 2013, and February and July 2014. Secondary data were collected through desktop review of available academic literature, articles in the press, some translated legislation, relevant Hluttaw proceedings, rules and regulations, and the Myanmar government gazette.

3 See Chapter 1 of this volume for a discussion of the lands grabs literature, which focuses mainly on 'large-scale land acquisition', 'land deals' or 'land grabs' by foreign investors who purportedly wish to grow food, feed and fuel in the global South for export back to the global North.

4 For a discussion, see Huxley 2004, 2008; Harding 2014.

5 The ruling military junta changed the country's name from Burma to Myanmar in 1989. This chapter refers to the country as Myanmar but retains the language used by individual sources in references.

6 As Westerners, we often forget that prior to colonization, colonized lands also enjoyed their own adjudication systems – whether based on religion, customary practice or secular edicts. Myanmar is no exception. For a review of scholarship on Myanmar's legal system, see Crouch 2014; for a discussion on the nature of Myanmar's early legal system, see references contained therein, in particular Huxley 1997, 2001.

7 For our purposes, relevant statutes include but are not limited to the 1879 Land and Revenue Act, which regulates the assessment and collection of land taxes; the Transfer of Property Act 1882, which governs the sale, mortgage, lease, exchange and gift of moveable and immoveable property; the 1899 Lower Myanmar Town and Village Act, which regulates land rights in towns and villages and provides certain rights such as the right to cultivate and sell, and rights in relation to inheritance and government lands; the Land Acquisition Act 1894, which regulates the expropriation of land by the government for public and other purposes, and makes provisions for land valuation methods, appeal processes and so on; the Registration Act 1909; the Trusts Act 1920; the Special Company Act 1950; the Arbitration Act 1944; the Land Nationalization Act 1953; the Protection of the Right of Cultivation Act 1963, which protects farmers against confiscation of their land and farming equipment; and the Civil Procedure and Criminal Procedure Codes.

8 In late October 2014, the Myanmar government circulated for comment the draft National Land Use Policy (NLUP). It was not available for analysis in this volume. However, it has been widely criticised for failing to include input from groups that will be most affected while giving privileges to investors which could spark more land grabs. For a response to the draft NLUP, see the Transnational Institute's February 2015 publication at www.tni.org/work-area/burma-project.

9 Focus groups 4 and 5, Dawei, 5 July 2013; Focus groups 6 and 7, Kyuak Phyu, 12 and 13 July 2013.

10 Interviewee 12, July 2014.

References

Asian Human Rights Commission (2014) 'Burma/Myanmar: Over 450 Farmers Victimized by Military Land Grabbing', 30 July, www.humanrights.asia/news/urgent-appeals/AHRC-UAC-109-2014.

Burma Environmental Working Group (BEWG) (2011) 'Burma's Environment: People, Problems, Policies', www.bewg.org/en/reports/beppp.

Brand, M. (2015, forthcoming) 'Towards "Genuine Federalism"? Myanmar's Inexorable Path Towards Constitutional Devolution and Decentralised Governance', in A. Harding and K.K. Oo (eds) *Constitutionalism and Legal Reform in Myanmar*, Oxford: Hart Publishing.

Buchanan, J., Kramer, T. and Woods, K. (2013) *Developing Disparity: Regional Investment in Burma's Borderlands*, Amsterdam: Transnational Institute, Burma Centre.

Carter, C. (2003) 'The Clonability of the Singapore Model of Law and Development: The Case of Suzhou, China', in C. Antons (ed.) *Law and Development in East and Southeast Asia*, London: Routledge/Curzon.

Carter, C. (2011) 'A Tale of Two Chinese SEZs: From Exogenous to Sustainable Endogenous Growth?' in C. Carter and A. Harding (eds) *Special Economic Zones in Asian Market Economies*, London and New York: Routledge.

Chan, T., Chen, E.K. and Chin, S. (1986) 'China's Special Economic Zones: Ideology, Policy and Practice', in Y.C. Jao and C.K. Leung (eds) *China's Special Economic Zones: Policies, Problems and Prospects*, Oxford: Oxford University Press.

COHRE (2007) 'Displacement and Dispossession: Forced Migration and Land Rights', www.cohre.org/site/default/files/burma_displacement_and_dispossession_forced_migration_and_land_rights_nov_2007.pdf.

Crane, G. (1994) 'Special Things in Special Ways: National Economic Identity and China's Special Economic Zones', *The Australian Journal of Chinese Affairs* 32: 71–92.

Crouch, M. (2014) 'Rediscovering "Law" in Myanmar: A Review of Scholarship on the Legal System of Myanmar', *Pacific Rim Law & Policy Journal* 23(3): 543.

Displacement Solutions (2012) 'Myanmar at the HLP Crossroads: Proposals for Building an Improved Housing, Land and Property Rights Framework that Protects the People and Supports Sustainable Economic Development', displacementsolutions.org/files/documents/MyanmarReport.pdf.

Gallagher, M. (2005) *Contagious Capitalism: Globalization and the Politics of Labour in China*, Princeton, NJ: Princeton University Press.

Harding, A. (2014) 'Law and Development in its Burmese Moment: Legal Reform in a Developing Economy', in M. Crouch and T. Lindsey (eds) *Law, Society and Transition in Myanmar*, Oxford: Hart Publishing.

Henley, G. (2014) *Case Study on Land in Burma*, London: Overseas Development Institute.

Huxley, A. (1997) 'The Importance of Dhammathats in Burmese Law and Culture', *Journal of Burma Studies* 1.

Huxley, A. (2001) 'Pre-colonial Burmese Law: Conical Hat and Shoulder Bag', *ILAS Newsletter* 25, www.iias.asia/iiasn/25/theme/25T7.html.

Huxley, A. (2004) 'Case Note: California Refuses to Apply Myanmar Law', *Asian Law* 6(1): 88.

Huxley, A. (2008) 'Case Note: Comparative Law Aspects of Doe v Unocal Choice of Law Hearing', *Journal of Comparative Law* 1(1): 219.

International Bar Association Human Rights Institute (2012) *The Rule of Law in Myanmar: Challenges and Prospects*, London: IBA.

International Commission of Jurists (2012) *Right to Counsel: The Independence of Lawyers in Myanmar*, Bangkok, Thailand: ICJ.

Kachin Development Networking Group (2010) *Tyrants, Tycoons and Tigers: Yuzana Company Ravages Burma's Hugawng Valley*, Chiang Mai, Thailand.

Karen Human Rights Group (2012) *Losing Ground: Land Conflicts and Collective Action in Eastern Myanmar*.

Leckie, S. and Simperingham, E. (2009) 'Housing, Land and Property Rights in Burma: The Current Legal Framework', *Displacement Solutions & the HLP Institute*, displacementsolutions.org/wp-content/uploads/2010/01/Burma_HLP_book.pdf.

Litwack, J. and Qian, Y. (1998) 'Balanced or Unbalanced Development: Special Economic Zones as Catalysts for Transition', *Journal of Comparative Economics* 26(1): 117–141.

Lowrey, A. (2012) 'US Sanctions on Myanmar Formally Eased', *The New York Times*, 11 July, www.nytimes.com/2012/07/12/world/asia/us-sanctions-on-myanmar-formally-eased.html?r=0.

Oberndorf, R. (2012) 'Legal Review of Recently Enacted Farmland Law and Vacant, Fallow and Virgin Lands Management Law: Improving the Legal & Policy Frameworks Relating to Land Management in Myanmar', Food Security Working Group, www.forest-trends.org/documents/files/doc_3274.pdf.

OECD (2014) *OECD Investment Policy Review: Myanmar 2014*, Paris: OECD Publishing.

Saffin, J. (2015, forthcoming) 'Seeking Constitutional Settlement in Myanmar', in A. Harding and K.K. Oo (eds) *Constitutionalism and Legal Change in Myanmar*, Oxford: Hart Publishing.

Sit, V. (1985) 'The Special Economic Zones of China: A New Type of Export Processing Zone?' *The Developing Economies* 23(1) (March): 68.

Thabchumpon, N., Middleton, C. and Aung, Z. (2012) *Development, Democracy and Human Security in Myanmar: A Case Study of the Dawei SEZ*, Bangkok: ICIRD.

Transnational Institute (TNI) (2013) 'Access Denied: Land Rights and Ethnic Conflict in Burma', www.tni.org/work-area/burma-project.

United Nations Development Programme (UNDP) (2012) *Democratic Governance in Myanmar: Preliminary Situation Analysis*, New york: UNDP.

USAID (2013) 'USAID Country Profile: Land Tenure Profile: Myanmar', www.globalprotectioncluster.org/_assets/files/field_protection_clusters/Myanmar/files/HLP%20AoR/Land_Tenure_Profile_Myanmar_2013_EN.pdf.

Williams, D. (2015, forthcoming) 'A Second Panglong Agreement: Burmese Federalism for the 21st Century', in A. Harding and K.K. Oo (eds) *Constitutionalism and Legal Change in Myanmar*, Oxford: Hart Publishing.

Woods, K. (2011) *Emerging Agribusiness Trends in Myanmar: An Overview*, Amsterdam: Transnational Institute.

Woods, K. (2014) 'A Political Anatomy of Land Grabs', *Myanmar Times*, 3 March: 2.

Zaw, H.N. and Khaing, A.K. (2013) 'Military Involved in Massive Land Grabs: Parliamentary Report', *The Irrawaddy*, 5 March, www.irrawaddy.org/archives/28506.

8 Peninsular Malaysia's customary lands

How does legal paternalism facilitate land grabs?

Yogeswaran Subramaniam[1]

Introduction

Despite the existence of constitutional and statutory provisions in Malaysia that empower the federal and state governments to act for the 'protection, well-being and advancement' of the *Orang Asli*, this indigenous minority of Peninsular Malaysia continues to face the appropriation of large tracts of lands claimed to be their customary territories. The common law recognition of Orang Asli customary land rights by the Malaysian courts and Malaysia's unequivocal votes for the 2007 United Nations Declaration on the Rights of Indigenous Peoples (UNDRIP) have not alleviated matters for the Orang Asli. At odds with these developments, the federal and state governments persist with the use of their extensive legal powers over both the Orang Asli and Orang Asli lands to determine state priorities for land and resource ownership, management and use. The exercise of these powers has adversely affected the Orang Asli because their lands function as an important source of economic livelihood, a social safety net and, perhaps most of all, a necessary component of their culture, identity and overall well-being.

This chapter examines the role of paternalistic written laws in potentially facilitating the grabbing of lands and resources claimed as Orang Asli customary lands. For the sake of clarity, 'land grab', consistently with the definition adopted in this book, is used to describe the taking of Orang Asli land, not just in violation of a statutory provision, but includes also the act of appropriating Orang Asli inhabited or used lands *with impunity*, that is without adequate consultation, consent or compensation. The chapter begins with an introduction to the Orang Asli and their constitutional position before examining the statutory provisions affecting Orang Asli land rights. The Orang Asli land grab problem is then put into perspective for the purposes of this chapter. More recent positive jurisprudential, international and local developments concerning Orang Asli land rights and their impact upon existing laws are discussed before current government responses to the Orang Asli land problem are examined. The chapter concludes with observations on challenges to the effective protection and recognition of Orang Asli lands.

Orang Asli in context

This section provides a snapshot of the Orang Asli community vis-à-vis Malaysian society, highlighting their relatively vulnerable political, demographic and socio-economic position.

The term '*Orang Asli*' collectively refers to the 18 official ethnic Aboriginal sub-groups in Peninsular Malaysia, classified into three broad categories of *Negrito, Senoi* and *Aboriginal Malay* (Subramaniam 2012: 20–3). Literally translated, the term means 'natural people' and is now also taken to mean 'original' or 'first' people (Andaya 2002: 25; Carey 1976: 5). Similar to other indigenous communities worldwide, many Orang Asli struggle to maintain their culture and identity which are inextricably linked with their close physical, economic, social, cultural, territorial and spiritual relationship with the environment (Williams-Hunt 1995: 35–6). As will be observed below, Orang Asli are distinguishable from natives of Sabah and Sarawak and ethnic Malays who are defined and treated separately under the Federal Constitution.

In terms of political representation, there is only one Orang Asli senator in the federal and individual state legislatures who represents Orang Asli interests. There are also no Orang Asli who hold executive positions in either the Federal Cabinet or State Executive Councils. In 2010, Orang Asli numbered approximately 178,197, around 0.6 percent of the population of Malaysia (JAKOA 2011: 20). In addition to being politically and demographically weak, key socio-economic indicators reveal that the Orang Asli are arguably the most impoverished and marginalized community in Malaysia. In 2009, 50 percent of Orang Asli lived below the poverty level compared to the national average of 3.8 percent (Economic Planning Unit, Prime Minister's Department 2010: 149, 151, 162). Orang Asli, who mostly reside in rural areas, have a much higher poverty rate than the national rural poverty rate of 11.9 percent (Economic Planning Unit, Prime Minister's Department 2006: 358). The drop-out rate of Orang Asli students from school has also been relatively high. In 2008, around 48 percent of Orang Asli students who registered for secondary school in 2004 failed to complete their secondary education (JAKOA 2011: 47–9). In 2010, water and electricity supplies only covered 67.4 percent and 76.1 percent of Orang Asli villages, respectively (JAKOA 2011: 34–5). These percentages pale in comparison to the corresponding national rural averages of 97 percent and 98 percent (Omar 2008: 15).

Orang Asli in the Federal Constitution

Constitutionally, Orang Asli,[2] ethnic Malays,[3] natives of Sabah[4] and natives of Sarawak[5] are afforded varying degrees of special rights and privileges by virtue of their ethnicity. Article 153 of the Federal Constitution obliges the *Yang Dipertuan Agong* [6] to safeguard the 'special position of the Malays and natives of any of the States of Sabah and Sarawak', while Art. 161A extends to the natives of Sabah and Sarawak the same 'special privileges' as the Malays.[7] This special position includes reservations of positions in the public service, scholarships, and other educational and training privileges and licences (Federal Constitution, art. 153(2)). In respect of land, Malay reservations created immediately before Independence Day (31 August 1957) continue to exist unless a state enactment is passed to the contrary by a two-thirds majority in the relevant state legislative assembly and both houses of parliament (Federal Constitution, art. 89(1)).

The Orang Asli do not enjoy equivalent constitutional rights, but instead are dependent on the federal government for their overall welfare. Item 16 of List I of the Ninth Schedule to the Federal Constitution specifically empowers the federal government to legislate for the welfare of Orang Asli.[8] Article 8(1), the equal protection clause in the Federal Constitution, states '[a]ll persons are equal before the law and entitled to equal protection of the law'. Article 8(5)(c) of the Federal Constitution permits laws 'for the protection, well-being or advancement' of Orang Asli, 'including, the reservation of land' or the 'reservation to Orang Asli of a reasonable proportion of suitable positions in the public service'. Therefore, affirmative action within the ambit of Article 8(5)(c) would be constitutionally valid. However, despite enabling positive discrimination laws in favour of the Orang Asli, these constitutional provisions do not expressly *oblige* the state[9] to safeguard the position of the Orang Asli. In contrast, the state is *obliged* to safeguard the privileged status of the Malays and natives of Sabah and Sarawak on a potentially wider scope of protections. Malays and natives of Sabah and Sarawak also have constitutional protection against laws that touch upon their respective customs (Federal Constitution, arts. 76(2) and 150(6A)).[10] Islam, the religion of all Malays (as defined in the Federal Constitution),[11] is the 'religion of the Federation' (Art. 3(1)) and is constitutionally protected (Art. 76(2)). The Malay language is the national language (Art. 152). Orang Asli have no equivalent protection for their languages, laws, traditions, customs and institutions.

Despite the Federal Constitution containing explicit provisions which contemplate their welfare, Orang Asli are largely reliant on the good will of the state for their welfare as there are no mandatory constitutional provisions for their protection. Accordingly, their privileged status under the Federal Constitution is arguably inferior to that of Malays and the natives of Sabah and Sarawak.

Express statutory land rights

This section examines express statutory provisions governing the Orang Asli and their lands, suggesting that individual states in Peninsular Malaysia possess ultimate statutory authority over Orang Asli lands. Other statutory laws affecting Orang Asli lands do not even envisage Orang Asli as a distinct indigenous group.

The Aboriginal Peoples Act 1954 (Malaysia)

The Aboriginal Peoples Act 1954 (Act 134, APA) is the principal statute governing the administration and rights of the Orang Asli. The APA can be described as a double-edged sword, functioning not only to protect the Orang Asli but to secure and perpetuate control over them and their lands and resources.

The preamble describes the APA as an act for the 'protection, well-being and advancement' of the Orang Asli. Consistent with criticisms that the APA was a British act of 'patronising benevolence' (Carey 1976: 289) passed during the height of the Malayan communist insurgency when many Orang Asli were seen as communist sympathizers, the APA confers extensive federal executive power over the Orang Asli. These powers include the discretion to: 1 determine if a person is an Orang Asli (s.3(3)); 2 determine the appointment and removal of Orang Asli headmen (s.16); 3 exclude undesirable persons from any Orang Asli inhabited areas (ss.14, 15); and 4 restrict any written, printed or photographic matter deemed harmful to the Orang Asli by the state (ss.19(1)(l)). It has been contended that these legal powers enable the federal executive to maintain a stranglehold over Orang Asli (Subramaniam 2011: 45–7, 49–50, 54–6).

In respect of land, the APA provisions relating to all the three statutory categories of Orang Asli land may be regarded as a limited form of state-controlled occupancy and use of lands and resources. These categories are now examined in turn.

Aboriginal reserves

Section 7 of the APA is the main provision governing Aboriginal reserves. Although Aboriginal reserves offer a measure of protection while an area is categorized as such (s. 7(2)), an individual state authority can declare an area as an Aboriginal reserve by gazette notification (s.7(1)) and revoke wholly or in part or vary any such declaration by a similar notification (s.7(3)). Aboriginal reserves therefore provide relatively limited security of tenure as their protection is wholly dependent on the state executive fiat.[12]

Section 8 creates a 'special form of tenure' (Legislative Council, Federation of Malaya 1954: 2) for Orang Asli but again vests power to grant such tenure in the relevant state authority. Under s.8, the state authority may grant rights of occupancy within Aboriginal reserves to any individual Orang Asli or members of any Orang Asli family or community, but such interests 'shall be deemed *not* to confer any better title than that of a tenant at will' (s.8(2)). In other words, any rights of occupancy granted to Orang Asli can be terminated by a notification from the state authority.[13]

Aboriginal areas

Section 6 is the main provision relating to Aboriginal areas. Aboriginal areas cover a broader scope than Aboriginal reserves as they can extend to cover areas: 1 'predominantly' (as opposed to 'exclusively') inhabited by Orang Asli; and 2 with more than one Aboriginal ethnic group, subject to divisions into cantons (s.6(1)).

Although there is some protection against the creation of interests within Aboriginal areas (s.6(2)), the powers to declare, vary and revoke an Aboriginal area (ss.6(1) and 6(3)) and grant rights of occupancy (s.8) are again vested in the state authority.

Aboriginal inhabited place

The third and residual category of Orang Asli land under s.2 of the APA is an 'Aboriginal inhabited place', which encompasses any other places inhabited by Orang Asli communities that are neither Aboriginal reserves nor Aboriginal areas.

Orang Asli communities in Aboriginal inhabited places have minimal statutory protection. Section 10(1) of the APA allows an Orang Asli community resident in an area declared to be a Malay reservation, forest reserve or game reserve under any written law to continue residing on such areas. However, the state authority possesses the power to order any Aboriginal community out of such lands (ss.10(3) and 4).

Compensation and land rights under the APA

With respect to compensation for loss of lands, the state authority *may* grant compensation to any Orang Asli or Orang Asli community where any 'Aboriginal reserve' is excised or land within an 'Aboriginal area' is alienated, granted, leased or otherwise disposed of or if any right or privilege in any Aboriginal reserve is revoked wholly or in part (s.12). Compensation for loss of lands within an Aboriginal reserve or area therefore appears to be discretionary. However, the Court of Appeal has interpreted the word 'may' in s.12 of the APA to mean 'shall' and introduced the word 'adequate' before the word 'compensation' in the same provision.[14] The purposive approach taken in interpreting s.12 was said to bring the provision in line with Article 13(2) of the Federal Constitution, which states that '[n]o law shall provide for compulsory acquisition or use of property without adequate compensation'. The practical effect of this development is examined below.

Payment of compensation for aboriginal inhabited places under ss.10(3) and 10(4) is at the discretion of the state authority and only applies to Orang Asli communities residing within Malay reservations, forest or game reserves. In reality, Orang Asli in aboriginal inhabited places also occupy other categories of land including state land,[15] land reserved for other state purposes, mining land, protected parks and private land (SUHAKAM 2013: 130–53). These Orang Asli communities do not possess express statutory *rights* of occupancy. Nevertheless, Orang Asli occupying *state land* are entitled to just compensation for the loss of their fruit and rubber trees (APA, s.11(1)).

Three conclusions can be drawn from an examination of Orang Asli land rights under the APA. First, legal control over the ultimate occupancy, enjoyment and use of such lands lies with the individual state authority. Orang Asli also have no express participatory rights over decisions affecting their lands. Second, all three interests over Orang Asli land are terminable by the state authority. Third, the state authority possesses the power, except in the case of Orang Asli fruit and rubber trees growing on state land under s.11, to determine if compensation is payable for the loss of Orang Asli lands. Such extensive powers can function to wrest control of Orang Asli lands with little redress available to the affected Orang Asli.

Resource-based legislation

The National Forestry Act 1984 (Act 313) (Malaysia) (NFA) which governs the administration of forests and forestry development in Peninsular Malaysia confers limited privileges upon the Orang Asli depending on the individual state.

Section 40(3) of the NFA provides that the state authority may exempt forest produce[16] removed from alienated land by Orang Asli for any of the purposes specified under Section 62(2)(b). An exemption under s.62(2)(b) negates the requirement for a licence to remove forest produce under the NFA.[17] Subject to any contrary direction by the state authority, s.62(2)(b) provides that the state director of forestry[18] may also reduce, commute or waive any royalty in respect of, or exempt from royalty, any forest produce taken from any state or alienated land by any Orang Asli for temporary huts lawfully occupied by Orang Asli, domestic purposes or 'work for the common benefit' of Orang Asli. However, these 'privileges' require the individual state authority or government agency, as the case may be, to exercise its discretion to act in favour of the Orang Asli concerned.

In spite of the federal government's constitutional power to legislate affirmatively to protect Orang Asli interests, there are no other provisions in other land and resource-based legislation that protect the Orang Asli and their special relationship with their customary lands. Under these laws, the Orang Asli for the most part appear legally 'invisible' in matters affecting their customary lands and resources.

The Orang Asli land problem

Government stewardship over Orang Asli customary lands has done little to alleviate Orang Asli land woes. Under the current statutory reservation scheme, the statutory power to safeguard Orang Asli lands and resources is vested in the government, specifically the federal government, through its Department of Orang Asli Development (JAKOA) and the individual state authority.

Protection of Orang Asli customary land from appropriation in the context of the statutory scheme would translate to a gazette declaration of Orang Asli lands as a reservation. Non-protection of these lands would leave such lands and resources open to alternative utilization. Table 8.1 shows the most recent publicly available statistics on officially acknowledged Orang Asli lands.

'Officially acknowledged' Orang Asli lands do not cover the full extent of Orang Asli customary lands as the status and area of officially acknowledged lands are not necessarily determined in accordance with Orang Asli laws and customs (Williams-Hunt 2011). Instead, these figures are determined by: 1 JAKOA, when it classifies Orang Asli occupied lands or applies for the reservation of Orang Asli lands; and 2 the individual state authority, when it approves and gazettes these lands. These determinations often result in the 'under-gazettal' of Orang Asli lands as reservations. The Malaysian Human Rights Commission (SUHAKAM) estimates that official figures only represent 17 percent of the total lands claimed by Orang Asli (SUHAKAM 2013: 133).

Notwithstanding these qualifications, these figures still demonstrate that the state's performance in gazetting officially acknowledged Orang Asli lands has been dismal.[19] Only 14 percent of officially acknowledged Orang Asli customary lands are gazetted and, even then, they are subject to revocation, variation or, in local parlance, 'de-gazettal' (APA, ss.6(3) and 7(3)).

Lands approved but not gazetted by the state authority account for 21.8 percent of officially acknowledged Orang Asli lands. Following *Koperasi Kijang Mas v. Kerajaan Negeri Perak* (1991), this category of lands should in theory enjoy the full statutory protection of Aboriginal reserves and areas without the need for a gazette notification.[20] However, the enforcement of rights on approved Orang Asli lands that have not been gazetted would have to be done through the courts because these lands are not officially demarcated in the land registry and surveyed maps. The remaining unprotected and untitled lands (57.7 percent) occupied by Orang Asli would fall under the

Table 8.1 Orang Asli land status 2008

Number	*Land status*	*Area (hectares)*
1	Gazetted Orang Asli lands	19,713.65
2	Individually titled Orang Asli lands	1,148.40
3	Approved for gazetting but not gazetted yet	30,849.86
4	Agricultural land	1,270.51
5	Applications for gazettal	81,535.24
6	No formal application for gazettal	6,842.63
	Total	141,360.29

Source: Ministry of Rural and Regional Development, Malaysia 2013.

category of 'Aboriginal inhabited places', which merely confer statutory rights of permissive occupancy over prescribed forms of reserved lands that are, in any event, terminable at the state authority's will (APA, s.10). The invisibility of Orang Asli lands on the land register compounds these problems through the state's maintenance and creation of land interests that overlap with Orang Asli occupied land, including title grants, forest and wildlife reserves, licences and protected areas, which include national and state parks. In such instances, the individual state authority sees itself as having the necessary statutory authority to deal with Orang Asli occupied lands as it deems fit.

In order to gazette Orang Asli lands, individual states have also resorted to the general 'public purpose' land reservation provision contained in s.62 of the National Land Code 1965 (Act No. 56) (NLC). However, these reservations provide less security of tenure than reservations under the APA as they do not possess the limited statutory protection conferred upon Aboriginal reserves and areas gazetted under the APA.

As will be observed in the next section, the judicial recognition of Orang Asli customary land rights has not seen any effective executive and legislative response to the seemingly perennial problem of 'under-gazettal', 'non-gazettal' and 'de-gazettal' of Orang Asli lands. It will also be seen that Orang Asli peoples who resort to the courts to enforce their rights face formidable challenges.

JAKOA (before 2011, the Department of Orang Asli Affairs – JHOEA) often attributes the poor performance in protecting Orang Asli land to the fact that land matters fall under the constitutional jurisdiction of the individual state (JAKOA 2011: 56–7). The statutory power to gazette and de-gazette lands is therefore vested in the individual state authority. As a federal government agency, JAKOA contends that it has no jurisdiction over the individual state when it comes to land matters. While this excuse may be acceptable to a degree, there is equally little doubt that the overall poor performance in protecting Orang Asli lands suggests a lack of priority and concerted will from both federal and state governments to protect Orang Asli customary lands under the statutory scheme.[21]

The reality under the prevailing statutory scheme is that an individual state government can expeditiously generate state and private revenue from large tracts of 'unprotected' Orang Asli occupied lands. This statutory framework legalizes Orang Asli land 'grabs' and, perhaps more importantly, facilitates broader industrial and agricultural expansion and resource exploitation activities, an important aspect of Malaysia's overall strategy towards progress (Subramaniam 2013: 109–11). Current national development strategies for land and resource exploitation do not integrate the legal recognition of Orang Asli customary land rights, suggesting that broader national development still takes precedence over the interests of the weak and minority Orang Asli community (Subramaniam 2013: 112–4). In this sense, both written laws and policies combine effectively to legitimize state appropriation of Orang Asli lands. As highlighted below, federal and state government responses to positive developments concerning indigenous land rights suggest that there is lack of priority for the effective recognition of Orang Asli customary land rights.

Judicial developments

Unlike jurisdictions like Australia where common law developments culminated in the legislative recognition of native title through the passage of the Native Title Act 1993 (Cth), significant judicial developments recognizing Orang Asli customary land rights have not driven any executive and legislative acts towards formal recognition of these rights. These developments include:

1 the recognition of Orang Asli customary land rights at common law;
2 the imposition of a fiduciary duty on the federal and state governments to protect Orang Asli lands and not to act inconsistently with Orang Asli land rights; and
3 the recognition of the constitutional right to life, equality and property of Orang Asli in relation to their customary lands.

The common law

The Malaysian superior courts have recognized the pre-existing rights of Orang Asli to their ancestral and customary lands at common law, in addition to constitutional and statutory law.[22] Under arts. 160(2) and 162 of the Federal Constitution, the common law as applied in Malaysia forms part of 'law' in Malaysia and is therefore legally binding. Despite Sabah and Sarawak having their own separate land regimes which explicitly recognize native customary rights (and are not applicable to Orang Asli), common law principles are also applicable there, making common law cases from Sabah and Sarawak equally relevant in Peninsular Malaysia (Subramaniam 2012: 212–3).

The salient features of the common law doctrine are as follows:

1 the common law recognizes and protects the pre-existing rights of Orang Asli to their lands and resources.[23]
2 The radical title of the state is subject to any pre-existing rights held by the Orang Asli.[24]
3 Common law customary land rights in Malaysia do not owe their existence to any statute or executive declaration.[25] In Peninsular Malaysia, statutory rights under the APA and common law rights of Orang Asli are complementary in that they can exist in tandem.[26]
4 Proof of these rights is by way of continuous occupation,[27] and oral histories of the claimants relating to their customs, traditions and relationship with their lands.[28] 'Occupation' of land does not require physical presence but evidence of continued exercise of control over the land.[29]

5 These rights have their source in traditional laws and customs.[30] The precise nature of these rights is determined by the customs, practices and usages of each individual community where a communal customary title may be held to exist.[31]
6 Customary rights under the common law and any derivative title are inalienable except in accordance with the particular laws and customs of the rights holders.[32]
7 These rights can either be held communally or individually.[33]
8 Extinguishment of these rights may be by way of clear and unambiguous words in legislation or an executive act authorized by such legislation.[34] A reservation or trust of land for a public purpose may not necessarily extinguish these rights unless it is inconsistent with the continued enjoyment of these rights.[35]
9 If these rights are extinguished, adequate compensation is payable in accordance with Article 13 of the Federal Constitution.[36] However, 'foraging areas' and 'settlement areas' have been treated differently in terms of assessing 'adequate compensation'. In *Adong HC* (1997: 436),[37] the court assessed compensation for loss of foraging areas having regard to deprivations of: 1 heritage land; 2 freedom of habitation or movement; 3 produce of the forest; and 4 future living of the individual and his immediate family and descendants but below the market value of the land. In *Sagong HC* (2002: 621),[38] the court awarded 'market value' compensation for the loss of settlement areas.

The legal principles summarized above, from the Malaysian superior courts, have not prompted any legislative or executive acts towards giving legal effect to the recognition of Orang Asli customary land rights. Additionally, Orang Asli face significant challenges in instituting and maintaining common law claims due to a number of factors, including the lack of financial means, an acute shortage of legal aid and assistance, internal conflict, the risk of state and external interference, strenuous opposition from the government, evidentiary challenges, the relative risk and uncertainty inherent in the legalistic, adversarial and the non-participative nature of the court process (Subramaniam 2012: 67–9, 263–88). Compounding matters, the federal and most state governments constantly attempt to roll back the common law recognition of Orang Asli customary land rights, raising concerns that it is only a matter of time before the government succeeds in negating the only legal recourse that Orang Asli possess to enforce their customary land rights.

Fiduciary duty

The Malaysian courts have held that the federal and state governments owe Orang Asli a fiduciary duty by virtue of: 1 constitutional provisions for the protection, well-being and advancement of Orang Asli as per art. 8(5)(c) and item 16 of the Ninth Schedule of the Federal Constitution as well as the APA, which is legislation for the protection, well-being and advancement of the Orang Asli; 2 the establishment of the JHOEA for the welfare of Orang Asli; and 3 a 1961 Orang Asli Policy. Specifically, paragraph (d) of the 1961 policy states that: 1 the special position of Aborigines in respect of land usage and land rights shall be recognized; and 2 Aborigines will not be moved from their traditional areas without their full consent.[39] It is clear that the relatively vulnerable position of the Orang Asli under the Federal Constitution has had a strong influence in the determination that Orang Asli are owed a fiduciary duty by the state, particularly in respect of their customary lands.

The content of the fiduciary duty consists of the duty to protect Orang Asli welfare including their land rights and not to act in a manner inconsistent with these rights, and further to provide remedies where such infringement occurs.[40] The Federal Court has affirmed the fiduciary duty owed by the state to Orang Asli and natives of Sabah and Sarawak.[41] The Malaysian courts have also held that the federal and/or state governments breached their fiduciary duty by:

1 depriving Orang Asli of their lands without paying adequate compensation;[42]
2 not providing adequate notice before evicting Orang Asli from their lands;[43]
3 failing or neglecting to gazette Orang Asli inhabited land;[44] and
4 delaying the gazettal of Orang Asli inhabited land.[45]

In response, the federal government maintains that their fiduciary duty, if it exists at all, is limited to the welfare of the Orang Asli and does not in its opinion extend to land matters, arguing that these matters come solely under the purview of the individual state. On the other hand, the states contend that any duties owed to the Orang Asli are the responsibility of the federal government. This seemingly convenient compartmentalization and abdication of state obligations and narrow interpretation of the constitutional provisions relating to the overall 'welfare' and 'well-being' of the Orang Asli is inconsistent with decisions of the Malaysian superior courts. Further, such compartmentalization fails to consider the constitutional powers of the federal government: 1 to acquire state land for federal purposes (Federal Constitution, Art. 83); and 2 to decide matters relating to land via the National Land Council (Arts. 91, 92).[46]

Fundamental liberties

In addition to holding that Orang Asli customary land rights are rights to property protected under Article 13 of the Federal Constitution, the Malaysian courts have also interpreted the constitutional rights to equality (Art. 8) and life (Art. 5) liberally in favour of Orang Asli and native customary lands.

The Malaysian courts have described the Orang Asli as enjoying 'a special position' under Article 8(5)(c).[47] In holding that federal and state governments owe a fiduciary duty to the Orang Asli claimants, the court of first instance in *Sagong HC* held that Article 8(5)(c) is an exception to the equality provision in Article 8.[48] On appeal, the Court of Appeal held that the lower court's liberal interpretation of the Land Acquisition Act 1960 to award compensation for loss of customary land based on market value[49] was merely to give 'full effect to art. 8(5)(c) of the Federal Constitution which sanctions positive discrimination in favour of the Aborigines'.[50]

Article 5(1) of the Federal Constitution provides that '[n]o person shall be deprived of his life or personal liberty save in accordance with the law'. In *Ketua Pengarah Jabatan Alam Sekitar v. Kajing bin Tubek* (1997: 43), the Court of Appeal held that deprivation of the *Penan* (natives of Sarawak) community's livelihood and way of life amounted to a deprivation of life itself. In Sabah and Sarawak, the High Court has held that native customary rights equate to the right to life under Article 5(1), as they could 'be considered as a right to livelihood'.[51] In respect of the Orang Asli, the Court of Appeal has held that the dispossession from their land deprived Orang Asli of their livelihood and therefore, life itself.[52] Citing this decision with approval, the Federal Court has subsequently observed in respect of the rights of natives under Article 5(1) that '[the] issue of compensation for loss of livelihood is now well established'.[53]

UNDRIP and the SUHAKAM Report

Malaysia voted in favour of the 2007 UNDRIP both at the Human Rights Council and General Assembly levels. UNDRIP contains extensive provisions for the recognition of land, territories and resources,[54] and calls for, amongst other matters, the recognition of the following rights:

1 ownership, management and use of lands, territories and resources (Art. 26) with due respect to indigenous customs, traditions and land tenure systems (Art. 27);
2 free, prior and informed consent (Arts. 10, 28, 29 and 32) and effective consultation (Arts. 18, 27, 30(2) and 38) in respect of matters affecting indigenous lands, territories and resources;
3 the development of indigenous political, economic, social and cultural institutions (Arts. 5, 14(1), 18 and 23); and
4 self-determination, meaning, the indigenous right to pursue and determine their own economic, social and cultural development including the development of their lands on their own terms (Arts. 3, 23 and 32).

While the legal enforceability of UNDRIP in Malaysia is debatable, there is little doubt that it creates, at the very least, a moral obligation on Malaysia to take appropriate measures to work towards achieving the aspirations of

UNDRIP in the 'spirit of partnership and mutual respect'.[55] Yet there has been very little thus far in terms of law and policy reform that incorporate the UNDRIP standards.

In August 2013, SUHAKAM released a report on its 18-month National Inquiry into the Land Rights of Indigenous Peoples (the SUHAKAM Report). The report contains 18 recommendations for the recognition and protection of indigenous (including Orang Asli) land rights as well as policy and administrative reform. In response, the federal government formed a task force whose terms of reference include an assessment of the findings and recommendations of the SUHAKAM Report with a view to implement its recommendations (Pragalath 2013). An evaluation of the challenges faced by the federal and state governments in doing so are discussed in the next section.

Recent policy responses

To address the Orang Asli land problem, the federal government is currently in the process of negotiating the reservation of land it deems sufficient for Orang Asli with a view to possibly converting the status of such lands to individual title ownership in the future. These lands will mainly be used for residential and cultivation purposes. As part of this exercise, the National Land Council earlier passed the Orang Asli land titles policy (the Proposed Policy). Under the Proposed Policy, every Orang Asli head of household is to be granted between two and six acres of plantation lands and up to half an acre for housing depending on land availability as determined by the individual state (JAKOA 2011: 57–8).

According to JAKOA, the granting of individual titles under privatized cash crop development schemes would increase economic activity and income (JAKOA 2011: 57–8),[56] and as such, facilitate the entry of Orang Asli into the mainstream market economy. However, these titles appear to come at the ultimate price of Orang Asli customary lands. The Proposed Policy prohibits Orang Asli who receive benefits under the policy from making any further legal claims in relation to their customary land rights (POASM and Gabungan NGO 2010: enc. 1). Additionally, the Proposed Policy would only apply to about 50,000 hectares (ha), close to the aggregate area of gazetted Orang Asli lands and approved but un-gazetted Orang Asli lands (SUHAKAM 2013: 138). An estimated 85,987.34 ha (JAKOA 2011: 55–6) or about 64.68 percent of officially acknowledged Orang Asli land, excluding additional land claimed by Orang Asli to be their customary lands, therefore stands to be lost. State-appointed external contractors for land development and limitations in the use of Orang Asli land for residential plots and plantations, diminishes Orang Asli control over their customary lands. Despite opposition from Orang Asli,[57] a few states have already started to implement their own refined versions of the Proposed Policy without effective engagement with the Orang Asli (SUHAKAM 2013: 138).

As for the national task force established to examine the SUHAKAM Report, it is likely that any genuine attempt by the federal government to wrest the extensive statutory power of the state over lands and to negotiate competing interests over Orang Asli land equitably, which form part of the SUHAKAM Report recommendations,[58] would encounter resistance from the state governments and other affected stakeholders. As suggested earlier, state land and resource priorities do not appear to lie with the Orang Asli, their culture and attendant customary lands. State inertia towards effectively recognizing Orang Asli customary lands is further exacerbated by a complex web of factors involving:

1 historical and cultural prejudices against the politically and numerically inferior Orang Asli;
2 hierarchical, differentiated and contested definitions of indigeneity in Malaysia; and
3 Malaysia's push for economic progress, which is linked to ethnic Malay-centric affirmative action (see Subramaniam 2013).

Conclusion

While the federal and state governments may not view the appropriation of Orang Asli lands as a 'land grab', it is equally evident that the legal stranglehold that the state possesses over Orang Asli land for their 'protection' and the non-recognition of Orang Asli customary land by the federal and state authorities legitimize and facilitate the taking of Orang Asli lands with relative impunity. Although land reforms that empower Orang Asli over the remainder of their customary lands and enable the gradual transition of state-Orang Asli relations from that of protectionism to partners with mutual respect may be desirable, the possibility of such reforms appears improbable when pitted against the national development agenda, resource use priorities and the weak demographic, political and socio-economic position of the Orang Asli. At this juncture, it would seem that the best the Orang Asli can hope for in terms of the recognition of their customary lands may be a negotiated legal, political, economic and pragmatic compromise, which may short change them yet again.

Notes

1 This chapter is current as at January 2014.

2 Article 160(2) of the Federal Constitution merely defines an 'Aborigine' to mean an 'aborigine of the Malay Peninsula'. Instead, s. 3 of Aboriginal People Act 1954 Act 136 (Malaysia) (APA) provides for the definition of an Orang Asli. It defines an 'aborigine' to mean: 1 any person whose male parent is or was a member of an Aboriginal ethnic group, who speaks an Aboriginal language and habitually follows an Aboriginal way of life and Aboriginal customs and beliefs, and includes a

descendent through males of such persons; 2 any person of any race adopted when an infant by aborigines who has been brought up as an aborigine, habitually follows an Aboriginal way of life and Aboriginal customs and beliefs and is a member of an Aboriginal community; or 3 the child of any union between an Aboriginal female and a male of another race, provided that the child habitually speaks an Aboriginal language, habitually follows an Aboriginal way of life and Aboriginal customs and beliefs and remains a member of an Aboriginal community.

3 A 'Malay' means a person who professes the religion of Islam, habitually speaks the Malay language, conforms to Malay custom and; 1 was before Merdeka Day (31 August 1957) born in Malaya or Singapore, or is on that day domiciled in the Federation or in Singapore; or 2 is the issue of that person (see Art. 160(2) Federal Constitution).

4 Article 161A(6)(b) of the Federal Constitution provides that a 'native' in relation to Sabah is a person who is a citizen, is the child or grandchild of a person of a race indigenous to Sabah, and was born (whether on or after Malaysia Day (16 September 1963) or not) either in Sabah or to a father domiciled in Sabah at the time of birth. For a discussion of land grabs issues in Sabah, see Chapter 9 of this volume.

5 Article 161A(6)(a) of the Federal Constitution provides that a 'native' in relation to Sarawak is a person who is a citizen, is the grandchild of a person of the *Bukitan*, *Bisayah*, *Dusun*, Sea *Dayak*, Land *Dayak*, *Kadayan*, *Kalabit*, *Kayan*, *Kenyah* (including *Subup* and *Sipeng*), *Kajang* (including *Sekapan*, *Kejaman*, *Lahanan*, *Punan*, *Tanjong* and *Kanowit*), *Lugat*, *Lisum*, *Malay*, *Melano*, *Murut*, *Penan*, *Sian*, *Tagal*, *Tabun* and *Ubit* race, or is of mixed blood deriving exclusively from these races.

6 The King of Malaysia, who is appointed on a rotational basis every five years from among the nine hereditary Malay rulers (Federal Constitution: arts. 33–8, Third and Fifth Schedules).

7 This article was introduced when Sabah, Sarawak, the Federation of Malaya and Singapore formed Malaysia in 1963.

8 Article 74(1) of the Federal Constitution empowers the federal government to legislate on matters enumerated in the federal list (Ninth Schedule List I) and concurrent list (Ninth Schedule List III).

9 In this context, the fiduciary duty owed by the state to Orang Asli discussed below may not be a *constitutional* fiduciary duty but a *common law* fiduciary duty supported by constitutional and legislative provisions and other sources.

10 There are constitutional rights for the resolution of such disputes by the Syariah courts (Federal Constitution, art. 121(1A)) in respect of Malays and native courts (Art. 72(20) and Ninth sch., List IIA, Item 13) in respect of natives of Sabah and Sarawak.

11 For a definition of 'Malay' under art. 160(2) of the Federal Constitution, see *supra* note 2.

12 However, see *Kerajaan Negeri Selangor v. Sagong bin Tasi* (*Sagong CA*) (2005): 312–4, where the Court of Appeal held that the federal and state governments were under a duty to gazette the Temuan Orang Asli claimants' lands, by virtue of their common law fiduciary duty owed to the claimants in that case.

13 The concept of a tenancy at will at common law has been applied by the Malaysian courts (see e.g. *Tan Khien Toong v. Hoong Bee & Co.* (1987) 1 M.L.J. 387: 391; *Cheah Leong Keah v. Mydin bin Tamby Bappoo* (1932) 1 M.L.J. 98: 99).

14 *Sagong CA*, 2005: 309–10.

15 'State land' means all land in the individual state (including so much of the bed of any river, and of the foreshore and bed of the sea, as is within the territories of the state or the limits of the territorial waters), other than: 1 alienated land; 2 reserved

land; 3 mining land; or 4 any land that under the provisions of any law relating to forests (whether passed before or after the commencement of the act) is for the time being reserved forest. National Land Code (Act No. 56 of 1965) (Malaysia): s.5.

16 'Forest produce' is defined in s.2 of the NFA to include: '(a) the following when found in or brought from a permanent reserved forest: guano, peat, rock, sea-sand, sea-shells and the surface soil; (b) the following when found in or brought from a permanent reserved forest or State land: (i) trees and parts or produce not hereinafter mentioned of trees; (ii) plants including climbers, creepers and grasses, and all parts or produce of such plants; (iii) silk, cocoons, honey and wax and edible birds' nests; (c) the following whether found in or brought from a permanent reserved forest, State land, mining land, reserved land or alienated land: timber, fuel wood, charcoal, *getah* [rubber], *getah taban* leaves, wood oil, bark, extracts of bark, *damar* and *atap.*'

17 Section 40 provides for the requirement of a licence for the removal of forest products.

18 This act applies throughout Peninsular Malaysia through its adoption by the individual states. Despite the uniformity of the act throughout Peninsular Malaysia, forestry matters nevertheless fall under the state legislative list (Federal Constitution, Ninth Schedule List II – State List, Item 3).

19 For historical figures on the status of Orang Asli lands, see Nicholas 2000: 32–40.

20 *Koperasi Kijang Mas v. Kerajaan Negeri Perak* (1991) 1 CLJ 486, see page 487 of the judgment.

21 For example, the federal–state power divide was not an impediment to the passing of the proposed Orang Asli land titles policy by the National Land Council in 2009 (see below).

22 *Adong bin Kuwau v. Kerajaan Negeri Johor* (Adong HC), 1997; *Kerajaan Negeri Johor v. Adong bin Kuwau* (Adong CA), 1998; *Sagong bin Tasi v. Kerajaan Negeri Selangor* (Sagong HC), 2002; *Sagong CA*, 2005).

23 *Adong HC*, 1997: 430; *Adong CA*, 1998 2: 162–3; *Superintendent of Lands v. Madeli bin Salleh*, 2008: 692 (Federal Court).

24 *Sagong CA*, 2005: 301–2; *Madeli*, 2008: 692.

25 *Sagong HC*, 2002: 612; *Superintendent of Land & Surveys, Bintulu v. Nor Anak Nyawai* (Nor Nyawai), 2006: 270.

26 *Adong HC*, 1997: 431; affirmed, *Adong CA*, 1998: 163.

27 *Nor Nyawai*, 2006: 269.

28 *Sagong HC*, 2002: 610, 621–4.

29 *Madeli*, 2008: 694–5.

30 *Madeli bin Salleh (Suing as Administrator of the Estate of the Deceased, Salleh bin Kilong v. Superintendent of Land & Surveys Miri Division*, 2005: 330.

31 *Sagong CA*, 2005: 301–2.

32 *Adong HC*, 1997: 430; *Adong CA*, 1998: 162.

33 *Sagong HC*, 2002 2: 613–4; *Madeli*, 2008: 693.

34 *Sagong HC*, 2002: 612; *Madeli*, 2008: 690, 696–7.

35 *Madeli*, 2008: 697–8.

36 *Adong CA*, 1998: 163–4; *Sagong HC*, 2002: 617; affirmed, *Sagong CA*, 2005: 309–10; *Madeli*, 2008: 691–2.

37 Affirmed, *Adong CA*, 1998: 163.

38 Affirmed, *Sagong CA*, 2005: 309–11.

39 *Sagong HC*, 2002: 619–20; *Sagong CA*, 2005: 311–4.

40 *Sagong CA*, 2005: 311–2.

41 *Bato Bagi v. Kerajaan Negeri Sarawak* (Bato Bagi), 2011: 326.

42 *Sagong CA*, 2005: 313–14, 319.

43 *Sagong HC*, 2002: 620.

44 *Sagong CA*, 2005: 314.

45 *Pengarah Tanah dan Galian Johor v. Khalip bin Bachik*, 2013: 812–3.
46 For further elaboration, see Subramaniam 2012: 145–9.
47 *Sagong HC*, 2002: 617.
48 *Sagong HC*, 2002: 619–20.
49 *Sagong CA*, 2005: 308–11.
50 *Sagong CA*, 2005: 311.
51 In relation to Sarawak, see e.g. *Nor Nyawai HC*, 2001: 266–7. In respect of Sabah, see e.g. *Andawan bin Ansapi v. PP* (unreported, David Wong Dak Wah J, Kota Kinabalu High Court File K41-128 of 2010, 4 March 2011): 7.
52 *Adong CA*, 1998: 164.
53 *Bato Bagi*, 2011: 305–6.
54 For commentary on UNDRIP, see e.g. Charters and Stavenhagen 2009; Allen and Xanthaki 2011.
55 UNDRIP, preamble para. 24, art. 38. In respect of UNDRIP and its enforceability in Malaysia, see Subramaniam 2012: 76.
56 The land would be cleared and cultivated by a third-party contractor. Orang Asli who are granted the titles would have to repay all costs associated with the issuance of such titles once the plantations become productive.
57 Orang Asli have resisted the introduction of these policies due to the potential further loss of customary lands and communal arrangements, lack of free, prior and informed consent and engagement, and selective consultation (for further discussion, see e.g. Subramaniam 2012: 61–3, 70–1, 188–9).
58 The SUHAKAM Report recommendations include, amongst other things, addressing indigenous land security of tenure, clarification of the concept of customary tenure, restitution for non-recognition of indigenous lands, the review of compensation, the recognition of indigenous lands in protected areas and active involvement of indigenous peoples in forest management (SUHAKAM 2013: 165–71).

References

Aboriginal People Act (1954) Act 136, Malaysia.

Allen, S. and Xanthaki, A., eds (2011) *Reflections on the UN Declaration on the Rights of Indigenous Peoples*, Oxford and Portland, OR: Hart Publishing.

Andaya, L.Y. (2002) 'Orang Asli and the Melayu in the History of the Malay Peninsula', *Journal of the Malaysian Branch of the Royal Asiatic Society* 75(1): 23.

Carey, I. (1976) *Orang Asli: The Aboriginal Tribes of Peninsular Malaysia*, Kuala Lumpur: Oxford University Press.

Charters, C. and Stavenhagen, R., eds (2009) *Making the Declaration Work: The United Nations Declaration on the Rights of Indigenous Peoples*, Copenhagen: IWGIA.

Economic Planning Unit, Prime Minister's Department (2006) *Ninth Malaysia Plan 2006–2010*, Putrajaya: Prime Minister's Department, Malaysia.

Economic Planning Unit, Prime Minister's Department (2010) *Tenth Malaysia Plan 2011–2015*, Putrajaya: Prime Minister's Department, Malaysia.

JAKOA (Department of Orang Asli Development) (2011) *Department of Orang Asli Development Strategic Plan 2011–2015* (Pelan Strategik Jabatan Kemajuan Orang Asli 2011–2015), Kuala Lumpur: Planning and Research Section, Department of Orang Asli Development.

Legislative Council, Federation of Malaya (1954) *Report of the Select Committee Appointed to Consider Aboriginal People's Bill, 1953, No. 2*, Kuala Lumpur: Government Printers.

Ministry of Rural and Regional Development, Malaysia (2013) 'Orang Asli Land Status Data, 2008' (Data Status Tanah Orang Asli, 2008), www.rurallink.gov.my/web/guest/hal-ehwal-orang-asli (accessed 18 August 2014).

National Forestry Act (1984) Act 313, Malaysia.

National Land Code (1965) Act No. 56, Malaysia.

Nicholas, C. (2000) *The Orang Asli and the Contest for Resources: Indigenous Politics, Development and Identity in Peninsular Malaysia*, Copenhagen: IWGIA Center for Orang Asli Concerns.

Omar, M. (2008) 'An Evaluation of the Social Impact of Orang Asli RPS' (Penilaian Impak Sosial Rancangan Pengumpulan Semula (RPS) Orang Asli), paper presented at National Conference 'Orang Asli After 50 Years of Independence of Malaysia: Contribution and Achievement of the Orang Asli in National Development', Muzium Seni Malaysia, University of Malaya.

POASM and Gabungan NGO (NGO Orang Asli Semenanjung Malaysia – Peninsular Malaysia Orang Asli NGO Network) (2010) 'Protest Memorandum Against Orang Asli Land Title Grant Policy approved by National Land Council in a Meeting Chaired by the Right Honourable Deputy Prime Minister of Malaysia on 4 December 2009' (Memorandum Bantahan Dasar Pemberimilikan Tanah Orang Asli yang diluluskan oleh Majlis Tanah Negara yang Dipengerusikan oleh YAB Timbalan Perdana Menteri Malaysia pada 4hb Disember 2009).

Pragalath, K. (2013) 'Task Force Will Not Mar SUHAKAM Report', *Free Malaysia Today*, www.freemalaysiatoday.com/category/nation/2013/08/28/task-force-denies-undermining-suhakam-report (accessed 18 August 2014).

Subramaniam, Y. (2011) 'Rights Denied: Orang Asli and Rights to Participate in Decision-Making in Peninsular Malaysia', *Waikato Law Review* 19(2): 44.

Subramaniam, Y. (2012) *Orang Asli Land Rights by UNDRIP Standards in Peninsular Malaysia: An Evaluation and Possible Reform*, PhD thesis, University of New South Wales.

Subramaniam, Y. (2013) 'Affirmative Action and the Legal Recognition of Customary Land Rights in Peninsular Malaysia: The Orang Asli Experience', *Australian Indigenous Law Review* 17(1): 103.

SUHAKAM (Human Rights Commission of Malaysia) (2013) *Report of the National Inquiry into the Land Rights of Indigenous Peoples*, Kuala Lumpur: SUHAKAM.

United Nations (2007) *Declaration on the Rights of Indigenous Peoples*, General Assembly resolution 61/295, UN GAOR, 61st sess., Agenda Item 68, UN Doc A/RES/61/295.

Wildlife Conservation Act (2010) Act 716, Malaysia.

Williams-Hunt, A. (1995) 'Land Conflicts: Orang Asli Ancestral Laws and State Policies', in R. Rashid (ed.) *Indigenous Minorities of Peninsular Malaysia: Selected Issues and Ethnographies*, Kuala Lumpur: Intersocietal and Scientific (INAS).

Williams-Hunt, B.T. (2011) 'FPIC and Orang Asli Lands in Peninsular Malaysia', paper presented at a Conference on Customary Lands, Territories and Resources: Bridging the Implementation Gap, Kuala Lumpur.

List of cases

Adong bin Kuwau v. Kerajaan Negeri Johor (1997) 1 MLJ 418 (High Court).
Bato Bagi v. Kerajaan Negeri Sarawak (2011) 6 MLJ 297.
Sagong bin Tasi v. Kerajaan Negeri Selangor (2002) 2 MLJ 591 (High Court).
Kerajaan Negeri Johor v. Adong bin Kuwau (1998) 2 MLJ 158 (Court of Appeal).
Kerajaan Negeri Selangor v. Sagong bin Tasi (2005) 6 MLJ 289 (Court of Appeal).
Ketua Pengarah Jabatan Alam Sekitar v. Kajing bin Tubek (1997) 3 MLJ 23.
Koperasi Kijang Mas v. Kerajaan Negeri Perak (1991) 1 CLJ 486.
Madeli bin Salleh (Suing as Administrator of the Estate of the Deceased, Salleh bin Kilong v. Superintendent of Land & Surveys Miri Division (2005) 5 MLJ 305 (High Court).
Pengarah Tanah dan Galian Johor v. Khalip bin Bachik (2013) 1 MLJ 799.
Superintendent of Lands v. Madeli bin Salleh (2008) 2 MLJ 677 (Federal Court).
Superintendent of Land & Surveys, Bintulu v. Nor Anak Nyawai (2006) 1 MLJ 256.

9 Land grabs in Sabah, Malaysia

Customary rights as legal entitlement for indigenous peoples – real or illusory?

Mariam N. Munang

> Indigenous peoples shall not be forcibly removed from their lands or territories. No relocation shall take place without the free, prior and informed consent of the indigenous peoples concerned and after agreement on just and fair compensation and, where possible, with the option of return.
>
> (Article 10, UN Declaration on the Rights of Indigenous Peoples)

Introduction

Indigenous peoples have a special connection with their ancestral lands. Their lands are their source of livelihood: traditionally their sites for hunting and gathering, today their lands are key to their economic participation primarily as farmers and cultivators. The UN Declaration on the Rights of Indigenous Peoples (UNDRIP) expresses the importance and significance between indigenous peoples and their ancestral lands. Amongst others, Article 10 of UNDRIP states that indigenous peoples cannot be forcibly removed from their lands.

In the state of Sabah, Malaysia, land grabbing affects almost exclusively the indigenous community. Sabah is situated in the north of the Malaysian part of the island of Borneo. It is the second largest state in the country with a population of 3.21 million.[1] An indigenous person of Sabah refers to a native of Sabah who is 'the child or grandchild of a person indigenous to the State, and was born (whether on or after Malaysia Day[2] or not), either in the State or to a father domiciled in the State at the time of birth'. The law does not define who an 'indigenous' person is, although the Kadazandusun Cultural Association (KDCA), the foremost association in Sabah promoting the cultural heritage of the indigenous peoples of Sabah, recognizes at least 40 indigenous communities, the largest of which are the Kadazandusun, Bajau and Murut (KDCA Constitution, Section 6). The Kadazandusun community alone makes up 24.5 percent of the total population of Malaysians in Sabah.

This chapter examines the traditional land ownership system practised by the indigenous peoples of Sabah and explores how gaps in the Sabah land laws open opportunities for land grabs to occur. First, native customary rights and customary tenure under the Land Ordinance (Sabah Cap. 68) ('the Land Ordinance') will be studied. It will be shown that the Land Ordinance recognizes customary tenure as legal entitlement to land and also that it provides mechanisms and procedures by which native customary tenure, being primarily unregistered tenure, may be strengthened. Case law that expands and refines the scope of customary tenure will also be assessed. The chapter then proceeds to study how the Land Ordinance, which also recognizes other more modern systems of land ownership, has gaps that allow land grabbing from indigenous peoples to occur. Further, it will also be shown how shortcomings in the application of the law make native customary rights as expressed under the Land Ordinance and case law insecure and illusory for many indigenous peoples.

History

Presently land ownership based on customary tenure and the Torrens system exist in parallel. To understand how this situation arose, it is necessary to have some understanding of the history of Sabah.

The indigenous peoples of Sabah have long practised native customary land rights which are governed by native customary law. In other words, their land tenure system is practised in accordance with their traditions and customs. There are three main features of the native customary land system. First, native customary law ownership rights may be acquired by clearing virgin jungle, planting land with fruit trees or using land as burial ground. As such, proof of ownership is displayed by markers on the ground rather than written documents. Second, the practice of shifting cultivation was widespread, which made it difficult for the authorities to identify uncultivated land. Land farmed on a long fallow system may appear uncultivated, although in fact it would remain the land of its farmer. Third, land was often held communally, meaning that the concept of private property and ownership was largely absent (Cleary 1992: 171). The Torrens land system was introduced into Sabah more recently in history by the British North Borneo Chartered Company. In 1881, the British North Borneo Chartered Company received Royal Assent to administer and develop North Borneo, as Sabah was then known. From 1882 to 1946, after which North Borneo was absorbed as a British colony, the North Borneo Chartered Company ruled North Borneo (Cleary 1992). In order to commoditize land, the Torrens land system of registered land ownership was introduced, with a land registration office maintaining a central land register. A registered title grants its holder indefeasible interest in the land (Jafry 2001: 2).

At the same time, the native customary land system was not abolished but was instead allowed to continue to be practised. This was due to the fact that the North Borneo Company was bound by its own charter, which under Article 9, stated:

> In the administration of justice by the Company to the people of Borneo ... careful regard shall always be had to the custom and laws of the class or tribe or native to which the parties respectively belong, *especially with respect to the holding, possession, transfers and disposition of lands.*
>
> (Cleary 1992: 171, emphasis added)

The balance struck by the North Borneo Company in giving careful regard to the holding, possession, transfers and disposition of lands by the indigenous peoples and commoditization of land was first to determine land that belonged to the indigenous peoples. Remaining lands were considered as 'government waste land' which could be alienated (Cleary 1992: 173).

The Land Ordinance was enacted by the North Borneo Company to give recognition to both native customary lands and registered land. Since Sabah gained independence in 1963, the Land Ordinance has not changed very much and so the present legal framework inherits this dichotomy between native customary lands and the Torrens system.

Native customary rights under the Sabah Land Ordinance

The Land Ordinance regulates the alienation and occupation of state land in Sabah. Under the Land Ordinance, native customary rights are expressly acknowledged. Section 15 of the Land Ordinance defines native customary rights as including land possessed by customary tenure, land planted with 50 or more fruit trees per hectare, isolated trees or plants kept and enjoyed as personal property, grazing land stocked with cattle or horses, cultivated land, burial grounds and shrines, and usual rights of way.

Although the various aspects of native customary rights as enumerated under Section 15 are to be read disjunctively, in practice, 'land possessed by customary tenure' is the most important grounds to prove the acquisition of native customary rights. Native customary rights were traditionally acquired by clearing virgin jungle; in other words, occupation of land by an indigenous group would only be lawful, in accordance with native custom, if they were the first people to settle on that land. Those settlers would then, amongst others, plant fruit trees, clear and cultivate the land to assert their rights as owners. It is these ownership rights acquired by virtue of being first settlers, that are codified as 'customary tenure'. Therefore, customary tenure is the most important aspect of native customary rights because actions under paragraphs (b) to (g) could not take place without the land being possessed by customary tenure in the first place.

Customary tenure is defined under Section 65 of the Land Ordinance as 'the lawful possession of land by natives either by continuous occupation or cultivation for three or more consecutive years'. Pursuant to Section 66, it confers upon the holder a 'permanent heritable and transferable right of use and occupancy in his land'. The importance of native customary tenure in terms of securing indigenous land ownership is clear when Section 88 of the Land Ordinance is considered:

> No new title and no dealing with, claim to or interest in any land *except land still held under native customary tenure without documentary title* shall be valid until it has been registered in accordance with the provisions of this Part [V: Registration].
>
> (emphasis added)

Therefore, once customary tenure is established, the Land Ordinance recognizes it as a legal claim even without documentary title. In place of documents, customary tenure is indicated by way of markers on the ground as provided for under paragraphs (b) to (g) under Section 15 of the Land Ordinance.

Scope of native customary rights

Native customary rights are recognized in common law

The Malaysian courts have considered native customary rights favourably, further strengthening indigenous peoples' ownership of their lands based on customary tenure. The landmark High Court case of Adong Bin Kuwau & Ors v. Kerajaan Negeri Johor & Anor was the first occasion on which the court positively recognized native customary rights under common law.[3] In this case an indigenous community brought a suit against the state which had alienated lands they claimed to have customary rights over to a state corporation. The state argued that the indigenous community was no longer staying in the area and thus the state was not prevented from entering the land. The court held that the plaintiffs had proprietary rights over the area based on customary rights. This decision was subsequently affirmed by the Court of Appeal in *Kerajaan Negeri Johor & Anor v. Adong bin Kuwau & Ors*. In recognizing native customary rights, the High Court at page 429 relied on the authority of *Mabo & Ors v. State of Queensland & Anor*, in which it was held that:

> common law recognizes a form of native title which, except where it has been extinguished, reflects the entitlement of the indigenous inhabitants in accordance with their laws or custom to their traditional land which is preserved as native title. Native title has its origins in and is given its content by the traditional laws acknowledged by, and the traditional customs observed by, the indigenous inhabitants of the territory. The nature of native title must be ascertained by reference to the traditional laws and customs of the indigenous inhabitants of the land.

In the subsequent case of Nor Anak Nyawai & Ors v. Borneo Pulp Plantation Sdn Bhd & Ors,[4] the High Court considered *Adong Kuwau* and its reference to *Mabo*, and held it as authority for the position that native customary rights as recognized by common law are not based on specific written laws that recognize them, and that native customary laws exist prior to colonial arrival and they continue to exist even though there is a change in sovereignty.

Native title can only be extinguished by clear and unambiguous provisions to that effect.[5] In *Nor Anak Nyawai*, the High Court recognized that the survival of the Iban tribe depended very much on their use of their ancestral lands. Thus, abolishing native customary rights would be tantamount to violating the right to livelihood of an indigenous group, which is protected under Article 5(1) of the Federal Constitution, which states that 'no person shall be deprived of his life or personal liberty save in accordance with law'.[6] Similarly in *Amit Salleh & Ors v. The Superintendent, Land & Survey Department Bintulu & Ors*, the High Court recognized that land ownership was crucial to the existence of indigenous peoples as a separate entity. It stated that native customary rights:

> entitled the natives to use and cultivate their land in such a manner that they may bring them income and along with it the betterment of their life. The economic use of the land to sustain their livelihood is synonymous with their existence as an entity. To take away these rights would mean depriving the natives of the main source of their survival. Their dependence on the land is something that no one can deny.[7]

Therefore, because of the dependency link between land ownership and survival of indigenous groups, the courts adopt a restrictive interpretation of any laws that might appear to extinguish native title. The extinguishment of native title is seen as a drastic measure and can only be expressed in clear language and cannot be derived by mere implication.[8]

In Sabah, the High Court in Rambilin Bin Awah v. Ruddy Bin Ambit recognized that native 'customs and laws' existed even before 1881 and the start of British North Borneo Company administration. Far from extinguishing native customary rights to land, these customs and laws serve to affirm their existence.[9] In *Rambilin*, the High Court examined various laws during the period of company administration and held that none of them had the effect of extinguishing native customary rights. This was because there was never 'clear language to that effect and nor [was] there a plain and clear intention to do so as required for the extinguishment of such customs and law'.[10] Even the Native Rights to Land Proclamation of 1889, which established that land was property of the state, did not preclude the coexistence of native customary land rights on state land.[11]

One piece of legislation that did expressly provide for the extinguishment of native customary rights to land was the 1913 Land Rules. Sections 66 to 71 provided for a settlement exercise to be completed for the whole of the state, during which all indigenous peoples claiming native customary rights over land must register their claims. Unclaimed land or land whose application was rejected would 'become absolutely the property of Government' (Land Rules 1913, Section 70). However, because such a settlement exercise was never in fact conducted, native customary rights in Sabah persist.[12]

Full rights of ownership

The High Court in Adong Kuwau reasoned that native customary rights grant the right to indigenous people to live on their land in perpetuity. This right has been acquired by virtue of their continuous and unbroken occupation and enjoyment of the rights of the land from time immemorial and thus their future generations would also be holders of this right.[13]

Native customary land rights include the right to move freely about their land, without disturbance or interference, and also to live from the produce of the land itself. Their right, however, does not extend to rights over the land itself in the modern sense, which would enable them to convey, lease or rent the land or any produce therein.[14] More specifically, the scope of native customary land rights varies depending on the use of land by the indigenous group. Often, indigenous peoples use vast areas of their traditional and ancestral land on which they do not stay, but depend to forage for their livelihood. The different land uses give rise to different rights: the right to own land, the right to settle on the land and the right to use natural resources found on the land.[15]

Within the settlement area, native customary land rights grant indigenous peoples full rights of ownership, rather than only the limited rights of settlement. This was decided by the High Court in the case of Sagong Bin Tasi & Ors v. Kerajaan Negeri Selangor & Ors. In this case, the state contended that the rights enjoyed by the Orang Asli community to occupy the disputed area were, in the first place, given by the state, and second, given only for the purpose of residence and settlement. Therefore, because the state did not grant full ownership to the community, the state could re-acquire the land for public purposes.[16] The High Court rejected such a restrictive view of the scope of native customary land rights. It held that within the settlement area the Orang Asli community had acquired the full range of rights as owners by custom and native title. The restriction of full rights of ownership to only the settlement area and not further, however, was seen as 'logical' in the appeal decision of *Nor Anak Nyawai*, in which the Court of Appeal stated that 'such a view is logical as otherwise it may mean that vast areas of land could be under native customary rights simply through assertions by some natives that they and their ancestors had roamed or foraged the areas in search for food'.[17]

Creation of native customary rights on state land does not require permission from the state

Section 6(1) of the Land Ordinance states that 'no unlawful occupation of State land or land reserved for a public [...] or residential purpose or occupation under temporary licence for however long a period shall establish any right, title or interest in [the land]'. It was argued by the state in the High Court case of *Rambilin*, that the occupation of state land by an indigenous person without prior approval from the state is unlawful within the meaning of Section 6 of the Land Ordinance, and thus the person is not entitled to claim native customary land rights. The High Court disagreed. It explicitly stated that indigenous peoples do not need to seek permission from the state to enter into any land, since nowhere in the Land Ordinance does it explicitly require permission for entry. The court found the absence of a provision to that effect as significant. It insisted that 'if it was intended that [...] native customary rights could only come into existence [...] if there was prior permission to enter the land, then it failed miserably as the law requires that the words used or the intention be plain and unambiguous'.[18]

Furthermore, the court pointed out that the very nature of indigenous custom excludes any such authorization. It observed that 'if the entry must in the first place be with the permission of the state, then no native can claim any native right since their custom, like, for example, shifting cultivation and taking forest produce, were practised without having to ask anyone for permission first'.[19]

The jurisprudence discussed has been to a large extent favourable to native customary rights. It gives substance to native customary rights as they are recognized in law. The courts have elaborated on the scope and limits of native customary rights and affirmed the right to compensation for the loss of ancestral land. Most importantly, the courts have recognized the important relationship that indigenous peoples have with their lands. By acknowledging that indigenous peoples depend on their lands for survival, the court advocates a broad interpretation of native customary rights and insists that native customary rights can only be extinguished in very specific circumstances.

Registration of customary tenure: application for native title

Whilst unregistered customary tenure is valid legal title under the Land Ordinance, the Land Ordinance also provides a mechanism by which customary tenure may be registered and native title issued. Unlike the other categories of titles provided by the Land Ordinance – namely, town land, country land and provisional lease (Land Ordinance, Section 49), which are granted for a term not exceeding 99 years (Sections 48 and 57) – native titles are held in perpetuity.

Registration of land held on customary tenure is done pursuant to Section 67(2):

> any native who holds his land under customary tenure without documentary title may be required by order of the Collector in writing to take out title by entry in the Native Title Register and to pay the prescribed fees for such title.

The term 'may' grants a discretionary power to the collector to require registration. However, the Land Ordinance does not specify the grounds upon which registration will be required. Nevertheless, Section 16 of the Land Ordinance implies that in all cases where native customary rights have been established under Section 15 of the Land Ordinance, the collector must either grant native title to the claimant or issue compensation. Section 16 reads:

> Native customary rights established under Section 15 shall be dealt with either by money compensation or by a grant of the land to the claimant and in the latter case a title shall be issued under Part IV [native lands].

Registration of land held on customary tenure can also be initiated independently of a request by the collector. Under Section 70(1) of the Land Ordinance, an indigenous person can make an application for native title to the collector. In both cases of land registration pursuant to Section 16 and Section 70(1) of the Land Ordinance, the applicant for native title may appeal the decision of the collector, as provided by Section 41(1).

The grant of native title accords the holder certain obligations. The size of native title land may not exceed 20 hectares (Land Ordinance, Section 70[3]) and may only be used for agricultural purposes (Section 70(2)), unless permission of the relevant authorities has been obtained. Upon the approval of the native title application, cultivation must be commenced within six months and the whole must be brought into cultivation within three years. If this requirement is not complied with, the uncultivated portions of the land may revert to the state (Section 70(4)). Furthermore, lands held on native title cannot be sold to non-indigenous persons. Sections 17(1) and 64(1) of the Land Ordinance prohibit all native title dealings between indigenous and non-indigenous persons, unless such transaction is sanctioned by the state. Requesting an exemption from this prohibition of native title sale to non-indigenous persons will require the indigenous native title holder to surrender that title in exchange for a different lease, either country land or town land (Section 17(2)).

Land grabbing

It has been demonstrated above that native customary land is given legal recognition by the courts which, having interpreted the law in favour of strengthening indigenous peoples' entitlements to their native lands, have shown themselves sympathetic to native customary land claims. However, land grabbing continues to affect and displace indigenous groups. This section will explore the procedures under the Land Ordinance and the gaps therein that make it possible for land grabbing to occur in spite of the law as set out above.

The typical land grab scenario in Sabah is this: a community in possession and occupation of their ancestral lands based on unregistered customary tenure one day discover that their lands have been entered into, usually by commercial enterprises, which, they then discover, have been issued with registered title as proof of their ownership of the very lands the indigenous people have occupied for generations.

The practical implications of this are far-reaching. The burden then shifts to the native community to prove its prior interest in the land, which necessitates judicial action. Judicial action is necessarily costly and lengthy – a cost not many communities are in a position to bear. On the ground, they may be forcibly removed from the land and their crops cleared. Many, if not most, indigenous communities rely entirely on working the lands for their livelihood and thus losing their lands would affect their very survival.

At the root of this problem is the fact that unregistered customary tenure, whilst recognized as a valid title to land, is in practice inherently insecure, especially in the land alienation process. There is simply no way to determine whether there are prior interests on the land unless a site visit is carried out to seek any markers on the ground indicating customary tenure. As will be shown below, the law falls short in not requiring such a comprehensive assessment to be done.

Land alienation procedure

Under Section 12 of the Land Ordinance, an application can be made to the director or the collector of land revenue for alienation of state land. Upon the receipt of any application for unalienated land, the collector publishes a notice, as required by Section 13 of the Land Ordinance, calling for submission of claims of native customary rights in such land. By calling for such claims, the law in effect gives priority to native customary claims over a subsequent alienation request. These claims must be made within a time period specified in the notice. If there is no such claim, the director will make a decision whether or not to alienate the land to the applicant on town land, country land or provisional lease terms, under Section 9 of the Land Ordinance.[20] The decision of the director under Section 9 is final and may not be appealed (Land Ordinance, Section 41).

The Section 13 notice is therefore an important safeguard to ensure that indigenous peoples owning lands based on customary tenure are given the opportunity to establish their claim before the collector proceeds with treating such lands as unalienable. It enables any indigenous persons who are already owners of that land based on unregistered customary tenure to make their interest in the land known to the collector.

In practice, the Section 13 notice is a notice posted in the Land Office (SUHAKAM 2013: Chapter 6.26). As soon as the notice is posted, the state takes the position that it has fulfilled its obligation under Section 13, and the burden then falls on any affected indigenous person to submit a claim. However, the indigenous person cannot be reasonably expected to be able to carry out this duty. Many indigenous land owners live on their land, itself often in remote areas so far removed from the Land Office that under no ordinary circumstance would they be able to come to know about the existence of the notice, or be able to state their claim to the land within the stipulated time.

The resulting situation is one where the collector, having not received any claims for customary tenure, assumes that the land is not occupied, and then proceeds to alienate the land to the applicant and issue title. Thereafter, the indigenous community that has been in occupation of their ancestral lands for generations suddenly discover, usually through face-to-face confrontation, that their lands now have new owners who can prove their ownership through registered title and written documents. The burden then falls on the indigenous group to challenge the alienation and prove their prior interest in the land.

The Land Ordinance does not otherwise prescribe the manner in which the Section 13 notice must be issued or the contents therein brought to the attention of any interested persons. By way of comparison, it is useful to look at the Land Acquisition Ordinance (Sabah Cap. 69), which has a provision that similarly requires the collector to issue a notice of intended acquisition. Under the Land Acquisition Ordinance, copies of the declaration announcing the acquisition must be posted on one of the buildings on the land, or exhibited at suitable places in the locality in which the land is situated, and where possible served on the owner of the land (Land Acquisition Ordinance, sections 3(2) and 7(3)). For obvious reasons it is more effective for a notice of land application to be posted *in situ*, rather than in the Land Office. This way, the affected indigenous community are more likely to become aware of a pending land application and so are able to take the necessary steps to come forward to make their prior interests known.

Application for native title

The possibility of applying for native title undoubtedly improves the security of land occupied under customary tenure. Although the Land Ordinance does provide a mechanism to apply for native title, in practice the application process is more difficult than it appears.

Upon an application for native title under Section 70(1) of the Land Ordinance, the collector still has the discretion, under Section 16, upon being satisfied of possession based on customary tenure, either to issue a native title or to reject the application and grant money compensation instead. The Land Ordinance does not specify the grounds upon which the collector may reject an application for native title when customary tenure has been established. The resulting situation facing an individual already enjoying the benefit of unregistered customary tenure is that he risks losing legal entitlement altogether should he be awarded compensation instead of being issued with native title. As a result, there is little incentive to seek to register unregistered possession. They continue to rely on possession based on unregistered customary tenure, and so are at risk of losing their lands when their lands are assumed to be unalienated in the land alienation procedure.

An application for land title will require action initially at the district level whose responsibility at this stage is mainly to communicate with other government departments, such as the Forestry Department, Agriculture Department and the Town Council. Then the application is forwarded to the headquarters of the Land and Survey Department, at which stage a decision whether or not to grant the application will be made, and if the application is approved, then the terms of registration will be determined. The application then reverts to the district office to carry out surveying work on the ground and prepare the title (Land and Survey Department, Sabah 2008).

Although the Land and Survey Department in its client charter has stated that it will strive to process land title applications within 24 months, often these applications take much longer, in some cases as long as almost 40 years. Apart from the considerable delays, there have also been reports of missing applications and even fraud (SUHAKAM 2013: Chapter 6). To make matters worse, it is very difficult to track the progress of a particular application. Therefore, if an applicant would like to determine the status of their application, there is simply no system that could readily provide that information. The procedure is unclear and opaque. It is also vulnerable to corrupt practices because there is no system for monitoring and providing accountability.

Conclusion

The right to property is protected under Article 13 of the Federal Constitution. It states that 'no person shall be deprived of property save in accordance with law', and that adequate compensation must be granted in compulsory acquisition exercises. In the case of land grabbing from indigenous communities, in spite of the formal recognition of their land title and rights to compensation, in practice they are left with little in the way of remedies and usually little or no compensation.

The irony of the land grab situation in Sabah is that although in law native customary tenure is a legal right and even has priority over any subsequent interest in the land, in practice, as we have seen, this right is insecure or illusory. This insecurity arises primarily from an evidential perspective: in the face of a registered title, the party claiming customary tenure bears the burden to prove that they had prior interest. Doing so is difficult, as customary tenure is evidenced by markers on the ground.

It has also been explained that there are problems with the administration of the land alienation procedure and native title application process. The Human Rights Commission of Malaysia (SUHAKAM) has documented various complaints and allegations of abuse, delays and irregularities (SUHAKAM 2013). Some of the problems reported to the commission indicate missing applications and, even more seriously, allegations of fraud.

The larger factor contributing to land grabs in Sabah is perhaps the problems with the administration of the land alienation and native title application processes. In this context the law could play a much larger role. It must extend further to guarantee transparency and accountability in the various procedures, to ensure that native customary rights as guaranteed under the law become real.

Notes

1 Population distribution by state, Department of Statistics, Malaysia, 2010.
2 16 September 1963, the day Sabah and Sarawak formally joined the Federation of Malaya to form Malaysia.
3 *Adong* and the following native customary land cases are discussed in greater depth in Chapter 8 of this volume.
4 The Court of Appeal in *Superintendent of Lands & Surveys, Bintulu v. Nor Anak Nyawai & Ors and another appeal* (2006) 1 MLJ 256, subsequently reversed the learned trial judge's finding of fact but endorsed the other expositions of the law by the learned judge in relation to native customary rights; see para. 30.
5 *Nor Anak Nyawai*, 2001: para. 83.
6 *Nor Anak Nyawai*, 2001: para. 78.
7 *Amit Salleh*, 2005: 13.
8 *Madeli Salleh*, 2007: 353.
9 *Rambilin*: 7, line 23.
10 Ibid.: 8, line 18.
11 Ibid.: 13, line 1.
12 *Rambilin*: 20, line 7.
13 *Adong*, 1997: 7.
14 Ibid.
15 *Sagong bin Tasi*, 2002: para. 47.
16 Ibid.: para. 21.
17 *Nor Anak Nyawai*, 2001: para. 30.
18 *Rambilin*: 24, line 1.
19 Ibid.: 21, line 22.
20 For a complete description of the land alienation procedure, see: *Sa-Mal (Sabah) Corp Sdn Bhd v. Director of Lands and Surveys, Sabah* (1994) MLJU 398, at p.236, paras. b–f.

References

Cleary, M.C. (1992) 'Plantation Agriculture and the Formulation of Native Land Rights in British North Borneo', *The Geographic Journal*: 158.

Jafry, M. (2001) 'Requirements of Law and Procedure Regarding Native Customary Land' (Kehendak Perundangan dan Prosedur Melibatkan Tanah Anak Negeri), Sabah Native Land Conference titled Land Utilisation as Catalyst for the Indigenous Business Community, Institute for Indigenous Economic Progress (Sabah), Kota Kinabalu.

Land and Survey Department, Sabah (2008) *Land Application Procedure*, Kota Kinabalu.

SUHAKAM (Human Rights Commission of Malaysia) (2013) *Report of the National Inquiry into the Land Rights of Indigenous Peoples*, Kuala Lumpur.

Legislation

Land Acquisition Ordinance (Sabah Cap. 69).
Land Ordinance (Sabah Cap. 68).
Land Rules 1913, North Borneo.
Native Rights to Land Proclamation of 1889 (North Borneo).

Cases

Adong Bin Kuwau & Ors v. Kerajaan Negeri Johor & Anor [1997] 1 MLJ 418 (High Court).

Amit Salleh & Ors v. The Superintendent, Land & Survey Department Bintulu & Ors [2005] 8 CLJ 1.

Kerajaan Negeri Johor & Anor v. Adong bin Kuwau & Ors [1998] 2 MLJ 158 (Court of Appeal).

Mabo & Ors v. State of Queensland & Anor (1986) 64 ALR 1 (High Court of Australia).

Nor Anak Nyawai & Ors v. Borneo Pulp Plantation Sdn Bhd & Ors [2001] 6 MLJ 241.

Rambilin Bin Awah v. Ruddy Bin Ambit (unreported, file number K22-71-2000).

Superintendent of Lands & Surveys, Bintulu v. Nor Anak Nyawai & Ors and another appeal [2006] 1 MLJ 256.

Superintendent of Land & Surveys Miri Division & Anor v. Madeli Salleh [2007] 6 CLJ 509.

Sagong Bin Tasi & Ors v. Kerajaan Negeri Selangor & Ors [2002] 2 MLJ 591.

Sa-Mal (Sabah) Corp Sdn Bhd v. Director of Lands and Surveys, Sabah [1994] MLJU 398.

10 Perspectives on land grabs in Vietnam

Toan Le

The rapid development of Vietnam's economy has been attributed to neo-liberal economic reform and industrialization policies that Vietnamese leaders introduced in the bleak days of near economic collapse nearly 30 years ago (Le 1993: 97–106). At the same time as delivering increased wealth to the Vietnamese people, however, economic reforms have produced land conflicts that are increasingly difficult to resolve (Gillespie 2011: 241; Kim 2011: 493). One of the most contentious explanations advanced for the cause of land conflicts in recent years is the belief that state officials are involved, have colluded in or acquiesced to land grabs (Hiebert 2012). Consistent with the themes explored in this book, this chapter analyses the how and why of land grabs in Vietnam. In particular, it focuses on the role of law in facilitating land grabs. In addition, the chapter examines the extent to which state officials are able to take advantage of socialist laws to act with an element of illegality, or at least specious legality, in cases involving the state's land acquisition powers. This is the case even though land recovery or land acquisitions are usually conducted in the name of the state's economic development and for the public good.

A key argument of the chapter is that the introduction of the socialist land system – which removed private land ownership rights and conferred the powers to manage land on the state – is a major cause of land grabs and land conflicts. Further, state laws that allow the appropriation of land for economic development purposes have enabled state officials at various levels to engage in dubious conduct to seek personal gain and placed the goal of economic development and the interests of investors above those of traditional land users. The lack of recognition of land users' rights and protections for land users, coupled with the government's total control of land, has created conditions ripe for unscrupulous investors and officials to take advantage.

The rest of the chapter is structured as follows. The next section provides a critical analysis of how and why socialist laws facilitate and legitimize land grabs in Vietnam. It begins with a discussion of development of the notion of land ownership and control in Vietnam. This discussion is relevant to show how socialist changes of land ownership laws challenged the accepted ideas about land ownership. The discussion then focuses on the changes under socialist rule to the land ownership system in Vietnam, and case studies will be used to show how those changes are incompatible with the accepted understanding of land ownership in the general populace, and how the changes facilitated land grabs and fuelled land conflicts. The following section then provides a summary of the analysis and concluding remarks. The chapter concludes that rising tensions between the state and the people require a solution be found to ensure that the people's right to transfer land – a right specifically provided for under Vietnamese land law – is not negated when the people's land is acquired by the state and allocated to investors for economic development projects.

Analysis of land grabs in Vietnam

The purpose of this section is to analyse critically the phenomenon of land grabs in socialist Vietnam and, in particular, the role of the law in facilitating land grabs and resulting in an increase in land disputes between state and non-state actors (World Bank 2011: 2). The key arguments presented here are that socialist land reform challenged the accepted understanding of private land ownership, and the land disputes that arose from land grabs in the socialist period from 1945–2014 are a consequence of incompatible thinking between the state and the general population on private land rights. Further, it is argued that the different modes of thinking on land rights and land ownership are influenced by historical events that shaped long-standing beliefs and practices.

Before examining how the socialist laws facilitated land grabs and how socialist land regulation challenged the accepted understanding of private land rights, it is useful to consider briefly the historical origin of the different regulatory approaches to land in Vietnam and how those regulatory approaches shaped the Vietnamese people's attachment to private land ownership.

The imperial and French governments' regulation of land rights

The regulation of land rights in Vietnam can be divided into three distinct periods: imperial, French and socialist. In respect to land rights regulation in the imperial and French-dominated periods, the discussion makes two main points. First, the development of land policies in imperial times shows that over time the imperial governments accepted the idea of private land ownership. Second, the idea of private land ownership not only survived in the French times, but private ownership rights were legislated and French titles were introduced to protect the land ownership rights of land users.

Recognition of exclusive property rights and private land ownership in imperial times

From 905 to 1884, Vietnam was ruled by feudal dynasties. In these times, the principal interests of the emperors were the expansion of territory and the collection of taxes to fund the administration (Bassford 1984: 16). Consequently, vacant land was worthless to both the emperor and his people. Thus while all land in theory belonged to the emperor, in practice it was the basic policy of the emperor to provide land to occupiers who converted the land to economic production and paid the required taxes to their village (Dao 1993: 86). This system of land regulation led to a conception developed in the Vietnamese village that equates land ownership to the occupation of land and payment of tax.

The idea of private land ownership is built upon under French rule (1884–1945)

With the signing of the protectorate treaty on 6 June 1884, the French gained legal authority to rule and took Tonkin as a protectorate (Nguyen 1985: 147–48). It had occupied Cochin China and ruled it as a colony 20 years earlier. The French administrators vowed to transform Vietnam into a country 'worthy of a great colony' and the reform of land tenure rights was a part of the administration's grand design (Gillespie 1998: 563). Recognizing the undesirability of foisting French laws upon the Vietnamese population, the ideas of land grants to individuals from the times of the emperors survived French rule. The French also introduced French titles and modernized the land registration system. The French administrators' interpretation of the theory that all land belonged to the emperor was, however, 'mistaken' or simplistic (Thompson 1937: 183). Consequently, its land policies were unpopular as it had the effect of assisting French colonials and wealthy Vietnamese landlords to appropriate a large amount of agricultural land (Dao 1993: 84–90). Further, the French land system was unpopular as it imposed exorbitant taxes on poor peasants, effectively forcing those peasants to sell their lands cheaply (Nguyen 1987: 113). The Viet Minh movement, led by the charismatic Ho Chi Minh, cleverly linked the 'unjust' appropriation of land that occurred under French rule with the political cause to regain independence for Vietnam.

In summary, the discussion shows that the ideas of private land ownership were developed at the village level, accepted by the emperors, and then built upon by the French rulers in this period. In particular, the idea of land grants to individuals from the time of the emperors survived French rule. French titles were introduced in this period and the idea of private land ownership in the general populace not only survived, but thrived throughout the French rule.

How socialist land regulation challenged the accepted notion of private ownership and facilitated land grabs

The regulation of land under socialist rule can be divided into three distinct periods. First, from 1945 to 1985, regarded as the high socialist period, the revolutionary government briefly provided land to the tiller before it embarked on the collectivization of land and vested land ownership in the state. Second, from 1986 to 2002, regarded as the economic renovation period, the socialist government searched for a solution to merge socialist ideology to the demands and pressures from non-state actors for private land rights. Third, from 2003 to the present, the government continued to respond to land disputes involving the state powers to appropriate land for economic development projects by officially expanding the bases upon which the government could recover land. In analysing the development of land laws in the three distinct periods, case studies will be used to show how the socialist laws facilitate land grabs.

From 'land returned to the tiller' to the abolition of private land ownership in the high socialist period (1945–85)

Socialist rule in Vietnam officially began in 1954 in North Vietnam with the signing of the Geneva Agreement. From 1945, however, Ho Chi Minh had formed a revolutionary government in North Vietnam. In the period of its rule from 1945 to 1954, the land policy in North Vietnam focused on two points. First, the government sought to provide relief in taxation to the landholding peasants. Second, land reform was implemented to transfer the ownership of land from the rich landholding class, mainly made up of Vietnamese capitalists and rich peasants, to the poor peasants (Le and Nguyen 2014: 282). In this period, the government cleverly linked its quest for a 'people's democratic revolution' (*cách mạng dân chủ dân tộc nhân dân*) with the promise of land returning to the tiller. The political slogan '*người nông dân được ruộng*' promises the return of land ownership to the peasant classes. The words '*được ruộng*' in the Vietnamese language mean 'to have ownership of farmland' (Nguyen 1987: 230).

After the 'land to the tiller' reform programme was implemented, the government launched a second revolution to nationalize land in state ownership and imposed a collective farming system. The land collectives were first imposed in North Vietnam from 1955 without informed consultation, and then rolled out in South Vietnam from 1975 after the end of the Vietnam War (Ngo 1993: 166). Under collective farming, peasants' rights of ownership to their land are transferred to farm cooperatives.

The nationalization of land triggered the beginning of a long-standing contest between the state and the Vietnamese people on the place of private land ownership within the socialist land system. Although few land disputes were reported in the period of nationalizing land ownership, the viewpoints of peasants on land collectivization and the peasants' preference for private land ownership were expressed in subtle forms. Cartoons that appeared in leading newspapers, for example, cleverly used drawings of managers of farming cooperatives living in two-storey houses next to cottages occupied by peasants to depict the 'unjust enrichment' of managers under the policy of collectivization. Some peasants reacted by neglecting their work in collective land and other peasants showed their opposition more strongly by abandoning the land completely and switching to trade (Huu 1958: 2).

In response to the opposition of peasants, Kim Ngọc, a provincial leader in Vĩnh Phúc Hanoi, entered into a secret agreement to give the peasants a fixed production quota (Dang 2008: 175). The insistence by peasants that they work on land that they own and control illustrates their desire for the return of pre-socialist land regulatory approaches that recognize a role for the private ownership of farmland. The desire of the peasants is captured in two common Vietnamese sayings. The first saying, that 'no one cares for land with a common father' (*cha chung không ai khóc*), captured both the reasons why farmers were not motivated to work in collective farming and their desire for private land ownership. The second saying, 'what my father owns, I own' (*tôi là chủ của tài sản ông bà để lại*), illustrates that the idea of private land ownership by inheritance is strongly developed in the mind-set of the Vietnamese people.

The national government policy response shows that the general population's viewpoints on land ownership were not acted on. In 1980 the government formally abolished private land ownership and vested land effectively in the state. Article 20 of the 1980 Constitution states, however, that 'land is owned by the entire people' (*sở hữu toàn dân*), to reassure the people of their entitlement to the 'ownership' of land.

In this period, reports of state officials abusing the 'people land ownership' system for private and family gain surfaced with such regularity that it prompted some policy adjustments. From 1981 to 1986, the national leaders formally allowed the private contracting of output to households, providing the first move towards compromise. The national leaders, however, refused to recognize private land ownership on the grounds that this right is incompatible with the idea of public land ownership in socialist ideology. This conflict in viewpoints between the state and the people remained sharp and led many peasants to not invest in agriculture. As a report of the Department of Agriculture Land states:

> Transfer and inheritance rights have not been legally guaranteed the accumulation of land and capital necessary for production has met with difficulties. Many better off peasants' households are still wary of investing in agriculture because of lack of legal protection.
>
> (Ngo 1993: 186)

In summary, socialist land reforms challenged the accepted notion of private ownership. The state's abolition of private ownership highlighted the role of law in facilitating land grabs. The responses of the peasants show they held opposing viewpoints on land ownership to the state. The contest in viewpoint shows no sign of resolution.

State land ownership in a market economy: how the state's commitment to the socialist ideology of 'the people's land ownership' facilitated land grabs (1986–2002)

State leaders had an opportunity to reconsider the role of private land ownership at the sixth National Party Congress, held in 1986. At this congress, the political veteran Trường Chinh, who presided as the interim general secretary of the Communist Party of Vietnam (CPV), urged his fellow comrades to accept the sensitive concept of the market and market mechanism (Van Arkadie and Mallon 2003: 66). Vietnamese leaders resolved to cautiously accept the market, but took no steps to accept private land ownership.

In 1987, the first land law was enacted to regulate land in the market economy transformation period. The preface to this Land Law provided a first insight into the degree to which the state would intervene in the market economy and how private land rights would be developed. It stated: 'this law provides the framework to manage the usage of land … to serve and protect socialist Vietnam.' Article 1 then reaffirms that the state has total management powers over land, including its allocation. The 1987 law recognizes the right of households and individuals to use land, but it states that the right has no market value and cannot be transferred. In respect of the state's authority to appropriate land, Article 15 provides that 'the state organization that allocated land has the power to appropriate the land'. People whose land is appropriated by the state are allocated alternative land on a needs basis.

Shortly after the enactment of the 1987 Land Law, tense protests in South Vietnam's delta river region exploded from 1988 (Le and Nguyen 2014: 284) as some farmers demanded the return of their land. Further, there were allegations that the socialist laws in relation to land ownership provided the opportunity for state officials to engage in corrupt behaviour in respect to the allocation of 'land belonging to the entire people'. In Instruction no. 47-CT/TW, which outlined the response of the state to the land protests, the new CPV General Secretary Nguyễn văn Linh admitted that some farmers regarded land that their families previously explored and exploited economically, as their own. However, Linh quashed any hope that private land ownership would be returned to the farmers (FBIS 1988).

In summary, Vietnamese leaders remain wedded to the idea of 'the people's ownership of land'. The 1987 Land Law, despite granting land use rights to households, prohibited its transfer and declared it to have no market value. The 1988 land protests involved issues that related to actions concerning the illegitimate taking of land which socialist laws are alleged to facilitate. The government response showed that it ruled out the return of land ownership to the peasants, ensuring that land conflicts continue to dominate the relationship between the state and the general population.

In 1991, Linh as the CPV general secretary specifically ruled out for a second time the recognition of private land ownership reform in the Political Report he delivered to the Congress (Huy 2012). Concurrently, however, the government was under pressure to allow land use rights to be transferable in order to attract foreign investors (Kokko 2004: 86).

In 1993, the government enacted a new land law. Its most remarkable feature is provisions that establish a land market, enabling Vietnam's market economy to function more effectively. The law granted land users the right to exchange, transfer, inherit, lease and mortgage land. Further, the government recognized that land has a price, and this price is used to calculate compensation for land appropriated by the state. In the government paper presented to Vietnam's National Assembly (NA), the former deputy prime minister of Vietnam, Nguyễn Công Tạn, stated 'our people continue to say "a centimeter of land is a centimeter of gold"' (Government of Vietnam 1993: 455). The minister's statement indicates that the government was attempting to merge socialist ideology with market practices. However, while the new law provided land users with marketable land rights, it also included provisions that effectively neutered the land rights allocated. First, although land was accorded a price following the reform, the price was to be set by the local government and was set very low (World Bank 2011: 76).

Second, under Article 20 of the 1993 Land Law, agricultural land is to be allocated to land users for only 20 years. This meant that land use rights that were allocated in 1993 would expire in 2013. Several delegates in the NA raised concerns about the impact that this provision would have on the investments in farmland and farm equipment made by peasants (Huy 2012). Perhaps anticipating the likely unpopularity of a 20-year limit, Article 20 also provides that '[a]t the expiry of the duration, if the land user wishes to continue using the land, the State shall satisfy that wish, provided that the land user has strictly obeyed the legislation relating to land during the period of occupancy'.

Third, Article 27 provides that 'in necessary circumstances the government may appropriate land to be used for the purposes of defence, security, national interest and public interest', without defining those terms. It is to be noted that the purposes for which the 1993 law allows the government to recover land do not specifically include economic development projects. Indeed, in an interview, a senior law drafter of the 1993 Land Law explained that in relation to land required for economic development projects, the drafters had envisaged that investors would negotiate directly with the land users (Dang, personal interview, 2013). In other words, the legal drafters did not intend that the takings of land for economic development projects would be encompassed within 'national or public interest' purposes.

The political discourse shows that the motivating force behind granting transferable land rights in the 1993 Land Law was to attract foreign and domestic investors. In respect of this objective, the new law was a success, as Vietnam's Bureau of Statistics shows investment into Vietnam surged following the enactment of the 1993 Land Law (World Bank 2011: 14).

The perspectives of investors, as a lawyer interviewed indicated, was to access land and to maximize profit in the most cost-effective manner

(Nguyen, personal interview, 2013). The 1993 Land Law facilitated this access. In practice, there were two options open to investors: direct negotiation with the land user, or use lawyers and state officials as conduits to conduct the negotiations. Most Vietnamese investors in interviews conducted by this author expressed a preference to work through officials. The reason investors prefer to work with local officials is captured in one lawyer's explanation: 'local officials have local knowledge about each of the families' (Nguyen, personal interview, 2013). In their dealings with state officials, many domestic and foreign investors will comply with the formal and informal procedures of the people's committee as well as pay the necessary 'under the table' expenses (Ho, personal interview, 2013).

The peasant land users have a different perspective in respect to the 1993 Land Law. Poor peasants, peasants unaware of future town planning in their district or province, and peasants who are not able to fight for a prolonged period (Kim 2011: 496) were most vulnerable to underselling. As time passed, Vietnamese peasants became agitated at the 'injustice' of underselling and were suspicious of the relationship between local officials and investors (Brown 2012a, 2012b). A minority of peasants, however, refuses to sell land inherited from their forebears, or burial lands. The latter phenomenon suggests that the conflict relating to the different thinking on land ownership cannot be resolved by a socialist land system that offers marketable land use rights.

In 1997, widespread peasant dissatisfaction manifested itself in one of the most controversial protests in Thái Bình province in North Vietnam. This case shows how laws create the conditions for a minority of unscrupulous state officials to take advantage of the law for personal gain. The Thái Bình land protest, despite full media censorship at the time, has become one of the most talked-about land disputes by internet bloggers in the last few years. In addition to systemic official corruption, the Thái Bình villagers protested the lack of *công bằng* (popular fairness or justice) in the distribution and protection of tenure rights connected with rural land (Le and Nguyen 2014: 286). The magnitude of dissatisfaction was great as the protests drew an estimated 3,000 villagers from May to November 1997, who fought pitch battles with security police in the streets of Thái Bình (Human Rights Watch 1997). As a senior state official, sent to investigate the cause of the civil disruption, recalled in his report to his superiors, the protestors were merely venting their anger over legitimate corruption claims and did not aim to overthrow the local government (Lai 2012). Events following the Thái Bình land protests indicated that the government had not moved sufficiently to accommodate the peasants' views on state land ownership. In 1998 and 2001, the law was amended to allow investors to build infrastructure in exchange for land allocated by the state (Land Law 1998, 2001).

In summary, the 1993 Land Law in practice facilitated land grabs in two ways. First, while it provided land use rights, the combination of the state ownership regime, the restrictions imposed on tenure length and the expansion of state powers to acquire land increased the vulnerability of peasants to underselling their land to investors. Second, the 1993 Land Law and the amendments in 1998 and 2001 set up the state as a referee of the law and a player in the land acquisition process. The controversy of state officials aligning with investors to undertake land grabs continues to reverberate in Vietnamese society.

The 2003 Land Law and subsequent developments impact on land grabs

The 2003 Land Law aimed to create a land law to accelerate Vietnam's road to industrialization. The new law grappled with conflicting needs, on the one hand to extend investor rights in land transactions, and on the other the need to respond to peasants' demands for fair land compensation and resettlement following the loss of their land. The new law, however, officially expanded the bases upon which the government could recover land to include economic development projects. This development thereby legalized what officials had already been doing in practice. Article 40, for example, specified that land could be requisitioned by the state for 'economic development in cases of investment for the construction of industrial zones, high-tech zones, economic zones and large-scale investment projects as stipulated by the government'. A remarkable feature of the 2003 Land Law is that it provided for a new 'land conversion' mechanism. The new law provided for both compulsory and voluntary land conversion processes under which land could be recovered. In reality, most land recovered for economic development occurred through the compulsory conversion process as investors seek to avoid the situations where land users refuse to transfer land to investors or required an extremely high price for the land (World Bank 2011: 20).

Following the enactment of the 2003 Land Law, investment by the non-state economic sector and foreign investors surged to new records (World Bank 2011: 14). Concurrently, and perhaps not unsurprisingly, the number of petitions sent to the Ministry of Natural Resources and Environment on land disputes rose significantly (World Bank 2011: 17). The political sensitivity of the petitions and the increase in land disputes prompted a series of government responses. In 2007, for example, Decree 123 brought compensation rates into 'alignment with market prices'. In 2009, Decree 69 provided further guidance on improving the value of compensation, support and location for resettlement for people affected by land recovery by the state. These responses, however, did not prevent land disputes from arising. The government's move only helped to tidy up and provide redress after peasants were unfairly deprived of land access or had undersold their land. The response did not address the underlying issue of the government's power to set the price at which investors could acquire land.

Far from resolving the issues underlying land disputes, the incidence of disputes and degree of hostility shown by affected peasants intensified in subsequent years (Marr 2012). In 2012 and 2013, a number of high-profile land disputes erupted in North and South Vietnam, generating wide support for the protesters from the Vietnamese public. The following discussions provide an analysis of three case studies that illustrate how and why land grabs occurred in Vietnam, and the degree to which state officials intervened in the land conversion process to the disadvantage of peasant land users. There are also some insights into the influence that foreign investors exert on the intervention of state officials. The case studies show that socialist laws systemically result in outcomes that disadvantage the interests of land users.

The Ecopark land dispute

This case study shows how socialist laws facilitate land grabs. First, it illustrates the strong alignment in interests between the national and local governments with foreign and domestic investors in undertaking economic development, and that infrastructure building projects result in the appropriation of land from peasants without adequate consultation and compensation (BBC 2012). Second, it shows that government involvement in land grabs is occurring at various levels. This development indicates that socialist laws systemically result in outcomes of land grabs.

The Ecopark land dispute relates to a major urban economic development project in the city of Văn Giang-Hưng Yên, located 9 kilometres east of Hanoi (Reuters 2012). The Ecopark development project is an US$8 million commercial urbanization and tourism project tendered to the domestic partner Viet Hung Urban Development and Investment Joint Stock Co. The development covered 173 hectares (ha) of land and affected more than 4,000 households (Reuters 2012).

The critical periods leading to the dispute correlate with a number of key state government decisions that expedited the approval process. First, in March 2003, the Office of the Prime Minister approved the project as a significant economic and infrastructure development project. Less than three months later, on 28 June 2003, the Ministry of Natural Resources and Environment (MONRE) sent to the Office of the Prime Minister the paperwork requiring an order to acquire land compulsorily and allocate that land to the investors. The date of approval was 30 June 2003, just one day before the 2003 Land Law providing more rights to protect land users came into force. By 2009, as reported by the People's Committee of Hưng Yên website, the local government had allocated to investors 57.19 ha of land. Of that land, 49.87 ha was earmarked for urban development and 7.32 ha was for the development of connecting roads (Hoai 2012).

On 23 April 2012, violent clashes erupted as the Hưng Yên People's Committee proceeded to evict forcibly 166 families who owned 5.8 ha and who had rejected the offered compensation. These families and their supporters reportedly remonstrated with 2,000 police officers (Reuters 2012). On its website, the Hưng Yên People's Committee emphasizes that the evictions and the demolition of houses in Xuân Quan district to make way for the Ecopark were all in accordance with the policies of the national government (Pham 2012). The committee also claims that it had protected the safety of the people, and that it had the overwhelming support of cadres, Party members and the people of Văn Giang in general and in Xuân Quan district specifically (Pham 2012).

The land users, protestors and Vietnamese media, however, told the other side of the story. The first reason causing anger amongst the affected land users, many of whom are peasants, relates to the inadequate amount of compensation offered. The land affected by this project lies only 9 kilometres from the periphery of Hanoi. However, the compensation offered to the land users was based on the classifications used for rural land. According to a media report, houses in the Ecopark development area are selling in the range of $1,000–2,000 per square metre, while land users were offered compensation of $6 per square metre (Tam 2012). As one land user, Phạm Hoành Sơn, explained, the land acquisition process has produced an unjust outcome for him and other peasants as the amount of compensation offered was inadequate to establish a new life and living arrangements. He said: 'Nearly every peasant like ourselves had to borrow from the bank, from our siblings, from our village and cooperatives. We have not recouped any profit from farming at the time of the confiscation of our land, so how can we survive?' (Hoang and Le 2012).

A second reason causing the peasants' anger was that the local government did not adequately consult with the peasants on the confiscation of their land. On this issue, in a state-owned newspaper land user Phạm Hoành Sơn recalled: 'At the beginning, we were not provided any information. We went together into the district to ask the chairman and were advised he was also unaware of how our land was affected. It was only later that we knew we had lost our land' (Hoang and Le 2012).

The third reason for the peasants' anger was that the government order to acquire the land compulsorily was hastily approved and did not followed proper procedures. The lawyer Trần Vũ Hải has argued under the Party's resolution 91/2002/NĐ-CP, that MONRE is required to present the compulsory acquisition documents to the government and not to the Office of the Prime Minister as MONRE had done (Tran 2012). In a publicly recorded meeting held at MONRE with the people of Văn Giang-Hưng Yên and the legal team of lawyer Trần Vũ Hải, Professor Đặng Hùng Võ, who was a MONRE vice-minister when the order was sent for the prime minister's signature, took responsibility for the procedural errors (RFA 2012a). Professor Võ points out that as this was an infrastructure development project of national significance, the government had accelerated its completion. Võ's explanations have provided some clarification of the matter.

In summary, the Ecopark land dispute shows that land conflicts arise when officials at various levels place the desire for economic development and the interests of investors ahead of the interests of peasant land users. Furthermore, the wide powers of state officials at various levels to intervene in the land acquisition process and to set low compensation amounts leave Vietnamese land users vulnerable to receiving unfair compensation for dispossessed land. In addition, the case study shows that the problem for a government that is committed to the retention of a 'people's land ownership' system is that it cannot afford to create even the perception of the state intervening in the land conversion process to the disadvantage of land users.

The Đoàn Văn Vươn *(DVV) case*

The DVV case illustrates two points discussed in this chapter. First, the state land ownership system facilitated and legitimized land grabs by state officials. Second, socialist laws on land ownership are rapidly losing social relevance in the eyes of Vietnamese, including some former state servants.

In January 2012, a previously unknown man by the name of Đoàn Văn Vươn became an overnight hero to people in North and South Vietnam after he fended off local government security and militia forces as they attempted to acquire his land (Hiebert 2012). A former soldier, Vươn was leased 19 ha of coastal marshland to farm by the district government for 15 years. The period of the lease was one of the points that made this case controversial. In Vietnam, the period for which land is allocated is based on the classification of the type of land. According to the Land Law 1993, state officials may determine the period for leases of coastal marshland. In contrast, agriculture land leases were limited to 20 years. In Vươn's case, he had turned the marshland into a fish farm, which would fall into the category of agricultural land. In 2009, when the business began to turn a profit, the authorities requisitioned for the return of the land. The grounds cited for requisitioning the land was to establish an airport on the marshland. At this point, Vươn had expanded his landholding to over 40 ha with the knowledge of state officials, and he had sub-leased 4 ha of the land to another party.

Vươn protested against the land requisition order. He argued that his family had had to borrow a large sum of money to establish the fish farm and without the land rights to it, he could not see how he could repay the debt and make a living. After a series of meetings failed to broker a solution, the district government decided to send a team of police and the army to the farm in order to evict him (Hiebert 2012). On entering the farm, the police were met with gunshots and homemade bombs, which caused injury to six policemen. The authorities called in reinforcements of more than 100 policemen (Hiebert 2012).

Vươn's arrest made headlines, not least because he had a strong legal claim (Hiebert 2012). The story of Vươn's predicament reinforces the narrative constructed and accepted by most Vietnamese, that the law operates as an instrument to legitimize land grabs. Vươn's story made him a sympathetic character to the Vietnamese public, where the state land system is perceived to have systematically produced this outcome. Vươn's wife cleverly invoked the words of Ho Chi Minh to defend her husband's actions. In an interview with RFA Free Asian Radio on the eve of her husband's trial, Nguyễn thị Thương said:

> We maintain our position that we are not guilty and that all what we did was to protect our belongings. According to the words of Uncle Ho, 'When the enemy comes to your house, even the women fight'.
>
> (RFA 2012b)

The statement made by Thương indicates how the notion of ownership and control of land has been accepted in Vietnamese society. Vươn's plight unleashed unprecedented public response, prompting Prime Minister Nguyễn Tấn Dũng for the first time to question publicly the actions of the local authorities and order an investigation. In spite of the prime minister's intervention, however, Vươn was later tried and subsequently jailed for breaching the criminal code (BBC 2013).

In summary, Vươn's case illustrates the incongruence between the state and the broader public thinking on land tenure rights. The tension between state socialist laws and the public thinking is palpable as economic development clashes with the community's notion of fairness. The defence of Vươn by the media and Vietnamese people shows that the state's public ownership system is rapidly losing social relevance as the law does not perform the function of protecting land users against land grabs.

The Nông Trường Sông Hậu *(NTSH) case*

This case study illustrates two points. First, it illustrates how socialist laws create an environment in which unscrupulous state officials can engage in dubious conduct to re-take the management of the NTSH farm. Second, the case shows that the state is not monolithic. It has different actors some of whom recognize that the state land system has created opportunities for the improper use of state power to sully the reputation of the director of a state farm.

The NTSH case involved allegations against local officials attempting to take over a profitable state farming enterprise, NTSH, for private gain. In this case, the allegations of embezzlement against the director of NTSH were used to appropriate land. Trần Ngọc Sương took over the management of NTSH, a large state farm with export contracts, from her father, who had managed the state farm since 1978 (Truong 2010: 4). Sương's ordeal began in 2005 when the top leaders in Cần Thơ proposed to take over NTSH to make way for the development of a new industrial town which was to be funded by investment from Taiwan and the USA (Brown 2012a, 2012b). Sương, unsurprisingly, objected to and resisted the plans, but within a few years, an investigation in Cần Thơ concluded that she had been illegally operating a $483,000 slush fund, which was not reported in the accounts of the state farm (Tuoi 2011). In 2008, the local District Court indicted her on the charges and she was convicted in 2009. Sương, however, had the support of many employees and some of Vietnam's former top national leaders, including the late Prime Minister Võ Văn Kiệt and former deputy chairwoman of the State Nguyễn Thị Bình (Brown 2012a, 2012b). Her supporters argued that such slush funds were common to avoid 'red tape' and the fund was legal at the time. In May 2010, Vietnam's Supreme Court threw out the District Court's verdict on the grounds that central prosecutors had found procedural violations in making the verdict. In 2011, however, new charges in Cần Thơ were laid against her (Brown 2012a, 2012b). Sương's supporters again rallied to her defence and enlisted the critical support of the FatherFront state organization whose role is to act as an intermediary between the government and Vietnamese people. In a public letter, FatherFront emphasized Sương's contribution to the state and the employment of peasants, and argued that many parties were responsible for the establishment of the slush fund in 1994, which was not regarded as illegal at that time. It concluded that the prosecution of Sương 'is sullying the name of a farm that has a fine reputation among senior government officials and has gained outstanding achievements' (Brown 2012a, 2012b). On 19 January 2012, the Cần Thơ authorities finally succumbed to public pressure, and dropped the charges against Sương on the grounds 'of the contributions made by Sương and her family to the state' (Brown 2012a, 2012b). The stated grounds for dropping the charges were as notable as the final decision.

In summary, the NTSH case shows the ability of state officials to engage in conduct that raises suspicion about the proper use of state land acquisition powers. The case demonstrates that the state ownership land system can have the consequence of facilitating the acquisition of land for an improper purpose. This is the one of the key reasons why land reforms that do not accommodate other forms of ownership, including private ownership and control for land users, are unlikely to resolve the gap in thinking between the state and the people on the notions of private ownership and control.

Conclusion

This chapter has shown that the introduction of the socialist land system – which removed private land ownership rights – has facilitated land grabs and produced intractable disputes. The case studies, in particular the Ecopark and DVV disputes, have shown that socialist land laws are rapidly losing social relevance as the laws do not accommodate the public's notion of private land ownership and control – a notion that developed during imperial times and upon which the French built during their rule. In addition to the removal of private land ownership, socialist laws have facilitated land grabs as they have created the conditions for unscrupulous investors and officials to take advantage of peasant land users. This is seen in the NTSH and the Thái Bình land disputes. The development of the socialist land system from the past 50 years as discussed in this chapter indicates that the recognition of private land ownership is unlikely to occur in the near future. However, the intervention of the prime minister in the DVV case and of the FatherFront in the NTSH case indicates that the government is concerned that socialist laws have produced outcomes that adversely affect social, economic and political stability.

A solution to reduce land grabs will be difficult to find. Rising tensions between the state and the people, however, require that a solution be found to ensure the people's right to transfer land – a right that is specifically provided for under Vietnamese land law – is not negated when the people's land is acquired by the state and allocated to investors for economic development projects.

References

Bassford, J.L. (1984) *Land Development Policy in Cochin China under the French (1865–1925)*, doctoral thesis, University of Hawaii, Hawaii.

BBC (2012) 'Arrests after Police Evict Hundreds', *BBC News*, www.bbc.com/news/world-asia-17844198.

BBC (2013) 'The Criminal Verdicts for the Doan Van Vuon Brothers' (Y án với anh em Đoàn Văn Vươn), BBC News, 30 July, www.bbc.co.uk/vietnamese/vietnam/2013/07/130730_tienlang_appeal_trial.shtml.

Brown, D. (2012a) 'Vietnam's Contentious Land Law – Part 1', *Asian Sentinel*, www.asiasentinel.com/society/vietnams-contentious-land-law/.

Brown, D. (2012b) 'Vietnam Contentious Law – Part 3', *Asian Sentinel*, www.asiasentinel.com/society/vietnams-contentious-land-law-part-3/.

Dang, P. (2008) *Vietnam's Economic Thinking: A Hard and Incredible Period 1975–1989*, Knowledge Publishing House.

Dang, P. (2013) *Fence-breaking in the Economy in the Nights Before Economic Renovation* (*Pha rao Trong Kinh Te Vao Dem Truoc Doi Moi*), Hanoi: Tri Thuc Press.

Dao, M.Q. (1993) 'History of Land Tenure in Pre-1954 Vietnam', *Journal of Contemporary Asia* 23(1): 84.

FBIS (1988) 'Party Directive Addresses Land Problems', *FIBIS Daily Report*, 9 September.

Gillespie, J. (1998) 'Land Law Subsystems? Urban Vietnam as a Case Study', *Pacific Rim Law & Policy Journal* 7: 555.

Gillespie, J. (2011) 'Exploring the Limits of the Judicialization of Urban Land Disputes in Vietnam', *Law & Society Review* 45(2): 241–276.

Government of Vietnam (1993) *Submission Paper to National Assembly on the Land (Amendment) Law*, 16 June, Doc. 2913/KTN.

Hiebert, M. (2012) 'Land Disputes Stir Political Debate', Center for Strategic and International Studies, csis.org/publication/land-disputes-stir-political-debate-vietnam.

Hoai, N. (2012) 'Hung Yen Announced Completion of Land Eviction in Van Giang' (Hưng Yên công bố hoàn thành vụ cưỡng chế tại Văn Giang), *VNEconomy*, vneconomy.vn/thoi-su/hung-yen-cong-bo-hoan-thanh-vu-cuong-che-tai-van-giang-20120427100858252.htm.

Hoang, A. and Le, D. (2012) 'Agricultural Land, Examining the Issues Related to the Van Giang Land Eviction Events' (Ruộng đất, nhìn từ chuyện cưỡng chế ở Văn Giang), *Nong Nghiep*, nongnghiep.vn/nongnghiepvn/vi-vn/25/93949/thoi-su/ruong-dat-nhin-tu-chuyen-cuong-che-o-van-giang.html.

Human Rights Watch (1997) *C911: Rural Unrest in Vietnam*, 1 December, www.refworld.org/docid/3ae6a7e1c.html.

Huu, D. (1958) 'Why are People Abandoning the Fields' (Le Nao Lai Bo Ruong Dong), *Nhan Dan*, 12 February: 2.

Huy, D. (2012) 'The Winning Side: In Liberation' (Ben Thang Cuoc 1: Giai Phong), OsinBook, Smashwords.

Kim, A. (2011) 'Talking Back: The Role of Narrative in Vietnam's Recent Land Compensation Changes', *Urban Studies* 48(3): 493.

Kokko, A. (2004) 'Growth and Reform Since the Eighth Party Congress', in D. McCargo (ed.) *Rethinking Vietnam*, London: RoutledgeCurzon, pp. 69–90.

Lai, T. (2012) 'From Tien Lang, We Remembered Thai Binh', *New World*, thegioimoi.vn/Home/ArticleDetail/vn/7/364/tu-su-kien-tien-lang-nho-lai-su-kien-thai-binh.tgm.

Le, D.T. (1993) 'Economic Doi Moi in Vietnam: Content, Achievements and Prospects', in W.S. Turley and M. Selden (eds) *Reinventing Vietnamese Socialism: Doi Moi in Comparative Perspective*, Boulder, CO: Westview Press, pp. 97–106.

Le, T. and Nguyen, Q.H. (2014) 'An Historical Overview of Vietnamese Land Law and Dispute Resolution', in J. Gillespie and H. Fu (eds) *Resolving Land Disputes in East Asia: Exploring the Limits of Law*, London: Cambridge University Press, pp. 275–290.

Marr, D. (2012) 'Vietnam's High Profile Land Dispute', *Inside Stories*, 23 March, inside.org.au/vietnam-high-profile-land-dispute/.

Ngo, V.L. (1993) 'Reform and Rural Development: Impact on Class, Sectoral, and Regional Inequities', in W.S. Turley and M. Selden (eds) *Reinventing Vietnamese Socialism: Doi Moi in Comparative Perspective*, Boulder, CO: Westview Press, pp. 165–207.

Nguyen, N.L. (1987) *Peasants, Party and Revolution: The Politics of Agrarian Transformation in Northern Vietnam, 1930–1975*, doctoral thesis.

Nguyen, T.A. (1985) 'The Vietnamese Monarchy under French Colonial Rule 1884–1945', *Modern Asian Studies* 19(1): 147.

Nguyen, T.A. (2003) 'Village Versus State: The Evolution of State-Local Relations in Vietnam until 1945', *Southeast Asian Studies* 10(1): 101–122.

Pham, Q.T. (2012) 'Summary of Some Figures Relating to the Land Confiscation in Van Giang' (Tóm tắt vài con số về vụ cưỡng chế đất tại Văn Giang), *Bauxite Vietnam*, boxitvn.blogspot.com.au/2012/04/tom-ta-vai-con-so-ve-vu-vuong-che-at.html.

Reuters (2012) 'Vietnam: Land Dispute Sets Off Clash', *The New York Times*, www.nytimes.com/2012/04/25/world/asia/vietnam-land-dispute-sets-off-clash.html?_r=0.

RFA (2012a) 'Former Vice Minister Dang Hung Vo Say Sorry to the People of Van Giang' (Nguyên Thứ trưởng Đặng Hùng Võ xin lỗi người dân Văn Giang), *RFA*, 9 November, www.rfa.org/vietnamese/vietnamnews/form-mi-vo-vangia-11092012090917.html.

RFA (2012b) 'Wives of Resistance Farmers Issue Online Plea', *RFA*, www.rfa.org/english/news/vietnam/plea-03272013173911.html.

Ta, V.T. (1982) 'Vietnam's Code of the Le Dynasty (1428–1788)', *The American Journal of Comparative Law* 30(3): 523–554.

Tam, N. (2012) 'Experts' Opinions Relating to some Land Evictions' (Ý kiến chuyên gia về vấn đề các vụ cưỡng chế), *Tamnhin.net*, www.baomoi.com/Y-kien-chuyen-gia-ve-van-de-cac-vu-cuong-che/148/8878038.epi.

Thompson, V. (1937) *French Indo-China*, New York: The Macmillan Company, pp. 228–235.

Tran, V.H. (2012) 'Exchange with Dang Hung Vo', *Dan Luan*, 11 December, www.danluan.org/tin-tuc/20121112/binh-luan-cua-luat-su-tran-vu-hai-ve-nhung-y-kien-cua-giao-su-dang-hung-vo.

Truong, M. (2010) 'Ms Suong, Recalling the Stormy Days – Part 2' (Ba Sương, những ngày trong sóng dữ (kỳ 2)), *BaoViet*, vietbao.vn/Phong-su/Ba-Suong-nhung-ngay-trong-song-du-ky-2/20903303/262/.

Tuoi, T. (2011) 'Fatherland Front Pitches in on Slush Fund Case', *InfoVn news*, news.com.vn/tennis/34218.html.

Van Arkadie, B. and Mallon, R. (2003) *Vietnam: A Transitional Tiger*, Canberra: Asian Pacific Press.

World Bank (2011) *Compulsory Land Acquisition and Voluntary Land Conversion in Vietnam*, Hanoi: World Bank.

Decrees, legislation and government submission papers

Constitution of the Socialist Republic of Vietnam Constitution 1980.

Constitution of the Socialist Republic of Vietnam 1992, www.vietnamlaws.com/freelaws/Constitution92(aa01).pdf.

Decree 69/2009/ND-CP on Providing Additional Clarification for Land Use Planning, Land Prices, Land Recovery, Compensation, Support and Resettlement, August 2009, www.xaydung.gov.vn/web/guest/home/-/legal/2pBh/vi_VN/18/29654/37;jsessionid=C524F08B578EA01EB667E3E9A4584D3B.

Decree 123/2007/ND-CP on Providing Clarifications on the Methods to Evaluate Land and Land Price Frame, July 27 2007, hud.com.vn/en/node/1161.

Government of Vietnam (GVN), Submission Paper on the Draft Land Law The Socialist Republic of Vietnam June 16 1993, document number 2913/KTN.

Land Law 1987, Department of Agricultural Land Management, Hanoi.

Land Law 1993 of the Socialist Republic of Vietnam, www.tuenhan.vn/forum/showthread.php?675-Lu%E1%BA%ADt-%C4%91%E1%BA%A5t-%C4%91ai-1993-1998-2001-2003-2009.

Land Law 1993 of the Socialist Republic of Vietnam as amended in 1998, www.tuenhan.vn/forum/showthread.php?675-Lu%E1%BA%ADt-%C4%91%E1%BA%A5t-%C4%91ai-1993-1998-2001-2003-2009.

Land Law 2001 of the Socialist Republic of Vietnam as amended in 2001, www.tuenhan.vn/forum/showthread.php?675-Lu%E1%BA%ADt-%C4%91%E1%BA%A5t-%C4%91ai-1993-1998-2001-2003-2009.

Land Law 2003 of the Socialist Republic of Vietnam, www.vietnamlaws.com/freelaws/Lw13na26Nov03Land[X2865].pdf.

Land Law 2013 of the Socialist Republic of Vietnam, vietnamnet.vn/vn/chinh-tri/151507/toan-van-luat-dat-dai-sua-doi.html.

11 Transnational state responsibility for human rights violations resulting from global land grabs

Sumithra Dhanarajan[1]

Introduction

Globalization has been disruptive – in both positive and negative ways – of the international law regime. Global land grabs speak directly to this phenomenon. In their contemporary form, land grabs manifest the clash between international investment law and international human rights law. Telesetsky (2011: 290) states:

> On the one hand, international economic law enables these land leases while, on the other hand, foundational principles from international human rights law and international environmental law caution against proceeding with these leases unless the leases are conditioned to protect public, social and environmental values.

A particular challenge to the international human rights regime is the seeming impunity accorded to investor states that participate in these land grabs. The role they play in catalysing, actively aiding or directly perpetrating human rights abuses is known, but victims have too few avenues for redress. It is argued in this chapter that a progressive approach towards general principles of international law – specifically customary international law rules on state responsibility – may serve to address the clash to some degree, but more importantly, deliver rights-based solutions to this problem. Further, in circumstances where private corporations are involved in land grabs where human rights abuses take place, the state in which they are domiciled may have extraterritorial obligations towards the victims.

Global land grabs: definition, drivers and scale

As detailed by Carter in the introductory chapter of this volume, foreign investment in agricultural land on a large scale is not a new phenomenon. Yet the contemporary 'race for arable lands' (De Schutter 2011: 504) is unique for a number of reasons. Driven by anticipated food and energy security, these long-term, large-scale acquisitions and leases tend to arise from strategic public policy decisions to secure future food and energy needs (Mann and Smaller 2010) – the so-called food-feed-fuel complex – resulting from interconnected factors such as population growth and urbanization trends, exhaustion of certain fossil fuels, and climate change impacts upon agriculture.[2]

The 2008 global food crisis prompted an acceleration in the number of acquisitions and leases of arable land by governments and investors from states such as China, Saudi Arabia, Libya and South Korea (Martin and Ayalew 2011) into countries in sub-Saharan Africa, Central Europe, other parts of Asia and Latin America.[3] The investing countries are 'finance rich' but lack arable land and, importantly, access to water for irrigation (Smaller and Mann 2009); the investee countries are 'resource rich' but 'finance poor' thus attracted by such investments.

The private sector still accounts for the majority of such acquisitions and leases but there is a noteworthy trend of investments by states directly or through state-owned enterprises or sovereign wealth funds (Cotula *et al.* 2009). Even with private-sector investments, the state is often involved as a financier or creates the framework for investment through an international investment agreement.

The context within which these land deals are made is relevant. Generally, the negotiation processes as well as the terms of the investment contract are opaque (Cotula 2011). Local communities affected by the terms of the contract are rarely forewarned of the circumstances and are unlikely to have participated in the decision making. The contracts are often part of a broader trade and investment package whereby the specifics of the land acquisition may be traded by the host state for other perceived trade gains. The host state is often – though not always – one that is highly dependent on foreign investment and therefore amenable to contracts that heavily favour the investor. Human rights protection and enforcement mechanisms may be weak within these states, thus presenting circumstances that can be exploited by the investor (Telesetsky 2011: 290).[4] The land that is being sold or leased is mostly state owned. The state thus feels under little obligation to consult with communities, even though the land might be used or occupied by them.

The Tirana Declaration (2011) states that a land acquisition can be defined as a 'land grab' when: 1 violations of human rights occur, particularly the equal rights of women; 2 the principle of free, prior and informed consent (FPIC) is ignored; 3 there is a failure to assess thoroughly or account for social, economic and environmental impact; 4 contracts are made in a non-transparent manner and, further, do not contain clear and binding commitments on employment and benefit sharing; and 5 the acquisition lacks democratic planning, independent oversight and meaningful participation by the stakeholders affected.[5]

Human rights violations resulting from global land grabs

Where large tranches of arable land as well as fresh-water supplies are cordoned off from those whose lives are dependent upon it, there are bound to be human rights implications. Given the kind of land that is being acquired, smallholder farmers, pastoralists, indigenous peoples and nomadic peoples are amongst those who tend to be immediately impacted by these deals, though over the long term, the broader population may also suffer from human rights abuses. The potential negative impacts of dedicating extensive land areas to mono-cropping both on ecological systems as well as on the economic and social structures of rural society are well- documented.

In December 2009, the United Nations (UN) special rapporteur on the right to food noted the following human rights as being vulnerable to violation as a result of land grabs (Mann and Smaller 2010).

The right to food

Article 11 of the International Covenant on Economic, Social and Cultural Rights (ICESCR) encapsulates the right to an adequate standard of living, including the right to adequate food. It recognizes the fundamental rights of everyone to be free from hunger and places an obligation upon states parties to take measures, either individually or through international cooperation, to address this. The state is obliged to ensure that everyone under its jurisdiction has access to minimum essential food, sufficient, nutritionally adequate and safe to ensure their freedom from hunger.[6] The special rapporteur argued that states would be violating the right to food if they negotiated land acquisition agreements without ensuring that this would not result in food insecurity. He detailed instances that should be accounted for including macro-level impacts such as increased vulnerability resulting from dependency on international food markets because land in the host state is no longer available to the local population. He stated that in order to realize the right to food more effectively, host states and investors need to agree on certain conditions according to which the investment would be made, and provided examples of such conditions.

The right to adequate housing

Article 11 of the ICESCR and Article 25(1) of the Universal Declaration of Human Rights (UDHR) guarantee the right to adequate housing. The right specifically prohibits forced evictions (General Comment No. 4 (1991), para. 18) save in exceptional circumstances.[7] Where it is justifiable, it needs to be carried out in strict compliance with the provisions of international human rights law and in accordance with principles of reasonableness and proportionality. Forced evictions are 'the permanent or temporary removal against their will of individuals, families and/or communities from the homes and land which they occupy, without the provision of, and access to appropriate forms of legal or other protection' (General Comment No. 7 (1997) para. 4). The practice of forced evictions may also 'result inviolations of civil and political rights such as the right to life, the right to the security of the person, the right to non-interference with privacy, family and home and the right to the peaceful enjoyment of possessions' (ibid., para. 5).[8] Prior to carrying out any evictions, especially those involving large groups, states are obliged to consult with affected persons and explore all feasible alternatives for avoiding or minimizing the need to use force. Legal remedies and compensation must be available to affected persons (ibid., para. 14).

The right to water

The UN Human Rights Council (HRC) adopted a consensus resolution (A/HRC/15/L14), affirming that 'the human right to safe drinking water and sanitation is derived from the right to an adequate standard of living (ICESCR, Article 11[1]) and inextricably related to the right to the highest attainable standard of physical and mental health, as well as the right to life and human dignity'. The right to water 'entitles everyone to sufficient, safe, acceptable, physically accessible and affordable water for personal and domestic uses' (CESCR, General Comment 15: The right to water). Violation of this right in the context of global land grabs, as with the right to food, stems from evictions (Centre on Housing Rights and Evictions 2006), as well as diversion of fresh-water supplies to mono-cropping on the land acquired. Further, the terms of the investment contract may restrict the host state's future policy space to manage water security issues where such policy affects the leased or acquired land.

The rights of indigenous peoples

Access to land for indigenous peoples has been given specific protection under international law (General Comment No. 7 (1997), paras 27 and 28). Article 10 of the UN Declaration on the Rights of Indigenous Peoples (UNDRIP) guarantees indigenous peoples the right not to be forcibly removed from their lands or territories, and no relocation shall take place without their free, prior and informed consent, and after agreement on just and fair compensation and, where possible, with the option to return. Articles 25 and 26 recognize the spiritual relationship of indigenous peoples with their lands, and their right to own, use, develop and control them. States must therefore give legal recognition and protection to these lands, territories and resources with due respect to the customs, traditions and land tenure systems of the indigenous peoples concerned.[9]

Land rights

The right to land is not codified within the international legal framework but it has been recognized that access to land is an inherent component of other human rights, such as the right to food, to water and to housing, as well as the rights of indigenous peoples (Wickers and Kalhan 2010).[10] In the case of land grabs, the main issue is access for land users. Those who use the lands in question tend not to have formal property titles even where they may have acquired user rights. When host states negotiate the lease agreement, the land is often designated as 'reserve agricultural land' or 'idle' or 'degraded', ignoring the reality of its use (Mann and Smaller 2010: 23).

The right to self-determination and the exploitation of natural resources

De Schutter (2011) also notes potential violations to the right to self-determination as provided for in Article 1(2) of both the ICCPR and the ICESCR, further re-affirmed in Article 3 of UNDRIP. This right includes the rights of people to dispose freely of their natural wealth and resources. The right to self-determination has been recognized as a *jus cogens* right (General Comment No. 7 (1997), para. 30).

In addition, the right to an adequate remedy may be breached where the state responsible for the substantive human rights violation cannot be challenged (UDHR, Art. 8; ICCPR, Art. 2; the International Convention on the Elimination of All Forms of Racial Discrimination (CERD), Art. 6). Further, given the length of the leases and therefore the long-term implications, the principle of intergenerational equity is also pertinent.[11]

Despite enumerated rights, international human rights law as a means of protecting those affected by land grabbing has so far proven a rather blunt instrument. Statist interpretations of human rights duties reinforce a vertical articulation which means victims are wholly reliant on their states to afford them protection as well as access to remedy in the case of violations. Yet their governments may either have been party or at least privy to the abuses, or unwilling or unable to challenge the perpetrators upon whom they are dependent for the investment or who are politically more powerful. Further, international investment law, by virtue of the heavy protection it generally affords to the investor, may additionally limit the state's capacity to protect human rights in the context of land deals.

International investment law and land grabs

Foreign acquisitions of agrarian land are mostly regulated through international investment contracts and investment agreements. Within the host state, domestic law applies and may cover various issues including taxation, property law, water rights, labour standards and foreign direct investment requirements (Smaller and Mann 2009; see also Chapter 1 of this volume).

These laws are scant in many of the countries where land is being grabbed.

The investment contract between the investor and the host state is important, as it sets out the price, quantity and duration for the purchase or lease. It will also cover issues such as tax and other incentives for the investor, rights to export production, rights to import equipment and personnel, infrastructure and logistical requirements (Smaller and Mann 2009). It may include requirements for environmental or social impact assessments. It may also include stabilization clauses that 'either preclude the application of, or require compensation for the new or changed regulatory measures that affect the investments' (Smaller and Mann 2009). Investment contracts are often enshrined in legislation. In most cases, the terms of these contracts are heavily weighted towards the protection of the investor.

International investment agreements are treaties between states that are intended to provide investors from one state investing in another state with special protections under international law. Land deals are often governed by bilateral investment treaties (BITs). These protect the investor-nationals' interests and provide them with access to state-investor international arbitration in the event of injury. When negotiating BITS, the host state may make promises of non-interference with investments as part of their 'sales pitch'. These promises can sometimes transform into 'legitimate expectations' (Telesetsky 2011) which are legally binding.

Stabilization clauses are also included in BITs, and these can used to limit the implementation of new social and environmental legislation by host states (Shemberg 2008). This is a particular concern in the case of land deals, given the impacts that they have on human rights and the environment, especially in the context of deepening environmental problems due to climate change and water, food and energy insecurities, and given the long-term nature of the leases.

It is generally the case that international investment law instruments are somewhat 'human rights-blind', even though in theory, human rights obligations can be incorporated into them or raised during adjudication proceedings (Dumberry and Dumas-Aubin 2012). With regard to general principles of international law, Article 53 of the 1969 Vienna Convention states that if a treaty conflicts with a peremptory norm, it is void. Peremptory norms that are clearly accepted and recognized include the prohibitions of aggression, genocide, slavery, racial discrimination, crimes against humanity and torture, and the right to self-determination.[12] Other candidates for elevation to a *jus cogens* statute include permanent sovereignty over natural resources, pollution on an exponential scale and the destruction of the rights of indigenous peoples (Sornarajah 2010: 470). In may be argued that where international investment agreements have the effect of breaching peremptory norms in the expanded sense are void.

Soft law approaches

An array of soft law approaches, both state led as well as civil society led, have emerged as regimes of choice in the governing of the social and environmental impacts of land grabs.[13] Dominating the emergent regime complex[14] is the voluntary code of conduct. For example, the Principles for Responsible Agricultural Investment that Respect Rights, Livelihoods and Resources (PRAI), jointly formulated by the World Bank and other UN agencies,[15] contains seven principles[16] to which investors may voluntarily subscribe when conducting large-scale farmland acquisitions. These include recognizing and respecting rights to land and natural resources, accountability for food security, consultations with those materially affected by the deals, respect for the rule of law, generation of social and distributional impacts, and minimizing and mitigating environmental impacts. These principles have been criticized for being vague as well as for having the effect of legitimizing land grabs rather than scrutinizing their impact upon human rights (Wisborg 2013: 99–1222; Stephens 2013: 187–92). In particular, critics were concerned that state responsibilities for these impacts were not adequately addressed by the principles (ibid.).

In May 2012, the Committee on World Food Security[17] adopted the Voluntary Guidelines on the Responsible Governance of Tenure of Land, Fisheries and Forests to respond to some of the criticisms levelled at the PRAI and to be more attentive to human rights considerations. The resulting guidelines orientate around core concerns about how people can gain access to the land necessary for ensuring food security, how that access is defined and regulated by state law as well as customary law, and how access is protected and respected by the various stakeholders involved in large-scale land acquisitions (Paoloni and Onorati 2014).

According to Borras and Franco, the push to make codes of conduct the dominant paradigm may be in order to re-set the storyline on land grabs as positive development opportunities (Borras and Franco 2010). The purpose of the code is to help manage any risks emerging with regards to social and environmental impacts so that the development outcomes inherent in these investments can flourish. Yet, in some cases, the land deal cannot be 'made right' and the concern is that parties may massage the facts or the situation to fit the investment imperative.

The code of conduct model does provide some protection against human rights violations, but its voluntary nature means that there is no enforcement mechanism and reduced access to remedy in case of breach. Importantly, the existing instruments do not adequately address the notion of wrong-doing and responsibility on the part of the state entities involved in a transaction that has resulted in human rights abuse.

Transnational state responsibility for human rights violations

This concern about how to hold states responsible for human rights violations resulting from land grabs continues to vex human rights advocates. In 2011, the World Social Forum drew attention to the problem of having land governance and human rights protection placed under the jurisdiction of states that actually 'bear the greatest share of responsibility for these land grabs'. The forum declared that each state should be held responsible for the impact of its policies and companies abroad, and that international trade and finance regimes, which encourage speculation in natural resources and agriculture, should also be accountable to human rights.[18]

General principles of international law could play some role in addressing this problem, which seemingly falls through the cracks of the extant regime complex. At present, there are few effective means for establishing state responsibility for land grabbing. As stated previously, the practice of international investment law has failed to respond adequately to this problem. International human rights law also falls short especially with regard to human rights violations that take place outside a state's territorial jurisdiction (Joseph and Castan 2013: 103).

The application of customary international law on state responsibility, as codified by the International Law Commission's Articles on the Responsibility of States for Internationally Wrongful Acts (ARSIWA),[19] could address this gap to some extent. Where state responsibility for an internationally wrongful act has been determined, a number of remedies are available under customary international law. ARSIWA details entitlements to reparations in the form of restitution, compensation and satisfaction, each with a set of criteria for application (ARSIWA arts 34–37; Crawford 2013).

Here I consider three scenarios all involving the state responsibility of the investor state for human rights violations resulting from foreign land acquisitions. First, where the investor state invests directly or through its sovereign wealth fund in the land acquisition or lease in the host state, and either commits a human rights violation itself or the host state violates human rights in connection with the land grab. Second, where the investor state through a state-owned enterprise acquires or leases land in the host state and that enterprise perpetrates human rights abuses directly or in complicity with the latter. Third, where a private corporate domiciled in the investor state is involved in human rights abuses in a host state, either directly or in complicity with the latter.

Under customary international law, a state will incur international responsibility for a breach of an international legal obligation if the act in question can be attributed to it. The rules codified in ARSIWA establish that a state is responsible for the internationally wrongful actions and omissions of all its organs and officials (ARSIWA, art. 4). It is accepted that these rules apply to international human rights law, and a number of human rights treaty bodies have referenced them (McCorquodale and Simons 2007: 601–2). It is also generally accepted that state obligations under international human rights law are not territorially confined (ibid.: 602–3).[20]

Scenario one

Where the investor state has directly violated human rights in conducting the land grab, it can be found to have committed an internationally wrongful act under Article 2 of ARSIWA. Where a sovereign wealth fund is involved, it may be considered a government organ under Article 4 and therefore if its actions amount to an internationally wrongful act, this may be attributed to its home state. Sovereign immunity could pose a potential barrier to victims seeking to access remedies through domestic courts. Most states now embrace a restrictive doctrine of immunity so it may be possible to argue in the case of global land grabs that these are *acta jure gestionis* and therefore sovereign immunity may not be invoked.[21]

In most cases, however, it is unlikely that the human rights abuses will have been perpetrated directly by the investor state. Rather, the host state will have committed the human rights abuses to meet the terms of the investment contract. For example, the contract may stipulate that the land being acquired or lease is 'marginal' or 'unused', and therefore the host state needs to deliver the land in that condition, resulting in forced evictions; or that water usage rights must be given to the investor, which results in restricted access to water for communities.

In these cases, a finding of complicity could be looked into. Article 16 of ARSIWA prohibits a state from aiding and assisting another state in the commission of an internationally wrongful act. Responsibility attaches if the state has knowledge of the circumstances of the internationally wrongful act and the act would be internationally wrongful if committed by that state. The standard of proof embraces both constructive and actual knowledge. What needs to be shown, though, is that there is a causal relationship between the act of aiding or assisting and the committal of the internationally wrongful act. It could be argued that where the investor state has knowledge that including a particular provision in the investment agreement may well result in human rights abuses if those provisions are not explicitly restricted within a human rights framework (which may include impact assessments and monitoring, for example, or restrict the reach of stabilization clauses), this might amount to aiding and assisting. There may be some obstacles in terms of showing causality but the facts of particular cases may render these surmountable.

Finally, as a catch-all, Article 41 of ARSIWA places a duty on states to cooperate to bring to an end any serious breach of a peremptory norm – that is, a breach that involves a gross or systemic failure by the responsible state. The duty obliges the state not to recognize as lawful the situation created by the breach, and not to render aid or assistance.[22] In the case of land grabs, much rides of the definition of peremptory norms. An expanded definition that accounts for violations of the right to self-determination and of indigenous peoples' rights could bring Article 41 to bear in a way that obligates the investor state to stop the human rights violations even where it is not directly complicit in the activity. This might include, for example, declaring the investment agreement void since honouring the latter would amount to recognizing the situation as lawful.

Scenario two

State liability under the second scenario could arguably be established in three instances. First, where it can be shown that the state-owned enterprise has been empowered by the law of its state to 'exercise elements of governmental authority' and is 'acting in that capacity in the particular instance', Article 5 of ARSIWA provides that its actions can be attributed to the state. The commentary on Article 5 states that the conduct of the entity must concern governmental activity and not other private or commercial activity.[23] On this point, Crawford, citing *EDF (Services) Limited v. Romania* (ICSID, 2009),[24] notes that mere ownership of an entity by a state will not automatically convert that entity into an organ of the state (Crawford 2013: 118). McCorquodale and Simons, on the other hand, believe that the key factor for attribution is not the degree of ownership of the corporation by the state but whether it has been empowered to exercise governmental authority (McCorquodale and Simons 2007). The distinction they make is instrumental in establishing state responsibility with regard to particular kinds of land grabs that are conducted as part of a state-sponsored scheme to acquire land in another territory for the purposes of growing food or fuel either for its own population or as an agri-investment.

If the provisions of Article 5 are not met, it may be possible under Article 8 to demonstrate that the entity is in fact acting on the instructions of, or under the direction or control of, the state in carrying out the conduct, which may give rise to international responsibility.[25] To establish state responsibility, however, requires a finding that the entity was effectively under the state's control. Gibney (n.d.) states that the International Court in the Nicaragua case[26] more or less held that 'effective control' means 'absolute control'. This 'effective control' test has been reaffirmed in other cases.[27] McCorquodale and Simons suggest that although it is highly unlikely that a state would exercise this level of control over a corporation, it might be possible with respect to a wholly state-owned enterprise (McCorquodale and Simons 2007).[28] State-owned enterprises that have been established under law to execute government policy on food or energy security through the acquisition of land, and which conduct their activities in a way that demonstrate a clear governmental mandate, could thus fall within either Article 5's or Article 8's ambit.

The UN Guiding Principles on Business and Human Rights,[29] referred to in Chapter 2 of this volume, also support the idea that states have the duty to take steps to protect against human rights abuses 'by business enterprises that are owned or controlled by the state, or that receive substantial support and services from state agencies such as export credit agencies and official investment insurance or guarantee agencies, including, where appropriate, by requiring human rights due diligence' (UN Guiding Principles, 9). The accompanying commentary states that 'where a business enterprise is controlled by the state, or where its acts can be attributed otherwise to the state, an abuse of human rights by the business enterprise may entail a violation of the state's own international law obligations' (ibid., commentary, para. 4).

Scenario three

Whereas scenario two evolves around the state's responsibility for a wrongful act conducted by its agent in another state's territory, scenario three takes us beyond ARSIWA to look at the possibility of placing positive obligations upon the state to prevent or provide access to remedies for individuals in another state who are threatened by or suffer abuse through the activities of corporations domiciled in its own territory. The corporations considered here would not satisfy the Article 5 or Article 8 provisions on attribution so as to invoke the customary international law codified by ARSIWA. Yet, it would seem that where such corporations have a particular type of connection with the state, then this should trigger these obligations. It is not uncommon for land acquisitions by companies to have a degree of state support either via a BIT, through state financing, or through diplomatic support in enabling the corporation's investment contract with the host state, and I would argue that this amounts to such a connection.

A home state's positive obligations either to regulate a corporation's activities in a host state or provide the means for adjudicating human rights abuses that take place in the host state amount to forms of extraterritorial jurisdiction. What triggers these obligations under international human rights law is currently moot. As stated by Augenstein and Kinley, the state-centrism of international law determines – for the most part – that 'human rights protection outside the state's borders is traditionally considered to require special justification in the light of the sovereign territorial rights of other states' (Augenstein and Kinley 2015). Along these lines, the US Alien Tort Claims Act,[30] which had previously provided one of the stronger possibilities for extraterritorial jurisdiction, was recently limited by the US Supreme Court in the Kiobel case.[31] Likewise, the UN Guiding Principles do not confirm a state duty to provide for extraterritorial jurisdiction. Importantly, however, the accompanying commentary to the Guiding Principles state:

> At present, States are not generally required under international human rights law to regulate the extraterritorial activities of businesses domiciled

> in their territory and/or jurisdiction. *Nor are they generally prohibited from doing so, provided there is a recognized jurisdictional basis.*
>
> (UN Guiding Principles, 9, para. 4, emphasis added)

Some UN treaty bodies have also indicated their support for extraterritorial jurisdiction with regard to corporate activities in host states. For example, the CESCR has stated that states parties should 'take steps to prevent human rights contraventions abroad by corporations which have their main seat under their jurisdiction, without infringing the sovereignty or diminishing the obligations of the host States under the Covenant'.[32] Recently the CERD has also indicated that states should take appropriate legislative or administrative measures to prevent adverse impacts on the rights of indigenous peoples in other countries from activities of corporations registered in their state, and they recommend that states explore ways to hold such corporations accountable for their actions.[33]

As indicated by the CESCR in its comment, the question of sovereignty of the host state – its right to non-interference with regard to how corporations operate in its territory – is a critical barrier to the home state's exercise of extraterritorial jurisdiction. Augenstein and Kinley (2015) observe that in such cases, 'the recognition of extraterritorial positive obligations to regulate and control global corporate power is likely to result in normative competency conflicts between home and host states of "multi-national" corporations'.[34]

Yet, some scholars lobby strongly for a progressive international law position on this issue. Sornarajah posits that although *prima facie* it is difficult to establish the case, the circumstances demand that an 'interpretative development banalogy' (Sornarajah 2010: 161) should be used to extend and adapt creatively the reach of existing jurisprudence. His own starting point is that states have a general duty under international law not to act in a way that causes harm outside their territory. He then offers evidence that states have come to accept liability for the harmful actions of their nationals on the basis of this general principle: for example, the Basel Convention[35] where states accept a duty to prevent the transport of hazardous waste to other states by their nationals, and domestic legislation to prevent sex tourism. His view is that the notion of sovereignty whereby the prerogative lies with the developing state to risk receiving the harm is set aside (Sornarajah 2010: 163). International human rights law, in fact, requires a state to take measures to control, regulate, investigate and prosecute human rights abuses perpetrated by non-state actors whether within or without the territory of that state.[36]

Sornarajah suggests that these precedents, plus *erga omnes* obligations, could extend international law towards the recognition of state responsibility in respect of violations of *jus cogens* principles by its corporate nationals. It must be shown, however, that the state knowingly permitted the violating actions, or that the state gave active assistance, hence attributing the conduct to the state. Active assistance might be imputed where the state fails to provide civil remedies in its own jurisdiction to address the harmful acts of the corporation abroad (McCorquodale and Simons 2007: 165). Finally, there is a definite commitment on the part of all states to prevent human rights violations wherever they take place, a position that has been iterated in the international human rights treaties (Sornarajah 2010; ICCPR, Art. 3).

Augenstein and Kinley also propose a re-think of international law's approach to extraterritorial jurisdiction obligations. They position this proposition as means of reinforcing the necessary normative drivers behind the concept of universal human rights in the context of the current global political economy (Augenstein and Kinley 2015). In their view, 'the resilience of the state-centred world-view has hampered international legal reform and propelled the marginalisation of international human rights law' (Augenstein and Kinley 2015: 3). They suggest that a subject-based approach rather than a territorial-based approach to international human rights law would trigger a home state's extraterritorial obligations (and corresponding obligations towards the victims) in situations where that state has a degree of influence over the corporation that is perpetrating the human rights abuses (ibid.). In their view, the state obligation under this approach derives from the power the home state wields over the rights holder as opposed to international law presumption of territorial control over persons. Establishing this nexus offers a different route to attaching state responsibility for the consequences of the corporate-related human rights abuses connected to the land grab.

Concluding thoughts

This chapter has sought to establish the possibility for invoking state responsibility for an internationally wrongful act where an investor state has committed or has been complicit in the commitment of a human rights violation in the course of a land grab. Further, it has raised the possibility of positive extraterritorial obligations upon the home state where corporations domiciled in its jurisdiction perpetrate abuses.

With regard to the application of state responsibility under customary international law, the final analysis, however, has to be a political one that addresses the gap between law in books and law in action. A finding of state responsibility will, in theory, enable the home state, as the injured state, to bring a claim to the International Court of Justice. In practice, this is unlikely to happen, given that the home state is likely to be involved in the perpetration of the violation, or if it is not, power imbalances between the parties will manifest as an obstacle.

Having said this, there is a value in establishing that the principle of state responsibility is applicable in these situations. International human rights law continues to evolve and there are signs that the state responsibility doctrine is being absorbed, as is the notion of extraterritorial obligations. The arguments put forth in this chapter lend weight to this evolution. So much the better if it leads to securing protection and remedy for victims of violations as a result of land grabbing. Further, as codes of conduct develop, so too are they influenced by the hard law framework and the findings of this chapter could strengthen the case of accountability on the part of the investor state.

Finally, if it is the case that international law is not currently capable of reconciling clashes between different regimes – in the case of land grabbing, between international investment law and international human rights law – this may reinforce the view that global governance models for dealing with 'wicked' or complex problems are more efficient. Rather than accepting the marginalization of international law within this paradigm, or worse, its practical redundancy in the context of our current global political economy, perhaps as lawyers we should invest in actively seeking out opportunities to make it 'fit for purpose', particularly where its utility is in ensuring access to justice where it is most needed.

Notes

1 The author expresses appreciation to Professor Connie Carter, Professor Andrew Harding, Professor Koh Kheng Lian and Professor M. Sornarajah for helpful comments on an earlier draft.

2 Government mandates on the use of biofuels as part of dual climate change-energy security policies act as an additional driver. See Meinzen-Dick and Markelova 2009.

3 See *Special Rapporteur on the Right to Food, Large-scale Land Acquisitions and Leases: A Set of Minimum Principles and Measures to Address the Human Rights Challenge*, Human Rights Council, UN Doc A/HRC/13/33/Add.2 (28 December 2009).

4 Telesetsky cites Knaup and von Mittelstaedt, who quote a venture capitalist as saying 'When food becomes scarce the investor needs a weak state that does not force him to abide by any rules'.

5 ILC, Tirana Declaration: Securing Land Access for the Poor in Times of Intensified Natural Resources Competition (Rome, 2011), www.landcoalition.org/about us/aom2011/ Tiranadeclaration. This declaration was endorsed by the ILC Assembly of Members on 27 May 2011.

6 Committee on Economic, Social and Cultural Rights (CESCR), general comment No.12 (1999) on the right to adequate food (Art. 11), para. 14.

7 The CESCR has stated that 'instances of forced eviction … can only be justified in the most exceptional circumstances and in accordance with the relevant principles of international law'.

8 The comment also notes that the right not to be forcefully evicted is complemented by the guarantee against 'arbitrary or unlawful interference' with one's home guaranteed under Article 17(1) of the International Covenant on Civil and Political Rights (ICCPR).

9 Articles 13 to 19 of the International Labour Organization (ILO) Convention No. 169 (1989) concerning Indigenous and Tribal Peoples in Independent Countries contains relevant provisions. Further, Article 8 paragraph 2(b) of UNDRIP states that 'States shall provide effective mechanism for prevention of, and redress for … any action which has the aim or effect of dispossessing [indigenous peoples] of their lands, territories or resources'.

10 Land rights are also invoked through ILO Conventions 117 and 169 on Social Policy (Basic Aims and Standards) and Indigenous and Tribal Peoples. ILO

Convention No. 117, The Social Policy (Basic Aims and Standards) Convention of 1962 covers measures to improve the standard of living for agricultural producers including control of the alienation of land to non-agriculturalists, respect for customary land rights and supervision of tenancy arrangements. The ILO Convention on Indigenous and Tribal Peoples, No. 169 of 1989, recognizes the special relationship between indigenous people and their lands and requires states to adopt special measures of protection on their behalf; provides safeguards against the arbitrary removal of indigenous people from their traditional land, with procedural guarantees; and includes provisions related to the transmission of land rights and respect for customary procedures. The Convention on the Elimination of all forms of Discrimination Against Women (CEDAW) requires that state parties 'shall ensure women the right to … equal treatment in land and agrarian reform as well as in land resettlement schemes …'

11 The Rio Declaration on Environment and Development, princ. 3, UN Doc. A/CONF.151/26 (Vol. I) (1992) states: 'The right to development must be fulfilled so as to equitably meet developmental and environmental needs of present and future generations.' See also Weiss 1992. The landmark constitutional rights case that refers to this principle is *The Philippines: Supreme Court Decision in Minors Oposa v. Secretary of the Department of Environment and National Resources (DENR)*, 30 July 1993, 33 I.L.M 173 (1994).

12 See *East Timor (Portugal v. Australia)*, Judgment, ICJ Reports 1995, p. 90, at p. 102, para. 29; *Legality of the Threat or Use of Nuclear Weapons*, Advisory Opinion, ICJ Reports 1996, p. 226, at p. 258, para. 83; and *Application of the Convention on the Prevention and Punishment of the Crime of Genocide*, Preliminary Objections, Judgment, ICJ Reports 1996, p. 595, at pp. 615–16, paras 31–32.

13 For an evaluation of these approaches through a human rights lens, see Wisborg 2013; Chapter 2 in this volume.

14 For the application of regime complex theory to global land acquisition governance, see Stephens, 2011.

15 The International Fund for Agricultural Development, the UN Conference on Trade and Development, and the UN Food and Agriculture Organization (FAO).

16 See siteresources.worldbank.org/INTARD/214574-1111138388661/22453321/Principles_Extended.pdf.

17 The Committee on World Food Security (CFS) was established initially as an intergovernmental body to serve as a forum for review and follow-up of food security policies, but in its current form it includes other stakeholders from civil society. As such, its current membership is inclusive of member states of FAO, the International Fund for Agricultural Development (IFAD), the World Food Programme (WFP), non-member states of FAO that are member states of the UN, representatives of other UN agencies and bodies, civil society and nongovernmental organizations (NGOs) and their networks, international agricultural research systems, international and regional financial institutions, and representatives of private sector associations and private philanthropic foundations. See www.fao.org/cfs/cfs-home/en/.

18 Supra, note 13. World Social Forum (2011) 'Dakar Appeal against the Land Grab', FIAN International, www.fian.org/news/press-releases/dakar-appeal-against-the-land-grab.

19 Articles on the Responsibility of States for Internationally Wrongful Acts, ILC *Ybk* 2001/II(2), 26.

20 Citing *Saldano v. Argentina*, where the Inter-American Commission held that a state party to the American Convention may be responsible under certain circumstances for acts and omissions of its agents that produce effects or are undertaken outside state territory; the Human Rights Committee's observation that Israel has obligations under the ICCPR in relation to individuals within its Occupied

territories and Belgium has obligations in relation to its forces operating as UN peacekeepers in Somalia. See *Victor Saldano v. Argentina*, Petition, Report No. 38/99, Inter-Am. C.H.R., OEA/Ser.L/V/II.95 Doc. 7 rev. at 289 (1998). Also NRC Gen. Comment 31: 'A State party must respect and ensure the rights laid down in the Covenant to anyone within the power and effective control of that State Party even if not situated within the territory of the State Party'.

21 Normative hierarchy theory could also mean that a state's jurisdictional immunity is abrogated when the state violates human rights protections that are considered peremptory international law norms. For a discussion, see Caplan 2003.

22 See ILC Commentary at 112, paras (7) and (8). The commentary to ARSIWA lays out the definitions of 'serious', 'gross' and 'systemic', which in essence amount to a consideration of the responsible state's intent to violate the norm; the scope and number of individual violations; and the gravity of their consequences for the victims.

23 ILC Commentary 43, para. (5).

24 *EDF (Services) Limited v. Romania*, ICSID Case No. ARB/05/3, 8 October 2009, § 190. In this case, two state-owned corporations with legal personality under Romanian law that was separate and distinct from that of the state, were held not to be considered as state organs.

25 Under Article 8: 'The conduct of a person or group of persons shall be considered an act of a State under international law if the person or group of persons is in fact acting on the instructions of, or under the direction or control of, that State in carrying out the conduct.'

26 *Military and Paramilitary Activities in and against Nicaragua (Nicaragua v. USA) (Merits)* [1986] ICJ Rep 14.

27 *Case Concerning the Application of the Convention on the Prevention and Punishment of the Crime of Genocide (Bosnia and Herzegovina v. Serbia and Montenegro)*, (Judgment) 2007: 398–407] *Prosecutor v. Tadic*, Case IT-94–1, International Criminal Tribunal for the former Yugoslavia (ICTY), Appeals Chamber (1999), 38 ILM 1518 at 132, where the court required 'specific instructions or directives aimed at the commission of specific act to show effective control'.

28 They also suggest that with regard to export credit agencies, because of their mandate to support and develop trade and investment opportunities for corporate nationals and their regulation by law, combined with their activities in developing business opportunities for their home state, it could mean that their actions can be attributable to the state.

29 Guiding Principles on Business and Human Rights: Implementing the United Nations 'Protect, Respect and Remedy' Framework, UN Doc. A/HRC/17/31 (21 March 2011) (by Professor John Ruggie), www.ohchr.org/Documents/Publications/GuidingPrinciplesBusinessHR_EN.pdf.

30 The Alien Torts Claims Act (ATCA) (28 U.S.C. § 1350) grants US district courts original jurisdiction of any civil action by an alien for a tort only, committed in violation of the law of nations or a treaty of the USA. The act allows US courts to hear human rights cases brought by foreign citizens for abuses committed outside the USA. The use of the act requires a finding of complicity with a state. See *Filartiga v. Peña-Irala*, 630 F.2d 876 (2d Cir. 1980); *Sosa v. Alvarez-Maehain*, 542 U.S. 692 (2004); *John Doe I v. Unocal Corp*, 395 F,3d 932 (9th Cir, 2002). For more information on the act and related cases, see www.business-humanrights.org/Categories/Lawlawsuits/Lawsuitsregulatoryaction/AlienTortClaimsActUSA.

31 In *Kiobel v. Royal Dutch Petroleum Co.,* 133 S.Ct. 1659 (2013), the claimants argued that they had standing to sue Shell (a British/Dutch company) in the USA for aiding and abetting human rights violations in Nigeria against Ken Saro Wiwa. Shell argued that the ATCA is not an exception to the presumption that US law has no extraterritorial effect, and should not be applicable to actions outside the

USA. The Supreme Court held that a US federal court cannot hear a claim under the ATCA where the claim arises out of conduct in a foreign country, reasoning that federal common law should not be interpreted to apply to conduct on foreign soil because US law is presumed not to apply extraterritorially.

32 UN CESCR, Statement on the obligations of States Parties regarding the corporate sector and economic, social and cultural rights, 20 May 2011, UN Doc. E/C.12/2011/1, para. 5. The CESCR has also affirmed that state obligations under the ICESCR extend to the extraterritorial operations of domiciled corporate entities, in its Concluding Observations in respect of Germany (EC/C.12/DEU/CO/5 of 2011), para. 10; Austria (E/C.12/AUT/CO/4 of 2013), para. 12; and Norway (E/C.12/NOR/CO/5 of 2013).

33 See Concluding Observations for Canada, CERD/C/CAN/CO/18, para. 17; Concluding Observations for the United States, CERD/C/USA/CO/6. para. 30; and Concluding Observations for the United Kingdom, at www2.ohchr.org/english/bodies/cerd/docs/UK_COBs_CERD79.pdf.

34 To make this point, the authors cite Ryngaert 2013, 207–10.

35 The Basel Convention on the Control of Transboundary Movement of Hazardous Wastes and their Disposal (1989) 28 ILM 657. See Sornarajah 2010: 162.

36 McCorquodale and Simons (2007: 619) also take this position: 'because some home states have some means to control the extraterritorial activity of foreign subsidiaries of corporate nationals, where a state has "sufficient knowledge" of the human rights impact of such activity in the host state, the home state has a duty "to prevent and mitigate the risk by adopting legislation to this end". A failure to do so would amount to a breach of the international obligation to exercise due diligence, for which international responsibility arises.'

References

Augenstein, D. and Kinley, D. (2015, forthcoming) 'Beyond the 100 Acre Wood: In which International Human Rights Law Finds New Ways to Tame Global Corporate Power', *International Journal of Human Rights*.

Borras, S. Jr and Franco, J. (2010) 'From Threat to Opportunity? Problems with the Idea of a "Code of Conduct" for Land-Grabbing', *Yale Hum. Rts & Dev. L.J.* 13: 507.

Caplan, L.M. (2003) 'State Immunity, Human Rights and Jus Cogens: A Critique of the Normative Hierarchy Theory', *American Journal of International Law* 97: 74.

Centre on Housing Rights and Evictions (2006) 'Right to Water: Background Information', www.cohre.org/water.

Cotula, L. (2011) *Land Deals in Africa: What is in the Contracts?*, London: IIED.

Cotula, L., Vermeulen, S., Leonard, R. and Keeley, J. (2009) *Land Grab or Development Opportunity? Agricultural Investment and International Land Deals in Africa*, London and Rome: IIED/FAO/IFAD.

Crawford, J. (2013) *State Responsibility: The General Part*, Cambridge: Cambridge University Press.

De Schutter, O. (2011) 'The Green Rush: The Global Race for Farmland and the Rights of Land Users', *Harv. Int'l L.J.* 52(2): 504.

Dumberry, P. and Dumas-Aubin, G. (2012) 'When and How Allegations of Human Rights Violations Can Be Raised in Investor-State Arbitration', *Journal of World Investment & Trade* 13(3).

Gibney, M. (n.d.) 'Reconceptualising Human Rights', in *Essays in Honour of Katarina Tomasevski*, www.rwi.lu.se/ktfestschrift/On-line_festschrift_in_honour_of_Katarina_Tomasevski_files/Re-conceptualising%20Human%20Rights%20-%20Gibney.pdf.

Joseph, S. and Castan, M. (2013) *The ICCPR: Cases, Materials and Commentary*, 3rd edn, Oxford: Oxford University Press.

Mann, H. and Smaller, C. (2010) 'Foreign Land Purchases for Agriculture: What Impact on Sustainable Development?', *Sustainable Dev. Innovation Briefs* 8(3), www.un.org/esa/dsd/resources/res_pdfs/publications/ib/no8.pdf (accessed 17 October 2011).

Martin, A. and Ayalew, M.M. (2011) 'Acquiring Land Abroad for Agricultural Purposes: Land Grab or Agri-FDI?', *Surrey Law Working Papers* 08.

McCorquodale, R. and Simons, P. (2007) 'Responsibility Beyond Borders: State Responsibility for Extraterritorial Violations by Corporations of International Human Rights Law', *MLR* 70: 598.

Meinzen-Dick, R. and Markelova, H. (2009) 'Necessary Nuance: Toward a Code of Conduct in Foreign Land Deals', in M. Kugelman and S. Levenstein (eds) *Land Grabs? The Race for the World's Farmland*, Washington, DC: Woodrow Wilson International Center for Scholars.

Paoloni, L. and Onorati, A. (2014) 'Regulations of Large-Scale Acquisitions of Land: The Case of the Voluntary Guidelines on the Responsible Governance of Land, Fisheries and Forests', *The Law and Development Review* 7(2): 369–400.

Ryngaert, C. (2013) 'Jurisdiction: Towards a Reasonableness Test', in M. Langford *et al.* (eds) *Global Justice, State Duties*, Cambridge: Cambridge University Press.

Shemberg, A. (2008) *Stabilisation Clauses and Human Rights: A Research Project for IFC and the UN Special Representative to the Secretary-General on Business and Human Rights*, International Finance Corporation and the UN Office of the High Commissioner for Human Rights, IFC: World Bank Group, www.ifc.org/wps/wcm/connect/9feb5b00488555eab8c4fa6a6515bb18/Stabilization%2BPaper.pdf?MOD=AJPERES.

Smaller, C. and Mann, H. (2009) *A Thirst for Distant Lands: Foreign Investment in Agricultural Land and Water*, Ottawa: International Institute for Sustainable Development (May).

Sornarajah, M. (2010) *The International Law of Foreign Investment*, Cambridge: Cambridge University Press.

Stephens, P. (2011) 'The Global Land Grab: An Analysis of Extant Governance Institutions', *International Affairs Review* XX(1), www.iar-gwu.org/sites/default/files/articlepdfs/Pheobe_Stephens_-_The_Global_Land_Grab.pdf.

Stephens, P. (2013) 'The Principles of Responsible Agricultural Investment', *Globalizations* 10(1).

Telesetsky, A. (2011) 'Resource Conflicts over Arable Land in Food Insecure States: Creating an UN Ombudsman Institution to Review Foreign Agricultural Land Leases', *Goettingen Journal of International Law* 3(1): 283.

Weiss, E.B. (1992) 'Intergenerational Equity: A Legal Framework for Global Environmental Change', in E. Brown Weiss (ed.) *Environmental Change and International Law: New Challenges and Dimensions*, Tokyo: United Nations University Press.

Wickers, E. and Kalhan, A. (2010) 'Land Rights Issues in International Human Rights Law', London: Institute for Human Rights and Business, www.ihrb.org/pdf/Land_Rights_Issues_in_International_HRL.pdf.

Wisborg, P. (2013) 'Human Rights Against Land-grabbing? A Reflection on Norms, Policies and Power', *J. Agric. Environ. Ethics* 26(11): 99.

UN documents

Articles on the Responsibility of States for Internationally Wrongful Acts, ILC Ybk 2001/II(2), 26.

CSECR, General Comment 15: The Right to Water.

ILO Convention No. 169 (1989) Concerning Indigenous and Tribal Peoples in Independent Countries.

Convention on the Elimination of all forms of Discrimination Against Women (CEDAW).

Guiding Principles on Business and Human Rights: Implementing the United Nations 'Protect, Respect and Remedy' Framework, UN Doc.A/HRC/17/31 (21 March 2011) (by Professor John Ruggie), www.ohchr.org/Documents/Publications/Guiding PrinciplesBusinessHR_EN.pdf.

ILO Conventions 117 and 169 on Social Policy (Basic Aims and Standards) and Indigenous and Tribal Peoples.

ILO Convention No. 117, The Social Policy (Basic Aims and Standards) Convention of 1962.

International Convention on the Elimination of All Forms of Racial Discrimination (CERD).

International Covenant on Civil and Political Rights (1966) (ICCPR).

Rio Declaration on Environment and Development, princ. 3, UN Doc. A/CONF.151/26 (Vol. I) (1992).

Special Rapporteur on the Right to Food, Large-scale Land Acquisitions and Leases: A Set of Minimum Principles and Measures to Address the Human Rights Challenge, Human Rights Council, UN Doc A/HRC/13/33/Add.2 (28 December 2009).

The Basel Convention on the Control of Transboundary Movement of Hazardous Wastes and their Disposal (1989) 28 ILM 657.

UNCESCR Concluding Observations in Respect of Germany (EC/C.12/DEU/CO/5 of 2011) paragraph 10; Austria (E/C.12/AUT/CO/4 of 2013, paragraph 12).

UNCESCR Concluding Observations for Norway (E/C.12/NOR/CO/5 of 2013).

UNCESCR Concluding Observations for Canada (CERD/C/CAN/CO/18).

UNCESCR Concluding Observations for the United States (CERD/C/USA/CO/6).

UNCESCR Concluding Observations for the United Kingdom CERD at www2.ohchr.org/english/bodies/cerd/docs/UK_COBs_CERD79.pdf.

UNHRC Resolution A/HRC/15/L.14.

UN Committee on Economic Social and Cultural Rights (UNCESCR) Statement on the Obligations of States Parties Regarding the Corporate Sector and Economic, Social and Cultural Rights, 20 May 2011, UN Doc. E/C.12/2011/1.

UN Declaration on the Rights of Indigenous Peoples (UNDRIP), GA Res 61/295, UN Doc.A/61/PV/107 (13 September 2007).

Universal Declaration on Human Rights (UDHR).

Other documents

Tirana Declaration: Securing Land Access for the Poor in Times of Intensified Natural Resources Competition (Rome, 2011), www.landcoalition.org/aboutus/aom 2011/Tiranadeclaration.

World Social Forum (2011) Dakar Appeal against the Land Grab, FIAN International, www. fian.org/news/press-releases/dakar-appeal-against-the-land-grab.

Statutory legislation

Alien Torts Claims Act (28 U.S.C. § 1350).

Cases

Philippines

Minors Oposa v. Secretary of the Department of Environment and National Resources (DENR), (30 July 1993), 33 I.L.M 173(1994)

USA

John Doe I v. Unocal Corp, 395 F,3d 932 (9th Cir, 2002).
Filartiga v. Peña-Irala, 630 F.2d 876 (2d Cir. 1980).
Kiobel v. Royal Dutch Petroleum Co., 133 S.Ct. 1659 (2013).
Sosa v. Alvarez-Maehain, 542 U.S. 692 (2004).

International

East Timor (Portugal v. Australia), Judgment, ICJ Reports 1995.
Legality of the Threat or Use of Nuclear Weapons, Advisory Opinion, ICJ Reports 1996.
Application of the Convention on the Prevention and Punishment of the Crime of Genocide, Preliminary Objections, Judgment, ICJ Reports 1996.
Military and Paramilitary Activities in and against Nicaragua (Nicaragua v. USA) (Merits) (1986) ICJ Rep 14.
Case Concerning the Application of the Convention on the Prevention and Punishment of the Crime of Genocide (Bosnia and Herzegovina v. Serbia and Montenegro) (Judgment) 2007 (398–407).
Prosecutor v. Tadic, Case IT-94-91, International Criminal Tribunal for the former Yugoslavia (ICTY), Appeals Chamber (1999) 38 ILM 1518.
Victor Saldano v. Argentina, Petition, Report No. 38/99, Inter-Am. C.H.R., OEA/Ser.L/V/II.95 Doc. 7 rev. at 289 (1998).
Lozidou v. Turkey (Preliminary Objections) (App no. 15318/89) (1995) 20 EHRR 99 (62).
EDF (Services) Limited v. Romania, ICSID Case No. ARB/05/3, 8 October 2009, §190.

Index